# History

## for the IB Diploma

# The Cold War and the Americas 1945–81

## John Stanley
### Series editor: Allan Todd

Cambridge University Press's mission is to advance learning, knowledge and research worldwide.

Our IB Diploma resources aim to:
- encourage learners to explore concepts, ideas and topics that have local and global significance
- help students develop a positive attitude to learning in preparation for higher education
- assist students in approaching complex questions, applying critical-thinking skills and forming reasoned answers.

CAMBRIDGE
UNIVERSITY PRESS

CAMBRIDGE UNIVERSITY PRESS
Cambridge, New York, Melbourne, Madrid, Cape Town,
Singapore, São Paulo, Delhi, Mexico City

Cambridge University Press
The Edinburgh Building, Cambridge CB2 8RU, UK

www.cambridge.org
Information on this title: www.cambridge.org/9781107698901

First published 2012

Printed and bound in the United Kingdom by the MPG Books Group

A catalogue record for this publication is available from the British Library

ISBN 978-1-107-69890-1 Paperback

Cambridge University Press has no responsibility for the persistence or
accuracy of URLs for external or third-party internet websites referred to in
this publication, and does not guarantee that any content on such websites is,
or will remain, accurate or appropriate.

This material has been developed independently by the publisher and the
content is in no way connected with nor endorsed by the International
Baccalaureate Organization.

# Contents

# 1 Introduction

This book is designed to prepare students for the Paper 3, Section 10 topic, *The Cold War and the Americas 1945–81* (in HL Option 3, Aspects of the History of the Americas) in the IB History examination. Although the Cold War developed in Eastern Europe and then spread to Asia, the Americas also became involved as the conflict progressed. The book examines the development and impact of the Cold War on the Americas, exploring key foreign and domestic policy developments from 1945 to 1981, focusing on the USA, Canada, Cuba and Chile. During the Cold War, some countries in the Americas were closely allied to the USA, while others took sides reluctantly. Some nations adopted socialist policies in reaction to what they regarded as US regional dominance. It should be noted that the events discussed in this book are far-reaching, and you are encouraged to carry out further research of your own to gain a full understanding of the period.

## Activity

Based on what you already know, define the term 'Cold War'. Draw up a timeline of major international developments in the Cold War from 1945 to 1981. When constructing the timeline, add any events or policies that affected the USA, Canada, Cuba and Chile. This timeline is something that you can start now and develop as you progress through this book.

*A map showing the Americas and other countries involved in the Cold War in the years 1945–81*

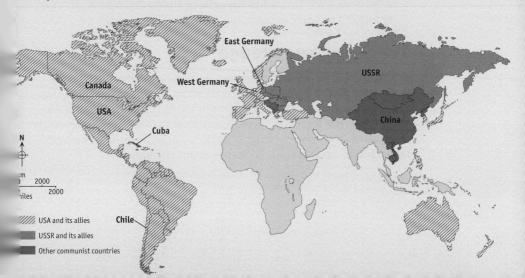

# Themes

To help you prepare for your IB History exams, this book will cover the main themes relating to *The Cold War and the Americas 1945–81*, as set out in the IB *History Guide*. In particular, it will examine the USA, Canada, Cuba and Chile in terms of:

- the development and impact of the Cold War on the foreign and domestic policies of the USA from 1945 to 1961; this includes Truman's policy of containment, the consequences of the Korean War, the rise of McCarthyism, Eisenhower's New Look and the growing importance of Latin America to the USA
- the continued impact of the Cold War on the USA from 1961 to 1981, with reference to the Cuban Missile Crisis of 1962 and the USA's involvement in Vietnam from 1964 to 1973; the book will also explore the Alliance for Progress, Carter's campaign for human rights, and increased US involvement in countries throughout the Americas
- Canada from 1945 to 1963, where the Cold War had an early impact with the Gouzenko spy scandal and then influenced policies concerning Canadian law and order, health, education, gender, language and ethnicity
- changes in Canada from 1964 to 1981, when the political climate was altered by Trudeau's foreign policy, the Quiet Revolution in Quebec and the 1970 October Crisis
- the impact of the Cold War on Cuba from 1945 to 1981 – a period that witnessed a shift in the balance of power in the Americas; the collapse of Batista's regime in Cuba led to the Cuban Revolution, and under Castro's leadership the country became a socialist republic
- the effects of the Cold War on Chile, including the activities of the anti-communist AChA in 1947, the election of the Marxist president Salvador Allende in 1970 and then the coup against Allende in 1973; this led to the exile of 20,000 Chileans and Pinochet's military dictatorship.

# Theory of knowledge

In addition to the broad key themes, each chapter contains Theory of knowledge (ToK) links to get you thinking about aspects that relate to history, which is a Group 3 subject in the IB Diploma. *The Cold War and the Americas* topic has several clear links to ideas about knowledge and history. The subject is highly political, as it concerns – amongst other things – aspects of and clashes about ideology.

The term 'ideology' refers to a set of ideas that form the basis of a political belief system or a political theory. The clash of ideologies relevant to the study of the Cold War and the Americas is that between capitalism and communism.

At times, the deeply political nature of this topic has affected historians writing about countries in the Americas during the period of the Cold War, the leaders involved, and their policies and actions. Clearly, questions relating to the selection of sources, and the way historians interpret these sources, have clear links to the IB Theory of knowledge course.

For example, when trying to explain aspects of particular policies, political leaders' motives, and their success or failure, historians must decide which evidence to select and use to make their case – and which evidence to leave out. But to what extent do the historians' personal political views influence them when selecting what they consider to be the most relevant sources, and when they make judgements about the value and limitations of specific sources or sets of sources? Is there such a thing as objective 'historical truth'? Or is there just a range of subjective historical opinions and interpretations about the past, which vary according to the political interests and leanings of individual historians?

You are therefore strongly advised to read a range of publications giving different interpretations of the theory and practice of the various economic, political and social policies that were carried out during the period covered by this book. This will help you gain a clear understanding of the relevant historiographies.

# IB History and Paper 3 questions

In IB History, Paper 3 is taken only by Higher-level students. For this paper, IB History specifies that three sections of an Option should be selected for in-depth study. The examination paper will set two questions on each section – and you have to answer three questions in total.

Unlike Paper 2, where there are regional restrictions, in Paper 3 you will be able to answer *both* questions from one section, with a third chosen from one of the other sections. These questions are essentially in-depth analytical essays. It is therefore important to study *all* the bullet points set out in the IB *History Guide*, in order to give yourself the widest possible choice of questions.

## Exam skills

Throughout the main chapters of this book, there are activities and questions to help you develop the understanding and the exam skills necessary for success in Paper 3. Your exam answers should demonstrate:

- factual knowledge and understanding
- awareness and understanding of historical interpretations
- structured, analytical and *balanced* argument.

Before attempting the specific exam practice questions that come at the end of each main chapter, you might find it useful to refer *first* to Chapter 8, the final exam practice chapter. This suggestion is based on the idea that if you know where you are supposed to be going (in this instance, gaining a good grade), and how to get there, you stand a better chance of reaching your destination!

## Questions and markschemes

To ensure that you develop the necessary skills and understanding, each chapter contains comprehension questions and exam tips. For success in Paper 3, you need to produce essays that combine a number of features. In many ways, these require the same skills as the essays in Paper 2.

However, for the Higher-level Paper 3, examiners will be looking for greater evidence of *sustained* analysis and argument, linked closely to the demands of the question. Examiners will also be seeking more depth and precision in your supporting knowledge. Finally, they will be expecting a clear and well-organised answer, so it is vital to do a rough plan *before* you start to answer a question. Your plan will show you straight away whether or not you know enough about the topic to answer the question. It will also provide a good structure for your answer.

It is particularly important to start by focusing *closely* on the wording of the question, so that you can identify its demands. Your answer needs to present a *well-structured* and *analytical* argument that is clearly linked to all these demands. Each aspect of your argument/analysis/explanation then needs to be supported by carefully selected, precise and relevant own knowledge.

In addition, showing awareness and understanding of relevant historical debates and interpretations will help you to access the highest bands and marks. This does not mean simply repeating, in your own words, what different historians have said. Instead, try to *critically evaluate* particular interpretations. For example, are there any weaknesses in some of the arguments put forward by particular historians? What strengths does a certain argument or interpretation have?

## Examiner's tips

To help you develop these skills, all chapters contain sample questions, with examiner's tips about what to do (and what *not* to do) in order to achieve high marks. Each chapter will focus on a specific skill, as follows:

- Skill 1 (Chapter 2) – understanding the wording of a question
- Skill 2 (Chapter 3) – planning an essay
- Skill 3 (Chapter 4) – writing an introductory paragraph
- Skill 4 (Chapter 5) – avoiding irrelevance
- Skill 5 (Chapter 6) – avoiding a narrative-based answer
- Skills 6 and 7 (Chapter 7) – skill 6 concerns using your own knowledge analytically and combining it with awareness of historical debate; skill 7 focuses on writing a conclusion to your essay.

Some of these tips will contain parts of a student's answer to a particular question, with examiner's comments, to give you an understanding of what examiners are looking for.

This guidance is developed further in Chapter 8, the exam practice chapter, where examiner's tips and comments will enable you to focus on the important aspects of questions and their answers. These examples will also help you avoid simple mistakes and oversights that, every year, result in some otherwise good students failing to gain the highest marks.

For additional help, a simplified Paper 3 markscheme is provided in Chapter 8 (page 219). This should make it easier to understand what examiners are looking for in your exam answers, and therefore help you reach the higher bands. The actual Paper 3 IB History markscheme can be found on the IB website.

This book will provide you with the historical knowledge and understanding to help you answer all the specific content bullet points set out in the IB *History Guide*. Also, by the time you have worked through the various exercises, you should have the skills necessary to construct relevant, clear, well-argued and well-supported essays.

# Background to the Cold War

The Cold War was the most significant extended political and diplomatic conflict of the second half of the 20th century. Lasting from 1945 to 1991, the Cold War was conducted between the United States and the Soviet Union, based in their respective capitals of Washington, DC and Moscow.

The name of the conflict comes from the fear that both sides had of fighting each other directly in a 'hot war', in which nuclear weapons might cause devastation far beyond anything previously experienced. Instead, the two superpowers – USA and the USSR – competed indirectly. Key tactics of the Cold War included economic sanctions, propaganda, non-co-operation, and strategic involvement in conflicts in different parts of the world. The term 'Cold War' was popularised in 1947 by Bernard Baruch, an advisor to US president Harry Truman, in reference to the frequent tensions arising between the USA and the USSR. These crises grew out of a long-standing unease between the communist Soviet Union and the capitalist United States, which began with the Bolshevik Revolution in Russia in 1917.

The Soviet Communist Party, under Vladimir Ilyich Lenin, considered itself to be the leader of an international movement to replace existing political structures. The ideological differences between the USSR and the mainly capitalist Western governments thus caused severe tension throughout the 1920s and 1930s. Communists in Russia and elsewhere claimed that their loyalty did not lie with their own country, but rather

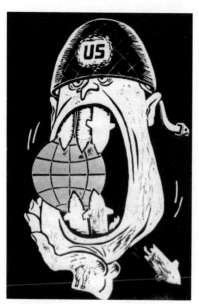

in establishing a political system that would benefit all nations. However, the Western powers believed that, in reality, all communists received their orders from – and were ultimately faithful to – the USSR.

Despite their differences, the two superpowers united in the struggle against Nazi Germany during the Second World War (1939–45). However, once Germany was defeated, political differences and ideological clashes surfaced once again. In 1945, the Allies held a series of conferences to discuss the division of Europe and the status of Germany after the war. It became clear during the conferences that the USA and the USSR had very different ideas about these issues.

*A Cold War cartoon from the 1960s*

Where do you think the Cold War cartoon on page 10 originated? Why do you think this? What is its message? How does the cartoonist convey this?

# Terminology and definitions

To fully understand the various political parties and ideological forces involved in the Cold War, you will need to be familiar with a few basic terms.

## Communism

Communism is a social and economic system in which all significant aspects of a country's economy are socially owned and managed. This means that they are run by the state or by local communities or co-operatives, rather than by the wealthy classes. Such social ownership is intended to create a classless society, in which wealth is shared out equally amongst the people. The writings of **Karl Marx** and Friedrich Engels brought communist ideas to prominence.

**Karl Marx (1818–83)** Marx was a German philosopher who argued that class struggle and conflict were the most (but not the only) important factors behind social and economic change, as well as intellectual and political development. Marx identified various stages in the development of human societies, working closely with his friend and collaborator Friedrich Engels (1820–95). They wrote *The Communist Manifesto* together in 1847. Marx then wrote an in-depth study of the workings of capitalism, entitled *Das Kapital* ('Capital'). He urged the industrial working classes in the developed countries of the period (Britain, Germany and the USA) to bring about socialist revolutions. Marx's ideas inspired many revolutionaries, including Vladimir Ilyich Lenin and Leon Trotsky.

Although communist parties are generally thought of as being on the left in political terms, it is important to remember that communist parties – like all political parties – are themselves divided into left, centre and right wings or factions. Another difficulty is that the term communism has meant – and still means – different things to different people, both to historians and to members and leaders of communist parties.

Communists believe that political parties are the result of class conflict. In a classless society, therefore, there is no need for different political parties. Consequently, a communist system is a one-party state in which the Communist Party rules on behalf of the people. The USSR was a communist state.

## Leninism

Leninist principles aim to guide society from capitalism to communism. Lenin felt that Marx's writings did not provide any guidelines for this transition, and believed that a small, professional group of revolutionaries was needed to overthrow the capitalist system by force. After this, a 'dictatorship of the proletariat' (that is, the rule of the working classes) must guide the state until a time when capitalism could be fully abandoned. As the working class was the majority of the population, this rule was expected to be *more* democratic than the rule of wealthy minority classes. This Marxist term did not have the usual connotations of undemocratic rule – Marx described Britain's liberal parliamentary democracy as 'the dictatorship of the bourgeoisie'. In practice, adopting Leninist ideas required taking control of all areas of life, and the 'dictatorship of the proletariat' later became increasingly undemocratic.

## Socialism

Socialism refers to an economic system in which the means of production are under the control of either the state or publicly owned co-operatives. Socialism can also refer to a political philosophy that encourages such a system. In Marxist theory, socialism is also regarded as a specific historical phase, marking a move away from capitalism but coming before full communism.

## Capitalism

Capitalism is a social and economic system based on private ownership of land, industries and banks. A capitalist society is often called a market or a free-enterprise economy, in which prices and wages are determined by supply and demand rather than by government policy. In the period under discussion, most – though not all – capitalist states had a liberal democratic political system. The USA, Britain, Canada and France were capitalist states.

## Liberalism

Liberals favour more gradual political change, using the process of law rather than revolution. The term liberalism refers to a belief in the importance of liberty and equal rights. A liberal democracy might be a constitutional republic like the USA or India, or a constitutional monarchy like Japan, Spain or the UK. Both these forms of government uphold the freedom to vote for a choice of political parties, freedom of speech and of worship, and a free press. A liberal democracy gives people the power to vote unpopular governments out of office.

# Dictatorship

Dictatorship is a form of government in which an individual and his/her followers direct the policy of the state. They often have the power to govern without public consent, and frequently control nearly every aspect of public and private behaviour. In this sense, dictatorship (government without the consent of the people) is a contrast to democracy (government whose power comes from the people).

## Discussion point

In small groups, decide on both the advantages and disadvantages of the capitalist and communist systems. Exchange your ideas. Which countries are still communist today? If, as Lenin suggested, communist groups have leaders, does this mean they are not truly communist?

# Summary

By the time you have worked through this book, you should be able to:

- understand and explain how the Cold War affected the domestic and foreign policies of the USA, Canada, Cuba and Chile between 1945 and 1981
- show awareness of the impact and significance of the early stages of the Cold War on both Canada and the USA, as the leading Western allies
- understand and account for the pressures on governments during the different phases of the Cold War
- understand the significance of leaders such as Truman, Kennedy, Trudeau, Batista, Castro and Allende, and their impact within their respective states
- understand and explain the growing importance of the Americas during the Cold War
- show a broad understanding of differing historical interpretations, both about the origins of the Cold War and about specific and controversial events in the four states being studied.

# 2 The USA and the Cold War 1945–61

## Key questions

- How are the government and political system in the USA structured?
- What was the early US response to the emerging Cold War 1945–50?
- What was the effect of the Korean War 1950–53?
- How did Eisenhower and Dulles change US–Soviet relations?
- What was the USA's response to Cold War developments in the Americas?
- What was the impact of the Cold War on aspects of US domestic policy?

This chapter examines the impact of the Cold War on the USA from 1945 to 1961, focusing on Truman's policy of containment, America's involvement in Korea, and the increasing importance of Latin America to the USA. It considers how domestic policy was shaped by a fear of communism, and how this affected law and order, education and civil rights, and led to 'McCarthyism'.

## Overview

- In the USA, the Second World War created jobs and laid the foundations for a huge post-war boom, as well as increasing the power of the federal government.
- Between 1945 and 1961, many Americans enjoyed a significant rise in living standards. However, 25% of the population still lived in poverty, and racism persisted.
- The USA was a nuclear superpower, locked in a stand-off with the USSR. Many people in the USA were anxious about the spread of communism in Eastern Europe, US–Soviet tensions in Berlin, the development of the Soviet nuclear bomb and the establishment of the communist People's Republic of China.
- Fear of communist infiltration increased as information about spying activity emerged. Suspicion grew about the worldwide aims of the 'Reds' (communists), and Senator Joseph McCarthy held investigations that were damaging to US society and culture.
- Presidents Truman and Eisenhower tried to limit Soviet power with a policy of containment. At the same time, the USA and the USSR had to find ways to co-exist to prevent a 'hot war' breaking out.
- This balancing act was tested by the Korean War between 1950 and 1953, and later when Cuba became a source of concern.
- The fight between 'free capitalist' and 'repressed communist' was not only central to US foreign policy, but also influenced domestic affairs.

*President Truman announces his new foreign policy in 1947*

# How are the government and political system in the USA structured?

## The US government and the Constitution

The USA is a federal state. Power is divided between the 50 states and the federal (central) government, which is based in the US capital – Washington, DC. The government of each state can decide its own laws in areas such as education and crime. The Constitution of the United States of America defines the three main branches of government, with power divided between the following:

- Legislature: a Congress or parliament of two houses – the House of Representatives and the Senate
- Executive: the policy-making branch, headed by the president
- Judiciary: the courts and judges, headed by the Supreme Court, which ensures that neither Congress nor the president exceed their powers.

Both legislative houses (the Senate and the House of Representatives) must agree laws before they can be passed. The number of state representatives (congressmen/women) is proportional to the population of the state, and these representatives face election every two years. The Senate is made up of 100 senators – two from each of the 50 states – who serve six-year terms.

The Executive branch is led by the president, who is elected every four years. He or she must be over 35 and US-born. Since 1951, presidents have been limited to no more than two terms in office.

The president can pass laws and run the country, but only with congressional approval. Congress can block a law proposed by the president if it can win a majority vote against the law. In turn, the president has the power to veto (overrule) congressional legislation.

Having three branches of government allows the US to be run by a system of checks and balances. For example, Congress is able to challenge the authority of the president (although it cannot *overrule* his authority). Joint sessions of the US Congress are sometimes held, such as during the State of the Union address – an annual speech in which the president delivers an assessment of the state of the country and outlines his legislative agenda.

What is meant by a 'system of checks and balances'?

*A joint session of Congress during President Eisenhower's State of the Union address in 1955*

The Supreme Court is made up of nine judges (justices), who hold office until they resign or die. They ensure that neither Congress nor the president exceed their powers. The president can appoint one of the nine Supreme Court justices if a vacancy occurs, and the political leanings of the Court can change.

The Constitution aims to prevent any one branch of government becoming too powerful. To maintain a balance of power, the Constitution deliberately grants members of the three branches different terms of office. The US Constitution was adopted in 1787, and over time additions and changes – known as Amendments – have been made. The first ten Amendments were introduced in 1789 and are collectively known as the Bill of Rights. By 2012, only 17 further Amendments to the Constitution had been passed, mainly because such changes can create a complicated form of government.

What are the key features of the US Constitution and the structure of the US government? How similar or different are they to the constitution and system of government in your own country or a country you have studied?

## Political parties and the electoral system

In the USA, the two main political parties are the Republicans and the Democrats. Minority parties receive only moderate support. Technically, presidents are chosen by the Electoral College, in which each state has a number of electors equal to its members in the House of Representatives plus its two senators. When members of the public vote for the president, therefore, they are effectively instructing the electors from their state to choose a particular candidate.

The US Constitution provides for this Electoral College rather than direct voting because the nation's founders feared that in the early years of the republic, direct voting could be manipulated by factions. These factions might affect the interests of the nation by pushing their own agenda. The existing system means that a presidential candidate can lose the nationwide popular vote, but still be chosen as president by the Electoral College. However, this has occurred only three times in US history – in 1876, 1888 and 2000.

# What was the early US response to the emerging Cold War 1945–50?

## Developments in Europe 1945–49

The Allied victory at the end of the Second World War was followed by a stand-off between the Soviet Union and the United States. These two nations had very different visions of the post-war world. As a result, the second half of the 1940s was characterised by several key policies and events that shaped the rest of the Cold War:

- The USA followed democratic and capitalist policies, while the USSR pursued a communist line.
- The USSR feared that opening up to trade would allow 'harmful' capitalist influences into the country.
- At the end of the war, Germany was divided between the USA, the USSR, France and Britain. The German capital, Berlin, was also split between these powers. This division was only intended to be temporary, but differences of opinion arose over Germany's longer-term future.
- The USA believed that German economic recovery was essential for the future stability of Europe as a whole. However, the USSR felt that a revived Germany would be an economic and political threat.
- Countries that had been liberated by the Soviet army at the end of the war were promised free elections. However, Soviet leader Joseph Stalin's understanding of 'free' elections differed from the expectations of the people in these countries.
- By 1948, the USSR's sphere of influence stretched from the Baltic Sea to the Adriatic Sea.

- The Berlin Blockade of 1948–49 was the first major Cold War crisis.
- The USA, Britain and France combined their German occupation zones to form the German Federal Republic (West Germany) in August 1949. In October 1949, the Soviets created East Germany from their zone of occupation.
- Two other key events occurred in 1949: the Soviet Union acquired the atomic bomb and China became a communist country.
- From 1945 to the end of the decade, the governments in Moscow and Washington increasingly regarded each other as a threat, both physically and ideologically. This eventually divided Europe into two blocs, separated by what Winston Churchill described as an 'iron curtain'.

*A map showing the Iron Curtain countries in 1955 (the USA and Canada were also NATO members); the division of Berlin is also shown (inset)*

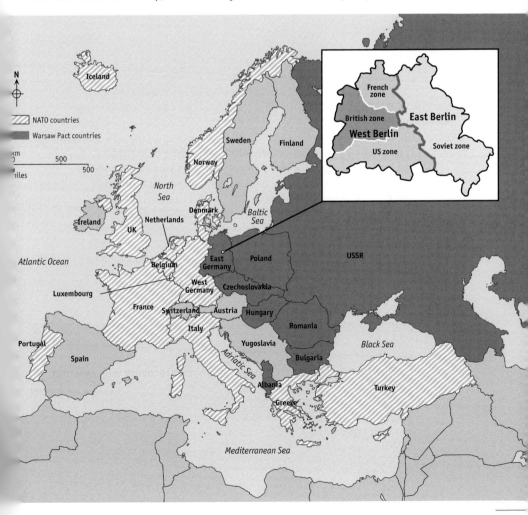

### SOURCE A

From Stettin in the Baltic to Trieste in the Adriatic an iron curtain has descended across the Continent ... in what I must call the Soviet sphere, and all are subject, in one form or another, not only to Soviet influence but to a very high and in some cases increasing measure of control from Moscow ... I do not believe that Soviet Russia desires war. What they desire is the fruits of war and the indefinite expansion of their power and doctrines.

Extract from Winston Churchill's 'Iron Curtain' speech, delivered at Fulton, Missouri, USA, 5 March 1946. From www.fordham.edu/halsall/mod/churchill-iron.asp

### SOURCE B

It may be that some quarters are trying to push into oblivion the sacrifices of the Soviet people which ensured the liberation of Europe from the Hitlerite yoke.

But the Soviet Union cannot forget them. One can ask, therefore, what can be surprising in the fact that the Soviet Union, in a desire to ensure its security for the future, tries to achieve that these countries should have governments whose relations with the Soviet Union are loyal?

Extract from Joseph Stalin's response to Churchill's 'Iron Curtain' speech, in an interview with Pravda magazine, March 1946. From www.fordham.edu/halsall/mod/1946stalin.html

According to Source A above, what does Churchill believe about both the present position and future role of the USSR in world affairs? Does Churchill's comment about an 'iron curtain' in Source A, and Stalin's response in Source B, reveal anything about the reasons for a breakdown in the relationship between the USSR and the West?

## Containment and the Truman Doctrine

Containing the threat from the USSR became a key feature of President **Harry S. Truman**'s foreign policy in 1947, when George Kennan – a political advisor based at the US embassy in Moscow – sent his famous 'Long Telegram' to Truman. In it, Kennan argued that the USSR considered itself to be at war with capitalism, and intended to spread communist ideology around the world. Some historians believe that the telegram defined the USA's role as a global power, and it was certainly significant in shaping US policy towards the USSR.

**Harry S. Truman (1884–1972)** Truman became president after Franklin D. Roosevelt's death in April 1945, and he adopted a more hardline approach to the USSR in the post-war peacemaking process than Roosevelt had. This was partly to assert himself in his new role and partly in response to growing pressure from anti-communist groups in the USA. Truman authorised the dropping of the atomic bombs on Japan in August 1945, and later committed US troops to war in Korea. His presidency (1945–53) coincided with the Marshall Plan (see page 23), the development of the Soviet atomic bomb, and anti-communist 'Red' hysteria in the United States.

*US president Harry S. Truman (centre), with British prime minister Clement Attlee (left) and Soviet leader Joseph Stalin (right), at the Potsdam Conference in August 1945*

The policy of containment was essentially a series of strategies to prevent the spread of communism. Containment was first tested in Greece, where Britain had been supporting the government against communist rebels. By February 1947, however, Britain was facing financial difficulties and the prime minister, Clement Attlee, told Truman that Britain could no longer provide aid to either Greece or its neighbour Turkey. On 12 March 1947, Truman made a speech asking Congress to approve $400 million in economic and military aid to Greece and Turkey, emphasising the communist threat to these strategically important states. Congress granted the aid.

Truman understood the USSR's desire to protect itself from outside threats after the Second World War. However, he was concerned by the nature of this self-protection, which took the form of rapid territorial expansion and increased military strength. The president's speech to Congress in March 1947, therefore, set the tone for a new US foreign policy, which came to be known as the Truman Doctrine.

Truman declared: 'I believe that it must be the policy of the United States to support free peoples who are resisting subjugation by armed minorities or by outside pressures.' He also stated that the world faced a clear choice: freedom with a capitalist democracy, or repression with communism – a global struggle between two very different ways of life. To prepare for this fight against communism new security departments were established, including the Central Intelligence Agency (CIA) and the National Security Council (NSC).

## Historical perspectives on the Truman Doctrine

Some historians have questioned whether the Truman Doctrine was an overreaction, and Christine Bragg argues that it was 'an attempt to talk up the threat from the Soviet Union'. Other historians have pointed out the hypocrisy of a US policy that offered support to *all* anti-communist regimes – even those that were undemocratic. Oliver Edwards draws attention to Truman's support for Greece and Turkey, regimes that 'imprisoned and intimidated their political opponents, exhibiting some of the very characteristics which Truman had attributed to communism in his speech'.

Communism was regarded as a totalitarian system – when a government has absolute control over all aspects of life, and suppresses opposing views. This interpretation dominated historical thinking in the West, justifying Western attitudes towards the USSR. Later, however, revisionist historians also considered economic factors. In particular, these included the USA's desire to develop world markets, which conflicted with the USSR's search for a socialist form of economic stability in a largely capitalist world. The debate over US–Soviet motives and actions at the start of the Cold War continues to this day.

To what extent was the Truman Doctrine a specific response to the situation in Greece and Turkey?

## Activity

Historians have attributed several motives to Truman for introducing his doctrine in 1947. These motives include:

- gaining global economic power
- demonising the USSR in the minds of the US public
- winning the presidential election
- basic diplomacy to protect Greece and Turkey
- a genuine reflection of Truman's personal views about the value of democracy
- a need to provoke the USSR
- taking pressure off Britain in the Mediterranean
- becoming the 'world's policeman'.

Working in groups of four, take two of these suggestions per group and carry out some further research. Then write an argument for and against each motive as a reason for the introduction of the Truman Doctrine.

# The Marshall Plan

In spring 1947, US secretary of state George Marshall visited Europe. He was dismayed by the economic depression, the problem of refugees and the lack of infrastructure he witnessed in many countries. Marshall was afraid that local communist parties might seize power in these weak and struggling states. Equally, without economic and political stability the USA might have no European market for its exports, which could lead to a recession in the US.

As a result of these concerns, Marshall devised the plan bearing his name. The Marshall Plan provided financial support to war-torn Europe and, at least in theory, all countries were eligible for this assistance. However, there were conditions attached that made it practically impossible for the communist states of Eastern Europe to apply for the aid. The most significant reason for this was that countries would have to tell the USA how they intended to spend the money, and agree to open up their economies, effectively allowing capitalism. The USSR took part in the first planning meeting for the Marshall Plan, but refused to share economic data on its resources and problems, or to allow the US to dictate how the aid would be spent.

Winston Churchill called the Marshall Plan 'the most unselfish act in history'. However, Soviet politician Vyacheslav Molotov viewed it as little more than 'dollar imperialism' – a way for the USA to exert influence in Europe by gaining economic control. Moscow therefore pressured the countries of Eastern Europe into turning down the offer of Marshall aid. The 16 nations that accepted it were given a four-year deal worth more than $17 billion, and by the 1950s they were all experiencing economic growth.

Many Americans regard the Marshall Plan as one of their country's most successful foreign policy initiatives, but it came at a great cost. Stalin had already established the Communist Information Bureau (Cominform) in September 1947, with the aim of controlling and co-ordinating communist parties throughout Europe. In reaction to the Marshall Plan, the USSR set up the Council for Mutual Economic Assistance (Comecon) in January 1949, to co-ordinate the economic development of communist countries.

> Why was the USA so concerned about the state of European countries in the years immediately after the Second World War? Did the Truman Doctrine and the Marshall Plan contribute to the development of the Cold War?

## The Berlin Blockade and NATO

At the Potsdam Conference in 1945, Germany was divided into four separate zones of occupation governed by France, Britain, the USA and the USSR. The Potsdam Agreement also created a four-power administration for the German capital, Berlin, which was located in the Soviet zone. The USA, Britain and France discussed converting their zones into a single, self-governing republic, and later – in January 1947 – the British and US zones were combined to form a single economic unit called Bizonia. However, Stalin opposed plans to unite Germany fully, and further discussions on unification broke down.

The Western powers then announced their intention to create Trizonia, in which France would join a Western currency zone in a further step towards a united West German state. On 18 June 1948, a new currency – the Deutschmark – was introduced, and five days later its use was extended to West Berlin. This was done without consulting the USSR. In response, on 23 June the Soviets blockaded Berlin, cutting off all road and rail access from the West.

US leaders feared that if they lost Berlin they would eventually lose the whole of Germany – and possibly even Europe. In reaction to the blockade, they launched the Berlin Airlift, in which Allied air forces flew supplies into the German capital. American, French,

Canadian and British planes dropped more than 2 million tonnes of goods throughout the 231 days of the blockade, which was eventually lifted on 12 May 1949.

For the USA, the next step was creating a military alliance that would further support efforts at containment. In 1949, 12 countries, including the USA, established the North Atlantic Treaty Organization (NATO). Based on the principle of collective security, the terms of NATO stated that an attack against one member nation would be viewed as an attack against all. In joining NATO, the USA entered a peacetime alliance. This was a major policy change for Washington – and a clear warning to Moscow that the United States was not standing in isolation.

When West Germany was admitted to NATO in 1955, the USSR created a rival military alliance – the Warsaw Pact. This included countries in the Eastern bloc, notably East Germany. By the mid 1950s, therefore, Europe was divided into two armed camps (see map on page 19).

## NSC-68 and 'roll-back'

In 1950, the recently formed National Security Council carried out a review of US foreign and defence policy. The resulting document – known as NSC-68 – committed the USA to assisting nations anywhere in the world that were threatened by Soviet aggression. This signalled a new direction: the policy of containment had focused on keeping communism within its existing post-war borders; NSC-68 spoke of 'rolling back' the frontiers of communism, and even liberating countries by force. Roll-back was a more aggressive foreign policy, and it was soon put to the test in Korea.

# What was the effect of the Korean War 1950–53?

In 1945, the Korean Peninsula was divided at the 38th parallel (a line of latitude around the Earth, see map on page 26). The USA controlled the south and the USSR controlled the north. By 1950, North Korea was under a Stalinist regime led by the communist Kim Il Sung. South Korea was governed by an authoritarian, US-backed regime under Syngman Rhee. Rhee openly stated that he would unite North and South Korea by force if necessary.

On 25 June 1950, North Korea attacked the South. This move took the US by surprise and led to accusations of Soviet aggression and expansionism, because it was widely believed that Kim Il Sung acted on Moscow's orders. However, not all historians agree with this. For example, US historian Bruce Cumings argues that Kim Il Sung's decision to invade was made by him alone, and not under pressure from Stalin.

Cumings points out that Kim had strong nationalist and revolutionary ideals, and notes that Stalin immediately withdrew Soviet advisors from North Korea when the war began, presumably to avoid being accused of involvement. This supports the idea that North Korea's leader acted alone in starting the Korean War.

Truman sent US air power and naval support to the South Koreans, and told the United Nations Security Council that he intended to force the North Koreans back to the 38th parallel. Truman appointed General Douglas MacArthur (US commander-in-chief in the Far East) as UN commander in Korea. After a summer of heavy casualties, in which North Korea almost succeeded in taking the South, MacArthur recaptured the South Korean capital, Seoul.

*The progress of the Korean War, 1950–53; US/UN troops eventually advanced as far as the Yalu River*

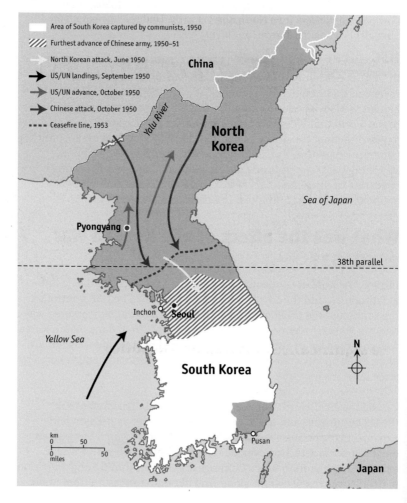

Despite Truman's original aim of simply driving the North Koreans out of the South, by October 1950 he had changed his plans and ordered MacArthur to invade the North. China warned Truman that it would intervene on behalf of North Korea if US or UN troops crossed the 38th parallel. MacArthur pushed on anyway, and by November 1950 he was within a few miles of the border between North Korea and China.

In response to this threat, China sent 250,000 troops across the border into North Korea, pushing UN forces back across the 38th parallel. In April 1951, MacArthur was dismissed as military commander. His replacement, General Matthew Ridgway, led UN troops back over the border into North Korea, halting a huge offensive that cost the Chinese 12,000 men on the first day alone. After this, China began to consider an armistice. However, it took two years of negotiations – and the deaths of thousands more soldiers on both sides – before an agreement was signed in July 1953.

*Military commanders from North Korea and the United Nations sign the agreement ending the Korean War in July 1953*

## The significance of Korea for US policy

Events in Korea tested Cold War boundaries. They proved to communist states that although the USA might hesitate to use nuclear weapons, it would still resist communist expansion with traditional methods of warfare. The USSR avoided direct involvement and, significantly, did not take advantage of the situation to threaten Germany while the Western powers were distracted by events in Korea. Despite this, the Korean War made both superpowers realise that they needed to be prepared for conflict.

The Korean War had a major impact on US foreign policy. In 1951, several defence treaties were signed, including the ANZUS Pact between Australia, New Zealand and the USA, and a series of US agreements with Japan and the Philippines. As historian Derrick Murphy comments: 'The Truman Doctrine, it seemed, was going to be applied to the East as well as to Europe ... both military and economic aid was sent to [US] allies in Japan, the Philippines and Thailand.' Such policies marked a significant move away from those outlined in Kennan's Long Telegram (see page 21), which had focused on political and economic methods for containment in Europe.

Perhaps most significantly for the USA, events in Korea caused a nervous US public to view China and the USSR as a potentially combined communist force, intent on world domination. This fear influenced the attitudes and events that developed in the USA as the 1950s progressed.

## How did Eisenhower and Dulles change US–Soviet relations?

### Eisenhower, Dulles and the New Look

**Dwight D. Eisenhower** replaced Truman as US president in January 1953. Soviet leader Stalin died in March the same year, and **Nikita Khrushchev** (see page 30) became first secretary of the Communist Party. These changes in leadership resulted in several policy shifts, as well as efforts towards improved relations between the USA and the USSR.

- The Soviets were concerned about their military spending and the gathering pace of the arms race. The USA exploded its first hydrogen bomb in November 1952; by July 1953, the USSR had also successfully developed and tested the H-bomb.
- Khrushchev knew that to improve the living standards of Soviet citizens, the USSR had to invest in agriculture, industry and technology. This was only possible by reducing defence spending.
- During Eisenhower's first months in office there was evidence of improved relations with the USSR. However, his secretary of state **John Foster Dulles** continued to encourage the policy of 'roll-back'.
- The heads of the US military services (the joint chiefs of staff) were asked to devise an effective yet economical way of dealing with future conflicts. Eisenhower believed in maintaining a constant level of military readiness.
- Eisenhower and Dulles both feared that resources would be drained by Soviet-inspired regional conflicts. They therefore urged the stockpiling of nuclear weapons rather than spending money on conventional weapons.

- As a result of this, the 1955 US defence budget (which became known as the 'New Look') reflected a concern for balancing military commitments with financial resources.
- The New Look policy emphasised the importance of relying more heavily on strategic nuclear weapons. This would be cheaper, providing 'more bang for the buck' (that is, a greater threat for less money).
- In addition, Dulles warned that the US would adopt a policy of brinkmanship (see Source C on page 30), and said that any aggressors would suffer 'massive retaliation'.

**Dwight D. Eisenhower (1890–1969)** Eisenhower was Allied commander during the invasion of Europe in 1944. As president (1953–61), he and his secretary of state, John Foster Dulles, developed the 'New Look' national security policy, encouraging US policy-makers to consider a *long-term* Soviet threat. Eisenhower's presidency witnessed the end of the Korean War and a deepening rivalry with the USSR in the space race. He authorised U-2 reconnaissance aircraft flights over the Soviet Union, and initiated the plans to invade Cuba that were later carried out by his successor, John F. Kennedy.

**John Foster Dulles (1888–1959)** Dulles was US secretary of state from 1953 until his death in 1959, and was a major influence on US foreign policy during the Cold War. He regarded politics after the Second World War as essentially an ideological fight between good and evil, and believed firmly in 'massive retaliation'. This policy committed a state to a disproportionate action in response to an attack – including the use of nuclear weapons.

*President Dwight D. Eisenhower (right) with his secretary of state John Foster Dulles, 1956*

**Nikita Khrushchev (1894–1971)** Khrushchev joined the Soviet Communist Party in 1918 and was elected to the Central Committee in 1934. He was party secretary of Ukraine, and was elected to the Politburo in 1939. He acted as a senior political commissar on the Stalingrad Front during the Second World War. One of Stalin's close advisors after 1945, Khrushchev was chosen as first secretary of the Communist Party on Stalin's death in 1953. He went on to rule the Soviet Union from 1955 to 1964, and later criticised Stalin for his crimes. Khrushchev was overthrown by Leonid Brezhnev in 1964.

### SOURCE C

The ability to get to the verge without getting into war is the necessary art. If you cannot master it, you inevitably get into war. If you try to run away from it, if you are scared to go to the brink, you are lost.

*John Foster Dulles, describing the policy of brinkmanship, 1956.*

### SOURCE D

When the administration was actually faced with rolling back the Russians in Hungary in 1956, they did nothing other than express loud protests. A similar response had followed in June 1953, when a strike by East Berlin construction workers turned into an uprising across East Germany which was suppressed by Soviet armed forces. Roll-back was nothing more than a paper-tiger and did little to impede improved East-West relations.

*Aldred, J. 2010. Aspects of International Relations 1945–2004. Cheltenham, UK. Nelson Thornes. p. 43.*

### Activity

Look at Sources C and D, and the text on pages 28–29. Write a list of any contradictions you find between the theory and practice of US foreign policy.

## Peaceful coexistence

From 1953, there was in fact greater compromise with the USSR than the US policies of New Look and brinkmanship might suggest. Eisenhower was skilled in personal diplomacy, and Khrushchev believed in flexibility. The Soviet leader also wanted to slow down the nuclear arms race and reallocate some of his defence budget to agriculture and industry. Khrushchev spoke of having 'peaceful coexistence' with the West. To show his sincerity he suggested making Austria a neutral state, removing all troops (like Germany, Austria had been divided into four zones of occupation after the war). Eisenhower agreed, and in May 1955 the Austrian State Treaty was signed.

Encouraged by Khrushchev's gesture, the Western powers removed their occupation forces from West Germany although some troops remained in Europe, largely to address the concerns of the French, who were still nervous about a German revival. However, in May 1955 West Germany was accepted as a member of NATO, as the USSR had feared. Unhappy about this development, Khrushchev announced the formation of the Warsaw Pact shortly afterwards. This treaty united the Soviet Union with the whole of the Eastern European bloc except Yugoslavia. Significantly, the Warsaw Pact included East Germany – demonstrating that the USSR had finally accepted the permanent division of Germany.

The countries of NATO now faced the USSR and all its Warsaw Pact allies – a Cold War stand-off that would last for another 35 years. Khrushchev felt that his vision of peaceful coexistence would ultimately prevail. He believed that the socialist system would prove to be superior to the capitalist system, and that eventually there would be a peaceful global transition to socialism.

> What did Khrushchev mean by 'peaceful coexistence'? What might have prompted him to talk in this manner?

## The 'spirit of Geneva'

In July 1955, the leaders of the USA, Britain, France and the USSR attended a summit in Geneva – the first time they had met since the Potsdam Conference in 1945. Although no significant agreements were reached at Geneva, the summit was carried out in a notable spirit of friendship.

At the Geneva Summit, Eisenhower and Dulles proposed two key ideas. First was the 'Open Skies' proposal, by which each side would allow the other to undertake aerial reconnaissance, as well as providing each other with details of military bases in their respective countries. Khrushchev rejected this suggestion, mainly because he knew that the USA already had advanced U-2 spy planes – high-altitude aircraft capable of operating beyond the range of fighter planes and Soviet ground-to-air missiles. Although no agreement was reached on this subject at Geneva, Eisenhower later ordered spy flights over the USSR – a decision that had serious consequences in 1960 (see page 32).

The second US proposal was the reunification of Germany, subject to free elections. As this implied full German membership of NATO, Khrushchev vetoed the proposal and argued that any reunified Germany should be wholly neutral and demilitarised. Khrushchev then suggested that *all* foreign troops should leave Europe and that both the Warsaw Pact and NATO should be disbanded. Unsurprisingly, the US rejected these proposals.

Despite the lack of progress, the press spoke of a 'Geneva spirit', and both Khrushchev's and Eisenhower's prestige was raised. The summit also encouraged the two leaders to meet for further discussions. However, the spirit of Geneva was soon destroyed by growing tension.

## Peaceful coexistence under pressure 1956–61

### The Hungarian Uprising

In October 1956, the USSR suppressed a revolt against the communist government in Hungary. Almost 40,000 Hungarians and Soviets died in the uprising, and 200,000 people were forced to flee Hungary and become refugees in other countries. Around 25,000 people were allowed to settle in the USA, but the US government refused to take action in the conflict itself. Eisenhower was about to face re-election, and Dulles knew that there was little the USA could do, as Hungary was firmly within the Soviet sphere of influence. This highlighted an important change in attitude in the United States – the government accepted that it could no longer realistically pursue a policy of liberating communist states.

### The Berlin crisis

Despite events in Hungary, 'peaceful coexistence' between the USA and USSR remained relatively undisturbed, although Khrushchev provoked a minor crisis over Berlin in November 1958. The Soviet leader called for the removal of all occupying forces, demanding that Berlin become a free city and that the Western powers formally recognise East Germany. Eisenhower was pressured to send in troops, but he did not want to destroy the fragile peace by forcing Khrushchev into a military response. As time passed nothing happened, and the crisis over Berlin disappeared.

### The U-2 spy-plane incident

In 1959, Khrushchev went on a successful visit to the USA and a follow-up meeting was planned to take place in Paris in May 1960. However, against this background of good relations the US was busy flying U-2 reconnaissance missions over Soviet airspace. Experts assured Eisenhower that if a plane was shot down, the high altitude and the fragility of the U-2 would ensure that the aircraft would disintegrate and the pilot be killed. The Soviets would therefore not be able to tell that it was a spy plane.

In May 1960, just as the Paris Summit was opening, Khrushchev was informed that a U-2 plane had been shot down over Soviet territory. The US immediately denied any wrongdoing, claiming that this was a weather plane that had entered Soviet airspace by mistake. Khrushchev replied that the pilot, Gary Powers, had been captured after parachuting to safety. Eisenhower could no longer deny the incident, and Khrushchev walked out of the summit. Eisenhower was deeply depressed by this turn of events, and US–Soviet relations declined dramatically in the final year of his presidency.

> Why was Eisenhower so embarrassed – and Khrushchev so angered – by the U-2 spy-plane incident?

# What was the USA's response to Cold War developments in the Americas?

## Cuba

Cuba was another major source of Cold War tension during the 1950s and 1960s. Since 1934, Cuba had been ruled by the US-supported military dictator General Fulgencio Batista. Much of Cuba's land – including most of its economically important sugar plantations – and many of its public utilities were owned by American companies. There was also a US naval base on the island, at Guantanamo Bay. Batista both worked with and exploited the rich and powerful Americans who made Cuba their playground.

In 1959, however, a radical left-wing lawyer named Fidel Castro overthrew Batista. Castro's new government initially sought aid from the US, but Eisenhower was concerned about its proposed agricultural land reform law. This limited all estates to a maximum of 1000 acres and stated that no agricultural land could be owned by foreigners, which would severely affect US interests in Cuba. Castro had also appointed a communist as the head of the National Institute of Agrarian Reform (see page 171).

In September 1959, Castro went to New York to address the United Nations. He stated that Cuba remained neutral in the Cold War, but despite this Eisenhower refused to meet the Cuban leader. Khrushchev seized this opportunity to befriend Castro, who was promised Soviet financial, military and technological aid.

Tensions increased in 1960 when US oil companies in Cuba refused to process Soviet crude oil, which was cheaper than the oil normally imported from Venezuela. Castro therefore nationalised the oil companies and Eisenhower retaliated by first suspending imports of Cuban sugar to the USA, and then stopping them altogether. The crisis deepened as Castro nationalised all US-owned companies in Cuba, and Eisenhower placed an embargo on almost all aspects of trade with Cuba. Castro then established diplomatic relations and negotiated a trade agreement with Communist China. He also secured an agreement with the USSR for the provision of $100 million so he could buy weapons and machinery, as well as extracting a promise from Khrushchev to purchase large quantities of Cuban sugar.

In response to all these moves, the CIA (see page 22) met with Cuban exiles to come up with a plan to destabilise the Cuban economy and government. An invasion force began training secretly in Guatemala, and as Eisenhower handed over the presidency to **John F. Kennedy** in January 1961, diplomatic relations between the USA and Cuba were broken off.

**John F. Kennedy (1917–63)** A Harvard graduate, Kennedy served in the US navy during the Second World War and was hailed as a war hero for his service in the Pacific. He entered politics in 1946, and was elected to Congress in 1952. Kennedy won the 1960 Democratic presidential nomination, and became the first Roman Catholic president. He adopted the 'New Frontier' approach, pushing the boundaries when dealing with problems at home and abroad, and when facing new challenges such as the space race. His presidency (1961–63) coincided with the gravest moment of the Cold War – the Cuban Missile Crisis. Kennedy was assassinated in Dallas, Texas, in 1963.

*John F. Kennedy delivers his inaugural address, 20 January 1961*

Kennedy therefore inherited a situation in which an increasingly independent Cuba was adopting communist-style policies. Given Castro's growing links with the USSR and China, it is unsurprising that Kennedy allowed the CIA's invasion plans to continue. The events that unfolded as a result of this would haunt his presidency (see page 58).

### Discussion point

Some historians have suggested that a lack of understanding, rather than pure animosity, lay at the heart of the declining relationship between Cuba and the USA between 1959 and 1961. To what extent do you agree with this assertion?

## The Rio Treaty 1947

As the Cold War began to develop, the US government grew concerned about the risk of pro-communist regimes being established elsewhere in the Americas – which the US regarded as its own 'back yard'. The Truman Doctrine thus set a precedent for supplying US aid to any regime, however repressive, that was fighting communism or experiencing internal unrest that might lead it away from the US sphere of influence.

The Inter-American Treaty of Reciprocal Assistance (the Rio Treaty) was signed in 1947, and provided a legal basis for US military intervention in any Latin American country. In 1948, the Organization of American States (OAS) was set up by the USA and the Rio Treaty members, with the stated belief that communism was incompatible with freedom. With the signing of the Mutual Security Act of 1951, the groundwork was laid for full US co-operation with Latin American states. Moscow watched as these alliances bound countries in the Americas closer to Washington and in opposition to the USSR.

Why was the USA so keen to sign the Rio Treaty and help set up the Organization of American States? How do you think the USSR might have viewed the establishment of the OAS?

Through these treaties, the USA ensured that its interests in Latin America were protected – often by military dictators. As a result, Washington freely provided assistance to any nation whose defence was believed to be important to the United States. One example of this is the level of US involvement in Chile from 1945 onwards, in particular Washington's attempts to prevent the Marxist Salvador Allende being elected president of Chile in 1964. When Allende eventually *was* elected in 1970, the USA attempted to destabilise his government by encouraging fear of communist revolution in the Americas. You will read more about this in Chapter 7.

Washington's hold over Central America was also demonstrated by the overthrow of Guatemalan president Jacobo Árbenz in 1954. In his 1951 inaugural address, Árbenz declared that he would reduce foreign dependency and modernise Guatemala. He passed laws to nationalise uncultivated land, and paid compensation for any land taken in this way. The US-owned United Fruit Company (UFCO) owned large areas of land in Guatemala – 85% of it unused. Árbenz seized this land and a dispute arose over the level of compensation that was offered.

US concerns grew over developments in Guatemala when Árbenz legalised the Guatemalan Party of Labour. John Foster Dulles believed that this was the start of a communist takeover. His brother, Alan Dulles – then the director of the CIA – was ordered to develop a plan to overthrow Árbenz, and in June 1954 two US-piloted planes bombed civilian targets and communications in Guatemala.

Fearing a US invasion, the army deserted Árbenz, who resigned and sought refuge in the Mexican embassy before fleeing to Mexico with his family. A US-backed dictator, Castillo Armas, was installed and many of his political opponents were executed.

# What was the impact of the Cold War on aspects of US domestic policy?

The move from a wartime to a peacetime economy was significant in shaping domestic policy in the USA. The late 1940s and 1950s were a period of huge economic growth in the country, and the US seemed to be enjoying great prosperity after the difficult years of the Great Depression and the Second World War. Truman and then Eisenhower presided over a country that controlled half of the world's manufacturing output, and where per capita income was double that of any other nation. Demobilisation also resulted in 9 million men returning from the armed forces to boost the US workforce or enrol in further education.

Transport and air travel created jobs in the burgeoning service and travel industries. Technology, space exploration and the media set up new career opportunities and led to a rise in disposable income for many people. In 1949, 1 million families in the USA owned a television set; by 1960 this had risen to 45 million. This period also witnessed the rapid growth of car ownership and credit availability. It was estimated that well over 50% of the population enjoyed a middle-class lifestyle and shared in a consumer boom greater than that of the 1920s.

SOURCE E

Post-war America saw increases in college and university funding, with ex-servicemen wanting to continue or resume their studies. Industry switched from war production to the manufacture of consumer goods. More houses were built, town suburbs developed and home ownership increased rapidly. By the mid 1950s and the early years of Eisenhower's presidency, America had continually rising per capita income and employment.

Bottaro, J. and Stanley, J. 2011. Democratic States. *Cambridge, UK. Cambridge University Press*. p. 117.

There were still problems, however. Poverty remained a fact of life for many people. Minorities continued to encounter racism. The Civil Rights Movement was beginning to emerge, but issues such as racial equality, gender equality and greater commitments to health and welfare spending were not high profile. Rebuilding life in the post-war world, and the constant fear of subversion, were the dominant forces in society. This was a conservative era crying out for patriotism in the face of communism – the perceived enemy.

## The Red Scare

After 1945, fears about communism grew in the USA. The Gouzenko spy scandal in Canada (see page 99) caused serious concern, especially as Canada had been involved in atomic research during the Second World War. A number of people in key positions in the USA and Britain were also suspected of involvement in Soviet espionage. After a raid on the New York offices of the pro-communist magazine *Amerasia* unearthed classified government documents in March 1945, a fear of communism taking hold in North America developed rapidly. This marked the start of the 'Red Scare'.

In March 1947, Truman signed Executive Order 9835, introducing formal loyalty tests for government employees. Any links with communists, or groups believed to have communist sympathies, led to dismissal – although a Loyalty Review Board was established to deal with appeals. Even expressing an interest in Russian art, history, music or literature was grounds for suspicion, as fears of communist infiltration spread across the USA. Within four years, 1200 federal employees had been dismissed and 6000 had left their jobs in protest over what they called 'questionable procedures'.

## SOURCE F

In 1948 the Truman administration prosecuted eleven leaders of the Communist Party (CPUSA) under the Smith Act of 1940 ... the eleven were convicted and sentenced to five-year jail terms as well as fines of $10,000, losing appeals all the way to the Supreme Court, where the vote was 7-2 against them. In retrospect it is known that the leaders of the CPUSA were guilty of aiding and abetting Soviet spying in the United States, but this can hardly justify their persecution on the grounds merely of their beliefs. The Supreme Court declared the Smith Act unconstitutional in 1956 after the Red Scare had waned.

Levine, P. and Papasotiriou, H. 2005. America Since 1945. Basingstoke, UK. Palgrave Macmillan. p. 57.

### Discussion point

Source F raises several questions. Was the government right to prosecute the 11 CPUSA members, or should it have accepted their individual rights to certain beliefs? To what extent was the state creating an impression of anxiety in order to carry out these prosecutions? Even if we agree with prosecution on the basis of national loyalty, is loyalty a legitimate and morally acceptable way of assessing if someone is really a threat? How far might opinion on this episode be influenced by hindsight?

Truman took several steps to improve domestic security. The 1947 National Security Act created the Department of Defense to oversee all armed forces. It also established the National Security Council (NSC) to advise the president on defence and security issues, and the Central Intelligence agency (CIA) to gather information.

The situation worsened for government employees when Eisenhower took over. Oliver Edwards points out that 'loyalty tests became even more stringent and workers in all federal departments or agencies could be summarily dismissed if "reasonable doubt" existed about their suitability for government employment'. Some people lost their jobs simply because they had left-wing friends or relatives.

White segregationists in the South accused civil rights supporters and leaders such as Martin Luther King (see page 46) of being communists. Opponents of homosexuality called gay men 'communist faggots', while church preachers were investigated for evidence of homosexuality in their sermons. The state monitored literary and other cultural activities for unpatriotic content.

Fear of subversion was demonstrated most notoriously by the House Un-American Activities Committee (HUAC), which played a key role in investigating communist activity.

## Investigating or attacking culture? The Hollywood Ten

HUAC was set up in 1937 with the purpose of investigating subversive activities in the USA, whether they were carried out by left- or right-wing political groups. By the mid 1940s, however, with communist paranoia widespread across the country, the committee became more focused in its investigations.

Those on the far right of the political spectrum pointed out that there were many Jewish German and East European refugees amongst the writers, producers and directors in Hollywood. Many early left-wing revolutionaries had been Jewish, and a link was implied between these Hollywood workers and European socialism and communism (despite the fact that artistic communities tended to have a liberal or left-wing bias anyway). In response to concerns from the far right about communism at the heart of the film industry, HUAC turned its attention to Hollywood.

It was known that 300 members of the CPUSA (the US Communist Party) were based in Hollywood, most of them screenwriters. In 1947, many leading figures in the film industry were summoned to hearings in Washington. Some allowed themselves to be interviewed, but ten of them refused to answer any questions. The 'Hollywood Ten', as they became known, claimed that the First Amendment to the US Constitution gave them the right to refuse interrogation about their beliefs.

The Committee for the First Amendment – formed in support of the Hollywood Ten – included many high-profile actors, including Humphrey Bogart, Lauren Bacall and Danny Kaye. Several members of the committee travelled to Washington to demonstrate their opposition to HUAC's hearings. However, cinemas soon began boycotting films associated with anyone who supported the Hollywood Ten. In fear of financial ruin and long-term damage to their careers, actors, directors and producers withdrew their support.

The ten men were found guilty of contempt of Congress, and sentenced to between six and 12 months in prison. After spending some time behind bars, the director Edward Dmytryk decided to testify again before HUAC. This time he answered all the questions. He named 26 former members of left-wing groups and claimed that he had been put under pressure to express communist views in his films. His testimony was extremely damaging to those he named.

The president of the Screen Actors Guild (the actors' union) at this time was Ronald Reagan, who was active in helping the FBI identify communist sympathisers. The Guild compiled a blacklist of suspected communists. These people found themselves unable to work at any studio in Hollywood; many of them left the USA to try and rebuild their careers in other countries.

*Seven of the Hollywood Ten arrive at court to face charges of contempt of Congress; Edward Dmytryk (far right) later decided to testify before HUAC*

## Theory of knowledge

### History and propaganda

Propaganda techniques have been employed by many political parties and organisations. Use the internet to find the poster for the 1949 film *I Married a Communist*. Consider the way film posters like this might be used to convey a particular message. How does the poster try to influence reason and emotion? Or might it just be aimed at advertising an exciting film? Research other examples. Were they effective? Do images like these always have greater impact than the written word?

## McCarthy and the politics of anti-communism

One of the most notorious figures in the Red Scare era in the USA was Wisconsin senator Joseph McCarthy. He encouraged anti-communist sentiment by declaring that the USA was being overrun by 'Reds' and that this was destroying the country's greatness. McCarthy's activities as chairman of the Senate Permanent Investigation Subcommittee – conducting witch-hunts to uncover communist subversion in all areas of public life – gave rise to a new word in the vocabulary of US politics: 'McCarthyism'.

## Start of the witch-hunts 1950

In 1950, McCarthy began holding hearings on alleged communist activities in areas including the military, government administration, the media, science and industry. The senator claimed that he had the names of 205 known communists in the State Department. When challenged on this, McCarthy revised the list to 81 names. Later, this number dropped to 57 and finally McCarthy changed the accusations from 'card-carrying communists' to merely 'subversives'. Even though some said that McCarthy had no real evidence, his claims gained a great deal of attention in the press.

## Spies and lies

In January 1950, Alger Hiss – a high-level official in the State Department – was found guilty of perjury for passing classified US information to the Soviet Union during the late 1930s. Only the statute of limitations (which sets a time limit on when legal proceedings for a crime can begin) prevented him being charged with treason.

The Hiss case was not the only one to be discovered at this time. In Britain, German-born Klaus Fuchs confessed to committing espionage while working in the USA on the Manhattan Project (a US-led atomic research project headed by scientist J. Robert Oppenheimer, which had been set up before the USA entered the war in 1941). Fuchs had worked with Ethel Rosenberg's brother, David Greenglass, and Ethel and her husband Julius were named as co-conspirators in the wartime spy network. The Rosenbergs were arrested on charges of stealing atomic secrets for the Soviets. Despite protesting their innocence, they were both executed in 1953. Soviet documents released in the 1990s confirmed that both Klaus Fuchs and Julius Rosenberg really had been involved in spying activities. However, Ethel Rosenberg's guilt remains uncertain to this day.

## McCarthy, the SISS and the Church

In 1950, the US Senate established the Senate Internal Security Subcommittee (SISS), to investigate threats to national security. Concentrating on spying, sabotage and cultural subversion, the committee became more active when McCarthy took control of it in 1953. McCarthy used the committee to further develop his investigations into the influence of communism in the USA.

McCarthy paid particular attention to the overseas library programme of the State Department, and books by authors considered to be pro-communist or morally inappropriate were removed from the shelves. There was minimal outward resistance to such censorship, since any officials who criticised this decision risked being accused of having communist sympathies themselves.

McCarthy gained a strong following in the Church, where clergy were often encouraged to denounce communism from the pulpit. Cardinal Spellman, the archbishop of New York, was strongly anti-communist and a McCarthy supporter, and informed the FBI about suspected communists. As the historian Paul Boyer notes, McCarthy also found favour with blue-collar workers (manual labourers) when he declared that a person was either a true American who detested 'communists and queers' or an 'egg-sucking phoney liberal'.

## McCarthy's downfall

By 1954, however, McCarthy's influence was declining. He was increasingly regarded as a trouble-maker who relied on people's fear of persecution to carry out his anti-communist activities without opposition.

McCarthy's fall from public favour was completed by his investigations into an alleged US army spy ring. Despite little evidence, McCarthy singled out a respected army dentist, demanding to know why he had been promoted to the rank of major when he had refused to answer certain questions on a loyalty form. This case culminated in the *Army versus McCarthy* hearings, which were televised before a nationwide audience approaching 20 million people. McCarthy's disrespectful conduct and lack of proof angered both the viewing public and many people in positions of authority. By 1955, McCarthy had been formally reprimanded by the Senate and his position as a prominent force in anti-communism had ended.

### Activity

Re-read the information on the Red Scare. Was McCarthyism a product of the external problems facing the USA? Or was it more a reflection of domestic attitudes and fears? Write two paragraphs, each one arguing for a different reason.

# Cold War influences on education and civil rights

## Education

At the start of the Cold War, schools, colleges and universities were carefully monitored for signs of communist propaganda.

By 1950, HUAC had asked for reading lists for students from over 70 educational institutions. By 1953, 39 states had created loyalty programmes that required teachers, professors and lecturers to sign an oath of loyalty or risk losing their job. In particular, university campuses were regarded as potential breeding-grounds for left-wing activity. At Yale University, college administrators worked with the FBI to spy on students, academics and applicants for jobs and fellowships. Three professors at the University of Washington were dismissed for alleged links with the CPUSA; they never found academic employment again. In California, more than 30 academics were dismissed from university and college posts.

This overseeing of education was based on the belief that 'the right message' about God-fearing American values (as opposed to the 'barbarity' of communist societies), must be heard at all times. The US Department of Education launched a campaign called Zeal for Democracy, in which local school authorities received government-created curriculum material aimed at raising awareness of the need to 'combat communist subversion'.

Those on the political right felt that the classroom should be a 'chapel of democracy', and many educated but controversial speakers and academics were banned from holding seminars or making lecture tours. Children's books, comics and student magazines contained articles with titles such as 'The Reds are after you' or 'Beware of commies, spies and foreign agents'.

Eisenhower's administration introduced even stricter loyalty tests. However, Eisenhower also realised that America would have to surpass the USSR in producing highly qualified scientists and technicians in the Cold War struggle – a fact that was emphasised by the Soviet launch of the first satellite, *Sputnik*, in 1957. The National Defense Education Act (NDEA) of 1958 issued a grant of almost $900 million, to be spent specifically on teaching languages and science, and to contribute towards student loans for people taking science-related courses.

The NDEA was created with two goals in mind. Firstly, it was designed to provide the USA with people who were specially trained in issues relating to defence. This included providing financial assistance to foreign-language scholars, area-studies centres and engineering students. Secondly, through the National Defense Student Loan Program, financial aid was provided to the growing number of students enrolling to study science at colleges and universities in the 1960s. In 1940, about half a million Americans attended college; by 1960, college enrolments had risen to around 3.6 million.

Thus, education in the United States became linked to wider Cold War concerns and policies. Shortly after the Soviets launched *Sputnik*, the influential political theorist Hannah Arendt commented that 'only in America could a crisis in education actually become a factor in politics'.

## Civil rights

The campaign for black civil rights began to evolve in the USA after 1945. Many African-Americans served in the armed forces during the Second World War, and witnessed the greater racial integration in Britain and Europe. The National Association for the Advancement of Colored People (NAACP) had existed since 1909, but its membership increased dramatically in the 1940s, and by 1946 it was represented in almost every state. In part, civil rights in the US came to the fore because of the onset of the Cold War and the Red Scare. As anti-communists demanded American freedom and democracy, it became clear that there were double standards that needed to be addressed in other areas of American society.

### SOURCE C

Liberal white people, especially in the north, were also conscious of the US role in the Cold War against the Soviet Union. How could the USA champion individual freedom in the world generally while denying it to an important minority in its own country? ... However, this could have a downside. The strong anti-communism of post-war and Cold War USA meant that campaigning groups and individuals could be accused of communism by leading figures such as Senator Joseph McCarthy; hence the NAACP was banned in Alabama in 1956, and even felt obliged to organise a 'purge' of its supposedly communist members.

Paterson, D. and Willoughby, S. 2001. *Civil Rights in the USA 1863–1980.* Oxford, UK. Heinemann. p. 107.

The Civil Rights Congress (CRC) was formed in 1946 when a number of organisations united to strengthen their campaign and petition the government more effectively in civil rights cases. Because several of its members had connections to the US Communist Party, the CRC was declared subversive and pro-Soviet by President Truman. During the Red Scare the CRC continued to criticise discrimination against black people, including segregated housing, the denial of voting rights, and unfair treatment by the legal system.

However, the climate of fear sometimes had a negative effect on key members of the Civil Rights Movement. One such example was an African-American lawyer and communist, Benjamin J. Davis. In 1943 Davis successfully ran for New York City Council, representing Harlem. He openly announced his Communist Party membership and gradually gained both black and white support. By 1946 he had links with the CRC and, with its support, was re-elected twice to his Harlem seat. Many hoped that his influence on such an important council as New York City might encourage growth on a wider scale and enable the CRC to make a major breakthrough on the national political scene, overcoming regional, ethnic and racial boundaries.

However, in the climate of the Cold War, New York City Council deliberately amended its rules for electing new members. Davis lost overwhelmingly to an anti-communist candidate in 1949, and was then convicted of conspiring to overthrow the federal government due to his association with the communists. He appealed against the conviction for two years, without success. Former supporters began to leave the CRC. In 1954, the US attorney-general declared the CRC to be a subversive organisation and it was dissolved in 1956 – just as the civil rights campaign in the South was emerging as a mass movement under the NAACP.

Strong anti-communist feeling made any protests or potential confrontations involving civil rights less likely, as people feared reprisal or implication by association. The more militant supporters of civil rights lost favour with both mainstream black America and the NAACP, which disapproved of violent methods. In order to secure a place in wider US society, civil rights leaders agreed that the success of the movement depended on it openly distancing itself from any communist associations.

## Discussion point

It has been said that the anti-communist mood in the USA in 1945–55 seemed to stifle reform of any kind. How might this have affected the progress of the Civil Rights Movement?

Many civil rights leaders and organisations were investigated by the FBI. Indeed, FBI bugging and telephone tapping of suspected radicals and supporters of African-American civil rights increased generally. The head of the FBI, J. Edgar Hoover, even had the home of famous Manhattan Project scientist J. Robert Oppenheimer bugged, after he was classified as a security risk because of his left-wing relatives and friends.

In 1955, a Baptist minister and civil rights campaigner, Dr Martin Luther King, came to prominence during a black boycott of segregated bus services in the town of Montgomery, Alabama. The boycott evolved into an African-American organisation that became known as the Montgomery Improvement Association (MIA). As a result of this, King became leader of the new Southern Christian Leadership Conference (SLCL) in 1957. He was soon placed under observation by the FBI.

The campaign for civil rights had to involve itself less in direct protest, and instead make legal challenges to segregation and discrimination, especially in areas such as education, voting and working conditions. Historian Mary L. Dudziak has shown how communist critics could easily point out how hypocritical it was for the USA to portray itself as the leader of the free world when so many of its citizens were discriminated against. In particular, Dudziak suggests that this pushed the US government into supporting civil rights legislation.

In 1957, nine black students enrolled at the previously all-white high school in Little Rock, Arkansas. After public protests at this integration, Eisenhower sent 1000 paratroopers to restore order and escort the black students to classes to ensure their safety.

In February 1960, a sit-in protest began at the Woolworth's lunch counter in Greensboro, North Carolina, when black students refused to leave a whites-only counter. This and similar protests highlighted the fact that meal segregation was a symptom of a much wider problem. Support groups sprang up in northern colleges and among white students, and the SCLC helped different civil rights groups and organisations. Peaceful protest moved towards co-ordinated challenge and, by 1961, 800 towns and cities had desegregated public areas.

The Greensboro sit-in marked a new phase in the Civil Rights Movement. The fact that it had taken place in North Carolina was of particular significance: this state was less racist than Alabama, Mississippi, Georgia or South Carolina. As a result, prominent white politicians were able to express sympathy for the students' cause. Terry Sandford, later elected governor of North Carolina, was particularly supportive. The instigators of the sit-in were college students who were articulate, idealistic and fired with a determination fuelled by the knowledge that they had no jobs to be dismissed from – and this brought a new dimension to the protest.

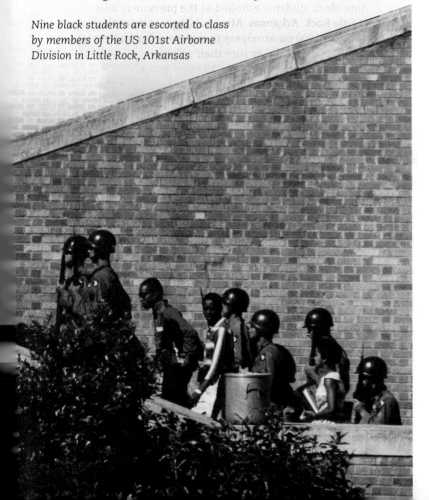

*Nine black students are escorted to class by members of the US 101st Airborne Division in Little Rock, Arkansas*

Black and white students across the USA were inspired by the Greensboro sit-in, and many similar protests occurred across the South. Young people were also motivated into forming groups determined to desegregate many other types of public facility. However, much of the Deep South remained untouched by this level of protest, and many people were highly outspoken against such attempts at desegregation.

In reality, the Cold War climate of the 1950s and early 1960s was not ideal for the rapid advancement of African-American rights. The Red Scare and anti-communist hysteria made members of the Civil Rights Movement reluctant to express objections or protest militantly. Legal campaigns did achieve some success, but association with the left and communists caused problems – as can be seen in the outlawing of the NAACP in Alabama. The FBI frequently monitored the SCLC, and many people in the USA saw a link between support for civil rights and disloyalty towards America.

### Activity

How did the Cold War climate of fear affect civil rights organisations? Re-read the text on civil rights and carry out some additional research of your own, then make a list of any ways you think civil rights actions succeeded between 1945 and 1960. Now swap lists with another student. Discuss your findings.

## America 1945–61 in retrospect

The obsession with communism, together with growing prosperity, prevented the development of liberal social reform until the 1960s. Paul Levine and Harry Papasotiriou argue that the USA from 1945 to 1961 was 'an era of social complacency and intellectual darkness' – everything the 1960s generation eventually rebelled against. Characteristics of this 'social complacency' included being afraid to speak up against blacklisting, racism, betrayal, small-town morality, increased political control of education, media propaganda, nuclear stand-offs and the role of women in society.

### Women's position in US society

An influential book published in 1947, *Modern Women: the Lost Sex*, argued that post-war problems such as alcoholism, teenage hooliganism and pregnancy outside marriage were a result of changes in family life. Women were blamed for choosing to pursue careers rather than traditional roles. Journals encouraged women to return to domestic life. Home appliances such as washing machines and fridges were advertised as 'every woman's dream', and an idealised middle-class suburban lifestyle was promoted, in which men worked while women shopped, baked and held Tupperware parties.

However, many women found the return to domesticity dull after the freedom that war work had opened up to them. By 1960, nearly 40% of adult women were members of the US labour force, and 25% of married women chose to work rather than remain at home. The rise in numbers of working women coincided with a growing sense of personal control over their lives. This sense of freedom was boosted substantially in 1960, when the contraceptive pill was made available for the first time, ushering in the era of women's liberation.

## Health reform

It can be argued that the major health and welfare reforms later instituted under President Lyndon B. Johnson (see page 84) ought to have taken place during the relatively more affluent 1950s, but there were problems with perception. Congress rejected laws proposed by President Truman that would have allowed federal aid for national health insurance. Historians have claimed that such a liberal welfare reform – with the state overseeing workers' contributions and deductions – might have appeared suspiciously like Eastern European state socialism with its centrally controlled economic policy.

The lack of reform largely continued under Eisenhower. His administration oversaw increased funding for the National Institute of Health in 1957–58, but the reintroduction of a national health insurance act – the Forland Bill of 1958 – met with conservative opposition. The conservatives felt that it would encroach on the rights of individual states, while some said that it was too socialist. The Forland Bill was defeated.

## 'The politics of tranquillity'?

The Red Scare and McCarthyism were ever-present in the late 1940s and early 1950s, but other factors may have shaped the apparent standstill on the home front. Rising income and affluence led many to look inwards and focus on their family, street and neighbourhood, ignoring events and influences in the wider world.

Many older Americans had grown weary of years of economic depression and war. Younger Americans were often apolitical, or were disillusioned veterans more anxious to find work, marry and start a family than take an active part in political reform.

Perhaps this was just not the time for argument or controversy. Americans often associate this era with a series of cultural icons such as Marilyn Monroe, Frank Sinatra, Ernest Hemingway and Joe di Maggio; or with the 'American Dream' of a suburban home, job security and a new car. These 'politics of tranquillity' were undermined during Kennedy's short presidency, due to the crises over Cuba and Berlin, which you will read about in the next chapter.

# End of chapter activities

## Paper 3 exam practice

### Question

'A nation filled with <u>anxiety</u> and <u>suspicion</u>.' <u>To what extent</u> is this a valid description of the USA from <u>1945 to 1961</u>?
[20 marks]

### Skill

Understanding the wording of a question

### Examiner's tips

The first step in producing a high-scoring essay is to look **closely** at the wording of the question, and every year students lose valuable marks by failing to do so. It is therefore important to start by identifying the **key or 'command' words** in the question. In the question above, these command words are as follows:

- anxiety
- suspicion
- to what extent ...?
- 1945 to 1961

Key words are intended to give you clear instructions about what you need to cover in your essay – hence they are sometimes called 'command' words. If you ignore them, you will not score high marks, no matter how precise and accurate your knowledge of the period.

For the question above, you need to cover the following aspects of the USA in 1945–61:

- **anxiety**: US concerns about Soviet gains in Eastern Europe; the Berlin Blockade; China coming under a communist regime; the USSR becoming a nuclear state; the war in Korea; the Soviet invasion of Hungary; the launch of *Sputnik*; Castro's revolution.
- **suspicion**: this requires discussion of *suspicion of people* – domestic espionage; spy networks; watching and informing on your neighbours; the Red Scare; McCarthy's purges; the media; academia; anyone who was 'different'. It should also cover *suspicion of politicians* – looking for evidence of leftist reforms and policies; civil rights campaigners, etc.

- **to what extent ...?**: this requires an analytical argument structured to show how you think the statement is *and* is not valid (the USA had many strengths during this Cold War period, and in some areas displayed confidence as opposed to anxiety); this should involve, where relevant, consideration and evaluation of different historical interpretations/views.
- **1945 to 1961**: a view of the whole period is the focus here. Be careful to select your examples from the time period specified in the question.

## Common mistakes

Under exam pressure, two types of mistakes are particularly common.

The first is to begin by giving some pre-1945 context, but then to continue writing a narrative account of this period. It is true that a brief reference to the situation just before 1945 will help to put your answer into context. However, the period before 1945 must not be any **significant** part of your answer. As the question focuses on 1945–61, such an answer would only score low marks, no matter how detailed and accurate your knowledge of the USA prior to 1945.

The other – more common – mistake is to focus **entirely** on the dates. This will almost certainly lead you to write a general account of what happened during this period. Such a narrative-based answer will not score highly, as it will not explicitly address the 'to what extent' part of the question. So, select **relevant** events from the period and use them to develop an argument that is **analytical** and uses **supporting evidence**.

Both of these mistakes can be avoided by focusing carefully on the wording of the question.

For more on how to avoid irrelevant and narrative answers, see pages 148 and 178 respectively.

## Activity

In this chapter, the focus is on understanding the question and producing a brief essay plan. Look again at the question, the tips and the simplified markscheme on page 219. Now, using the information from this chapter and any other sources of information available to you, draw up an essay plan (perhaps in the form of a spider diagram) that includes all the necessary headings for a well-focused and clearly structured response to the question.

# Paper 3 practice questions

1 'Fear of communism was the driving force behind US domestic policy from 1945 to 1961.' To what extent do you agree with this view?

2 For what reasons, and with what results, did Joseph McCarthy carry out an anti-communist campaign between 1947 and 1954?

3 Examine the impact of the Truman Doctrine and the policy of containment on US relations with Latin America in the period 1945–61.

4 How far did Eisenhower's Cold War policy differ from Truman's?

5 'Americans in the 1950s were living in an era of social complacency and intellectual darkness.' To what extent do you agree with this assertion?

# 3 The USA and the Cold War 1961–81

## Key questions

- How did Kennedy define US foreign policy from 1961 to 1963?
- Why did the Vietnam War have such a profound effect on the USA?
- How did US foreign policy change under Nixon in the 1970s?
- Why was Jimmy Carter an 'outsider' in foreign policy 1977–81?
- What were the implications of US foreign policy for the wider Americas between 1961 and 1981?
- How did the Cold War further influence domestic policy in the USA between 1961 and 1981?

This chapter examines the continued impact of the Cold War on US foreign and domestic policy from 1961 to 1981. It focuses on the Cuban Missile Crisis – considered by many historians to be the most dangerous moment of the Cold War – and on US involvement in Vietnam and the influence this had on US society. This chapter also discusses US foreign policy from Kennedy to Carter, notably Kennedy's Alliance for Progress, Nixon's covert operations in Chile, Carter's ethical foreign policy and the Panama Canal settlement.

## Overview

- In the 1950s, the US experienced previously unknown prosperity, and many working-class families enjoyed middle-class lifestyles. However, groups such as the African-American community remained marginalised.
- In 1961, Kennedy brought energy and a reforming government to the White House. His Alliance for Progress organisation sought economic and political co-operation between the USA and the rest of the Americas. Despite this, Kennedy faced major crises over events in Berlin and Cuba during his presidency.
- After Kennedy's death, Johnson and later Nixon presided over the Vietnam War – an event that polarised the USA and led to domestic upheaval.
- The desire for better relations with China and the USSR resulted in a period of détente (a lessening of tension and greater co-operation during the Cold War) in the 1970s; however, this decade also saw presidential disgrace for Nixon after the Watergate scandal.
- Carter's presidency offered a fresh start, with a search for international peace and an emphasis on human rights.
- Carter negotiated peace between Egypt and Israel, and the SALT II agreement with the USSR. However, he was criticised within the USA for returning the Canal Zone to Panama. Carter also faced the Soviet invasion of Afghanistan and the Iran hostage crisis.
- Carter's challenger for the presidency in 1980, Ronald Reagan, spoke of the USA's 'malaise' and the need to find 'morning' again in America. When Reagan became president in 1981, he addressed the USSR forcefully about the need to find a resolution to the two countries' Cold War differences.

## How did Kennedy define US foreign policy from 1961 to 1963?

By 1960, the USA was growing in wealth and consumer confidence. However, there were still many white people living in poverty, as well as a marginalised black community. These factors contributed to a growing sense of unease among younger people, who believed that the USA was drifting towards a more polarised society.

The McCarthy era had passed, but anxieties remained over the situation in Berlin (see page 24) and Soviet advances in science and technology. The Korean War and the USSR's suppression of the 1956 Hungarian Uprising caused the US government to focus on opposing communism anywhere in the world. The escalating war in Vietnam, anxieties over Cuba, and watchfulness towards events in China and the Americas characterised US foreign policy from 1961.

John F. Kennedy delivers a televised address to the nation about the Cuban Missile Crisis in October 1962

## Background to the Berlin and Cuba crises

Stalin's death in 1953, the 1955 Geneva Summit (see page 31) and Nikita Khrushchev's (see page 30) visit to the USA in 1959 all contributed to a 'thaw' between the superpowers and moves towards peaceful coexistence. However, relations only improved superficially.

By 1957, the USSR had developed inter-continental ballistic missiles (ICBMs), capable of travelling nearly 5000 km (3000 miles) in 30 minutes, leaving Earth's atmosphere and splitting into multiple nuclear warheads. China's nuclear capability was edging closer to completion, whilst Germany's future, the revolution in Cuba, and the U-2 spy-plane incident (see page 32) all heightened Cold War tensions. The situation was therefore already delicate when John F. Kennedy became president in 1961.

Kennedy's inaugural address was both a rallying cry and a warning about the communist threat. 'Let every nation know,' he stated, 'whether it wishes us well or ill, that we shall pay any price, bear any burden, meet any hardship, support any friend, oppose any foe to assure the survival and success of liberty.'

In preparation for this battle, Kennedy began to develop a strategy of 'flexible response' – increasing the country's stock of conventional weapons to enable it to fight limited wars wherever needed. This marked a shift from Eisenhower's policy of 'massive retaliation', which relied on a nuclear response. Kennedy continued with a moderate expansion of the USA's nuclear arsenal, but he wanted to limit the nuclear arms race.

## Activity

Using books, the internet and any other resources available to you, find out more about Kennedy's strategy of 'flexible response'. What does this term mean? What did this policy aim to achieve?

# The Berlin Wall

During Eisenhower's presidency, Khrushchev demanded that the West recognise East Germany (the German Democratic Republic) and accept the whole of Berlin as a free city and an independent political entity. However, Eisenhower ignored him. When Kennedy came to power, Khrushchev hoped that the new president's inexperience would work in the USSR's favour.

When the two men first met (in Vienna in June 1961), Khrushchev asked the Western powers to stop allowing West Berlin to be used as an escape route for East Germans, whose departure was causing a drain of skilled professionals – particularly doctors, engineers and teachers – in the GDR. Despite Khrushchev's hopes, Kennedy refused to make any concessions. As a result, in August 1961 the East German government erected a barbed-wire fence between the two parts of Berlin. When this failed to halt the flow of refugees to the West, work quickly began on a concrete wall.

Kennedy said of the situation in Berlin: 'It's not a very nice solution, but a wall is a hell of a lot better than a war.' What do you think Kennedy's comment suggests about the success or failure of his policy of 'flexible response'?

*Workers from East Germany building the Berlin Wall in November 1961*

# The Bay of Pigs invasion

In January 1961, diplomatic relations between Cuba and the USA were broken off (see page 34). On 15 April that year, the CIA assisted around 1400 anti-Castro Cuban exiles in making air attacks to destroy Castro's air force in preparation for a land invasion. The landings themselves took place two days later at the Bay of Pigs, on Cuba's south coast.

The invasion proved to be a humiliation for the USA. The US-armed exiles expected local support, but this failed to materialise. In addition, Kennedy refused to authorise support from the US air force, so the invasion force had little back-up. They were quickly halted by Castro's army. Ninety of the invaders were killed and the rest were captured.

## SOURCE A

The danger of Kennedy's preferred style of foreign policy exploded for all the world to see in the Bay of Pigs operation in Cuba. Ironically, the Castro revolution against the Batista regime represented at its inception, the kind of democratic insurgency against totalitarian forces that Kennedy wished to identify with. But Castro had turned against the USA, had allied with the Soviet Union and had become, as result, a primary target of American hostility.

*Chafe, W. H. 2003. The Unfinished Journey: America Since World War II. New York, USA. Oxford University Press. p. 194*

Despite the humiliation of this defeat, in November 1961 Kennedy authorised Operation Mongoose 'to help Cuba overthrow the communist regime'. This plan allowed for the use of military force, but its main intention was to weaken Castro's regime and encourage internal rebellion in Cuba. Kennedy knew that despite his hopes, such a rebellion was unlikely, so he also developed plans for another land-based invasion. In March 1962, a series of large military manoeuvres were carried out in the Caribbean (Operation Quick Kick). This show of US power persuaded Khrushchev that Cuba would be quickly defeated in the event of a US attack. As a result, the Soviet leader decided to place both long- and short-range nuclear missiles on the island.

### SOURCE B

The fate of Cuba and the maintenance of Soviet prestige in that part of the world preoccupied me ... We had to establish a tangible and effective deterrent to American interference in the Caribbean ... We knew that American missiles were aimed against us in Turkey and Italy, to say nothing of West Germany.

Khrushchev, N. 1970. Khrushchev Remembers. Quoted in Rayner, E. G. 1992. The Cold War. London, UK. pp. 50–51.

## The Cuban Missile Crisis

On 14 October 1962, a U-2 spy plane photographed the construction of one of the nuclear missile bases on Cuba. The US government was warned that the missiles would be operational within ten days and that, if activated, they could reach US cities. Kennedy immediately called a meeting of his National Security Council and, on 22 October, he made a televised announcement that he was imposing a 'quarantine' on Cuba. Kennedy chose his language carefully – using the word 'blockade' would have suggested an act of war. In fact several historians, including John Aldred and Mike Sewell, have questioned whether Kennedy's order to stop and search all ships bound for Cuba was technically an act of war anyway.

Kennedy's quarantine forced Khrushchev to respond. If the Soviet leader submitted to the quarantine and allowed all Soviet ships heading to Cuba to be searched, his own position would be weakened. However, refusing to honour Kennedy's demands might force the USA into a military response – a situation Khrushchev wanted to avoid. This became the most extreme example of Cold War brinkmanship.

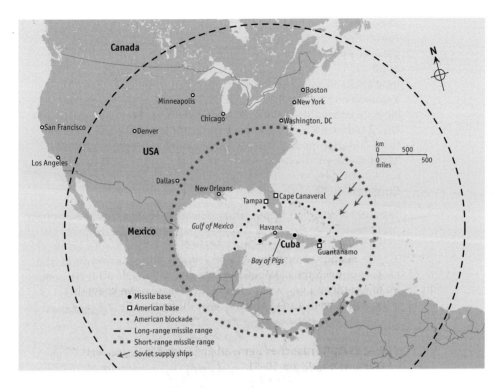

*The Cuban Missile Crisis, October 1962*

## The 'Thirteen Days'

Khrushchev argued that the missile sites being built on Cuba were 'solely to defend the island against the attack of an aggressor', and accused Kennedy of piracy by imposing the quarantine. Around 20 Soviet ships were heading for Cuba at the time, and Khrushchev warned that the USSR would not respect the blockade and would give 'a fitting reply to the aggressor'. The first Russian ship reached the quarantine zone on 24 October but, as an oil ship, it was allowed through. To international relief, the other Soviet ships stopped or turned around when they reached the zone later the same day.

On 26 October, Kennedy announced that he would invade Cuba if the missiles were not removed. Khrushchev sent a telegram to Kennedy, agreeing to dismantle the missiles if the US lifted the quarantine and promised not to attempt another invasion of Cuba. However, before Kennedy had a chance to respond, Khrushchev sent another, more aggressive, telegram. This demanded that the USA dismantle its Jupiter missiles in Turkey, which were very close to Soviet cities. Shortly afterwards, an American U-2 plane was shot down over Cuba.

Kennedy ignored both the U-2 incident and Khrushchev's second communication. Instead, after consulting his brother (the US attorney-general, Robert Kennedy), he sent a reply to the first telegram, agreeing to lift the blockade and stating that he would not invade Cuba as long as the missile bases there were taken down. In secret, Robert Kennedy met with the Soviet ambassador to the United States, Anatoly Dobrynin, and offered to remove the missiles in Turkey. On 28 October, Khrushchev gave the order to remove the missiles from Cuba. Kennedy lifted the blockade and the crisis ended after 13 tense days.

## Consequences of the crisis

The Cuban crisis led all the major powers to realise that some control over the nuclear arms race was essential. One significant consequence of the crisis, therefore, was the Partial Nuclear Test Ban Treaty of August 1963. This was signed by the USA, the USSR and Britain, and banned atmospheric and outer-space tests. The treaty did not cover underground testing, but it was an early step towards détente – a word used to describe a period of reduced tension and increased co-operation during the Cold War.

The crisis improved Kennedy's popularity – he became known as the man who successfully challenged the USSR. In contrast, Khrushchev lost prestige: many people believed that he simply responded to events rather than being in control of them.

## Historical perspectives on the Cuban Missile Crisis

Historian Mike Sewell considers the Cuban Missile Crisis to be the 'moment when the Cold War changed from being a confrontation focused on the perimeters of the USSR and China to a global one'. Certainly the crisis widened the scope for conflict. As the struggle for ideological influence reached the Caribbean, states in South America and Africa watched with growing concern.

While the resolution of the crisis was the starting point for improved superpower relations, Paul Levine and Harry Papasotiriou have noted that 'Soviet archives show that the primary Soviet objective was to deter an American invasion of Cuba rather than to change the strategic balance'. However, John Lewis Gaddis believes that the USSR intended 'to spread revolution through Latin America'. It has also been suggested that the crisis may have been part of a necessary response by the USSR to challenge China's growing influence in international communism.

Khrushchev may have begun placing missiles on Cuba in a deliberate attempt to show the USA that despite the widening gap between US and Soviet missile capability, the USSR was still a power to be reckoned with. The missile bases on Cuba could be easily seen by US spy planes, yet the Soviets did little to conceal them. Some revisionist historians have suggested that the episode was part of a wider plan by Khrushchev to force the USA to discuss missile reduction. This would enable the Soviet leader to divert defence spending into agriculture and industry, both of which were stagnating.

Some historians believe that in fact Khrushchev triumphed from the crisis: Cuba was secure, the USA promised not to invade, and Washington was left with a pro-Soviet neighbour. For the same reasons, many Americans felt that containment of communism had failed. During the crisis the USA had hinted at a greater military power than it really had, to pressure Khrushchev into withdrawing the missiles. In reality, the Cuban Missile Crisis made future nuclear war less likely, as both sides realised how close they had come to outright war, and became aware of the need to exercise some control over the nuclear arms race. Historian Richard Crockett later commented that 'détente itself showed the impress of the missile crisis'.

In Cuba, Castro was able to consolidate his power and – feeling betrayed by Khrushchev's handling of the crisis – he was determined to proceed with his revolution in his own way. According to J. M. Roberts, Castro was now viewed as 'a revolutionary magnet in Latin America' in consequence of 'a crisis which had by far transcended the history of the hemisphere'.

## Discussion point

When debating the Cuban Missile Crisis, historians examine the actions of the USA and Cuba, as well as evaluating Khrushchev's motives for intervention. Look at Sources A (page 57) and B (page 58) and the text in this section. Consider the following questions:

1 What were the immediate causes of the Cuban Missile Crisis?
2 Why did Khrushchev act as he did?
3 Was the outcome of the Cuban crisis a victory for the USA or the USSR?
4 What was the immediate impact of the crisis on the Cold War?
5 What message might the events of October 1962 have sent to the states of Central and South America?

# Why did the Vietnam War have such a profound effect on the USA?

## Kennedy's inheritance

Before the Second World War, Vietnam was part of the French Empire. In 1930, the Vietnamese nationalist Ho Chi Minh became the leader of the Communist Party of Indochina; in 1941, the Communist Party joined a wide variety of other political groups to form the Viet Minh. Led by Ho Chi Minh, the Viet Minh's aim was to gain independence from France – by armed force if necessary. During the Second World War, Indochina (Vietnam, Cambodia and Laos) was taken over by the Japanese, and from 1943 the Viet Minh carried out a military campaign against this occupation. Ho assumed that the US would support his fight for independence; however, the US was afraid that communism might spread beyond Indochina, and so it decided to help France regain dominance in the region.

France had been fighting a war against the Viet Minh for several years, and during this time the USA provided the French with $2.6 billion in aid. However, defeat at the Battle of Dien Bien Phu in 1954 marked the end of French ambitions in Indochina. At a peace conference in Geneva, Vietnam was temporarily divided into a pro-US South and a communist North.

> ### Discussion point
>
> If a country such as the USA or the USSR gives support and weapons to another state simply because that state opposes a common rival, a mutual enemy or a conflicting ideology, is that support morally devalued if the recipient state is repressive or dictatorial?

In 1956, the South Vietnamese president Ngo Dinh Diem refused to honour one of the terms of the Geneva peace agreement and hold unification elections, afraid that Ho would win. By 1958, the Viet Cong (South Vietnamese communists) were fighting a guerrilla war against the South Vietnamese government. Ho Chi Minh announced his intention to reunite Vietnam, and encouraged the Viet Cong to form the National Liberation Front (NLF) in union with other anti-Diem forces. The USA sent 2000 military advisors to help organise and train the South Vietnamese in their fight against this communist alliance. By 1963, the number of US advisors in the region had reached 16,000.

The events unfolding in Indochina caused serious concern in the West, where many believed in the 'domino theory' – the idea that if one country fell to communism, others would quickly follow like a row of dominoes. Kennedy believed that Vietnam was 'the cornerstone of the free world in Southeast Asia', and stated that other countries – Laos, Cambodia, Burma, Thailand and India – would be threatened if 'the red tide of communism overflowed into Vietnam'. Increasingly, Kennedy came to view the conflict in Vietnam as crucial to the USA's strength and influence in the wider context of the Cold War.

## The steps to war

Kennedy initially received conflicting advice about Vietnam. The French warned that committing to war would trap the USA in a 'bottomless military and political swamp'. However, other politicians and military advisors assured the president that the US was better equipped than France and could win the fight. Eventually, Kennedy financed an increase in South Vietnam's army from 150,000 to 170,000 troops.

In 1962, Kennedy introduced the policy of Strategic Hamlets to Vietnam. Vietnamese peasants were moved into almost 3000 fortified villages to protect them from attack by the Viet Cong. This policy failed badly: nearly half of these villages were destroyed and thousands lost their homes. Many people felt that Strategic Hamlets destroyed centuries of village life by moving peasants from their land and family burial sites. This caused thousands of South Vietnamese peasants to support the Viet Cong, and during the period that this policy was in operation, NLF membership increased by 300%.

At the same time, it was clear that Diem's regime was becoming increasingly corrupt. Applying a suitably 'flexible response', Kennedy and his top CIA and Pentagon officials did nothing when generals of the Army of the Republic of South Vietnam (ARVN) overthrew and then murdered Diem on 1 November 1963.

> Why did Kennedy place such importance on Vietnam? It has been suggested that Kennedy's opinion about Vietnam was influenced by the Cuban Missile Crisis. Why might there be a connection between these two events? How did Kennedy's administration apply a 'flexible response' to the corruption in Diem's regime?

## Historical perspectives on Kennedy and Vietnam

Clearly Kennedy had to consider the impact his decisions about Vietnam would have on his 1964 re-election. Derrick Murphy suggests that Kennedy bought time to install a South Vietnamese government that would eventually allow the US to withdraw. However, James N. Giglio argues that Kennedy was unlikely to have pulled out of Vietnam without first obtaining an honourable settlement.

It is likely that neither Kennedy nor, later on, Johnson had a contingency plan to deal with the consequences of increased military involvement in a far-away country with mountainous jungle terrain. However, Kennedy's sense of idealism may have triumphed over the practical problems of carrying out such a military campaign. Some have argued that Kennedy believed the communists posed a real challenge to the USA's status in the wider world in the early 1960s. Certainly China and the USSR dominated Southeast Asia, and the USA could not afford to surrender influence to the communist powers. Levine and Papasotiriou pursue this idea, suggesting that abandoning South Vietnam would destroy US credibility in the eyes of the world.

Whatever Kennedy's motives, he tied the USA to South Vietnam's fate. After coming to power, Johnson waited 16 months before committing troops to the region, but at this point he saw little alternative – the only way to save South Vietnam was by escalating the fight.

## Johnson's escalation 1964–68

By the time **Lyndon B. Johnson** took over the presidency in November 1963, 35% of South Vietnam was controlled by the Viet Cong. More troops were required to continue containment, and Johnson needed both congressional approval and public support to send them.

**Lyndon B. Johnson (1908–73)** Johnson was elected to the House of Representatives in 1937 and became a senator in 1948. Losing the 1960 Democratic nomination to Kennedy, he became vice-president and took over on Kennedy's death. Johnson began a 'war on poverty' as part of his Great Society program, but his achievements were overshadowed by the costly and increasingly unpopular Vietnam War. He remained president until 1969.

### The Tonkin Resolution and Rolling Thunder

An opportunity to win public support arose with the Gulf of Tonkin incident. In August 1964, the US destroyer ship *Maddox* was fired on by North Vietnamese patrol boats during an intelligence-gathering operation. As a result, Congress passed the Gulf of Tonkin Resolution, which gave Johnson the authority to 'take all necessary steps including the use of armed force' to protect South Vietnam. Effectively, Johnson could continue the fight without making any formal declaration of war.

### Activity

Some historians regard the Gulf of Tonkin Resolution as the trigger for the Vietnam War. Do you agree? Re-read the last few pages. Can you suggest an alternative starting point?

In 1965, Johnson launched Operation Rolling Thunder, which involved strategic air strikes on North Vietnam. In March 1965, the first ground forces – two battalions of US marines – landed at Da Nang. By 1968, US forces in the region numbered 540,000 and had largely taken over the South Vietnamese army's fight against the Viet Cong. The communists were aided by equipment from North Vietnam, which in turn received supplies from the USSR.

During the bombing raids, the North Vietnamese moved production out of the capital, Hanoi. In fact, US bombers hit few real targets in the cities, but the use of chemical weapons such as napalm to destroy the Viet Cong's jungle cover had a devastating effect on Vietnamese civilians. Over 3 million acres of vegetation were destroyed, ruining communities and livelihoods, and causing health problems. It is estimated that between 1965 and 1968, more bombs were dropped on North Vietnam alone than upon Germany, Italy and Japan combined during the Second World War. Such devastation unsurprisingly aroused a great deal of anti-US sentiment among the Vietnamese people.

The Ho Chi Minh Trail also allowed the continued movement of supplies to communist supporters in the South. This complex system of jungle tracks, footpaths, truck routes and river navigations meant that it was difficult for US troops to intercept supplies. Unfamiliar jungle terrain and climate proved hazardous to US soldiers facing Viet Cong experienced in guerrilla warfare. Booby-traps and ambushes frequently halted disheartened US troops.

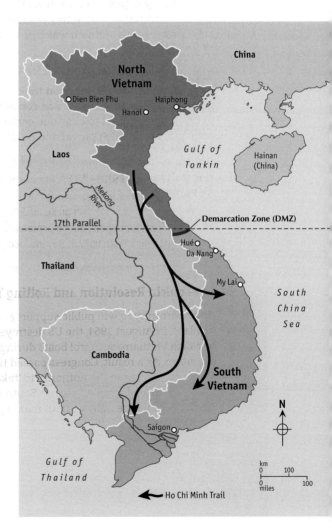

*A map of Indochina showing the Ho Chi Minh Trail, a major supply route from North to South Vietnam*

## The Tet Offensive

In January 1968, during the religious festival of Tet, the North Vietnamese and the Viet Cong launched an offensive. They attacked towns and US bases across the South, including the US embassy in the South Vietnamese capital, Saigon. By April, the US had regained nearly all land and bases lost, and around 50,000 communist troops had been killed. However, the Tet Offensive seriously challenged the USA's status as a superpower, and the American public began to question their country's involvement in Indochina.

The US news anchorman Walter Cronkite went to Vietnam to cover the war. On his return in February 1968, he commented that the USA was caught in a stalemate in the region. Cronkite noted that 'the only rational way out then will be to negotiate, not as victors, but as an honourable people who lived up to their pledge to defend democracy, and did the best they could'.

## Johnson steps down

In March 1968, Johnson announced that he would not run for re-election. His unpopularity was growing, and his final year as president echoed with the anti-war chant: 'Hey! Hey! LBJ, how many kids did you kill today?' The conflict was costing the US taxpayer $30 billion a year, and the bodies of around 300 US soldiers were being shipped home every week. Johnson ordered that the bombing be reduced, and peace talks began in Paris in May 1968. Despite little progress, in October the same year Johnson ordered a temporary stop to all bombing in North Vietnam.

*US soldiers carry a wounded comrade through jungle terrain in Vietnam*

Who do you think was more responsible for initial US involvement in Vietnam – Kennedy or Johnson?

## Nixon's peace 1969–73

Many people in the USA believed that by supporting the Republican **Richard Nixon** in the 1968 presidential election, they were voting to end the war. As a result, Nixon swept to victory. At first, he suggested that the USA and North Vietnam should withdraw their troops from South Vietnam at the same time. However, the North Vietnamese refused, and Nixon ordered bombing to begin again. At the same time, he began to encourage a policy of 'Vietnamisation'. By this, he meant reducing US troops in the region to force the South Vietnamese to take more responsibility for fighting the war (although Nixon still intended to provide financial aid). Between 1969 and 1971, US troops in Vietnam dropped from 539,000 to around 157,000.

**Richard Nixon (1913–94)** Republican Nixon was elected to Congress as a California representative in 1946, and became a senator in 1950. He was Eisenhower's vice-president and assumed the presidency himself in 1968. Nixon was a strong supporter of HUAC's anti-communist activities during the period of the Red Scare (see page 37), but he later became the first president to visit Communist China. He negotiated the USA's withdrawal from Vietnam, and pursued a policy of détente with the USSR. Re-elected in 1972, Nixon resigned in disgrace over the Watergate scandal in 1974.

### SOURCE C

Nixon had no secret plan for ending the war in Vietnam, but he knew what he did not like. The war had wrecked Johnson's ability to act freely in foreign affairs and the new president wanted to restore the authority of the White House.

Schulzinger, R. D. 2002. US Diplomacy Since 1900 (5th Edition). Oxford, UK. Oxford University Press. p. 289.

Vietnamisation may have been welcomed by citizens of the USA, but it turned South Vietnam into one of the most militarised nations on Earth. By 1972, there were more than 1 million troops in the country, as the South Vietnamese government attempted to take on the communists alone (although US supplies of military vehicles such as tanks and helicopters continued). The civilian People's Self-Defence Front had a membership of over 3 million by 1972.

Despite this response to its call to arms, the South Vietnamese
leadership was little more than an unstable military dictatorship
about to fall. What started as a civil war escalated into a major
Cold War conflict that South Vietnam was not equipped to pursue.

> Why did Nixon introduce Vietnamisation? Did this policy contribute to the
> USA's failure to save South Vietnam?

## Anti-war protests

Nixon sent troops to destroy communist supply bases in neighbouring
Cambodia in April 1970, attempting to stop the flow of North
Vietnamese soldiers and supplies into South Vietnam. However,
this violation of Cambodian neutrality provoked anti-war protests
on university campuses across the USA. On 4 May 1970, during a
demonstration at Kent State University in Ohio, National Guardsmen
killed four protesters (see page 87). This led to a huge anti-war
demonstration in Washington.

### Activity

US army morale and discipline declined dramatically between 1969
and 1971. Desertions increased by 400% in this period, and drug use
amongst US soldiers was widespread. But the reputation of the army
was truly shattered when information about the My Lai Massacre of
May 1968 reached the American public. Research the events in My Lai.
What happened? Who was involved? How were the perpetrators dealt
with by the US government? Why was it such a significant event?

## Moves towards peace

Peace negotiations dragged on. The USA proposed trade agreements
with the USSR on the condition that it pressured North Vietnam into a
settlement. However, in June 1972 the communists launched another
offensive, targeting towns in South Vietnam. In response, Nixon
ordered further bombing of the North. The US secretary of state, Henry
Kissinger, and his North Vietnamese counterpart, foreign minister Le
Duc Tho, finally agreed a ceasefire in January 1973. By the terms of the
ceasefire, the armies of North and South Vietnam would retain the
areas under their control when fighting stopped. This favoured North
Vietnam, which held large parts of the South, but at least the agreement
meant that the North accepted the existence of South Vietnam as a
separate political entity, rather than pushing for a unified Vietnam.

US forces were withdrawn and prisoners of war were released, but
the ceasefire did not last long. In April 1975, the North captured
Saigon. South Vietnam surrendered and Vietnam was reunited.

## The consequences of the Vietnam War

Any attempt by the new president, Gerald Ford, to use US forces to guarantee the survival of the dying Saigon regime would have been illegal due to the War Powers Resolution of 1973. This new law required any US president to obtain congressional approval for military action within 60 days of committing troops to any conflict.

In the course of the Vietnam War, 2 million Vietnamese died. The conflict also cost the lives of 55,000 US soldiers, and caused many people in the USA to turn away from foreign policy concerns and look inwardly to domestic and environmental issues. They were less supportive of the policy of containment and began to oppose interference in global affairs. Future debates about intervention in other countries, such as in the cases of Bosnia, Afghanistan and Iraq, have frequently invoked references to Vietnam.

> What was the significance of the 1973 War Powers Resolution?

# How did US foreign policy change under Nixon in the 1970s?

Nixon wanted to play a major personal role on the international stage, and to do so he planned to exploit the growing rift between the two main communist powers, the USSR and China. Nixon's career had been founded on his opposition to communism, yet he sought to improve US relations with these communist nations. Politically, Nixon wanted credit for easing tensions, which he hoped would win him re-election in 1972. However, his foreign policy was increasingly linked to the economic problems in the USA caused by the Vietnam War.

The president realised that the cost of the arms race and the recession of 1971–74 had weakened US economic dominance. Withdrawal from Vietnam could improve the economy, as well as laying the groundwork for improved relations with China and the USSR. Throughout the 1970s, Nixon was assisted in his plans by his national security advisor, **Henry Kissinger**.

**Henry Kissinger (b. 1923)** Kissinger was born in Germany to Jewish parents, who emigrated to the USA in 1938. He became a professor at Harvard University and later a government advisor. He was assistant to the president for national security affairs from 1969 to 1975, as well as secretary of state from 1973 to 1977, working with Nixon's successor, Gerald Ford. Kissinger shared the 1973 Nobel Peace Prize for his part in negotiating the ceasefire in Vietnam.

# Détente with China and the USSR 1970–79

In 1969, relations between the two main communist powers – the Soviet Union and China – erupted into open conflict in the form of border clashes. To take advantage of this communist in-fighting, Nixon opened lines of communication with China, and its communist leader Mao Zedong invited a US table-tennis team to the country for exhibition matches in April 1971. At the same time, Nixon sent Kissinger to hold secret meetings with Chinese officials and begin diplomatic discussions. In February 1972, Nixon himself made a historic visit to Beijing. As a result of these political manoeuvrings, the USSR also began to seek further agreements with the USA.

## The SALT talks

In May 1972, Nixon became the first US president to visit Moscow since the Cold War had begun. He negotiated agreements on science, the space race and trade. Two important treaties dealing with nuclear weapons were also signed – the Strategic Arms Limitation Treaty (SALT) and the Anti-Ballistic Missile Treaty. These paved the way for future accords, aiming to limit long-range nuclear weapons.

SALT I was particularly significant. By signing the treaty, the US accepted equal status with the USSR in nuclear capacity. SALT I also made future negotiations on the subject possible. SALT II talks began in Washington in June 1974. In Vladivostok, in November the same year, Gerald Ford and Soviet leader Leonid Brezhnev agreed a draft treaty to further slow down the arms race. Brezhnev believed that détente with the West was crucial to prevent the spread of capitalism and US imperialism into the Soviet sphere of influence.

### SOURCE D

Brezhnev saw Détente as a means of overcoming the Cold War and the route by which normal, equal relations could be restored between states … Détente would be resolved … through peaceful means via negotiation. The legitimate interests of each side would be recognised and respected by the other.

*Aldred, John. 2010. Aspects of International Relations 1945–2004. Cheltenham, UK. Nelson Thornes. p. 71*

SOURCE E

First, a nuclear war was utterly unacceptable, as the Cuban crisis had clearly demonstrated. Second, there was an enormous burden of military expenditures ... Third, the process of improving relations between the Soviet Union and Western Europe, especially with the Federal Republic of Germany ... would become extremely complicated if the United States were trying to impede it. Fourth, there was a sharp aggravation in Soviet-Chinese relations.

*Alexander Dobrynin, in his book* In Confidence: Moscow's Ambassador to Six Cold War Presidents. *Quoted in Sewell, M. 2002.* The Cold War. *Cambridge, UK. Cambridge University Press. pp. 97–98.*

SALT talks continued under **Jimmy Carter**, and concluded with the signing of SALT II in Vienna in June 1979. Carter called it 'the most detailed, far-reaching, comprehensive treaty in the history of arms control'. Both sides agreed to a maximum number of missile launchers and heavy bombers. However, tensions grew again after the Soviet invasion of Afghanistan in 1979, and Carter refused to ratify the treaty.

**Jimmy Carter (b. 1924)** Carter served in the US navy before running his family's peanut-farming business. He was Democratic governor of Georgia from 1971 to 1975, and defeated Gerald Ford in the 1976 presidential election. Carter's presidency (1977–81) marked a period of economic recession and energy crises. His greatest achievements were the SALT II nuclear arms reduction treaty, the signing of the Camp David Accords (see page 72), and the return of the Panama Canal (see pages 81–82). However, after the Iran hostage crisis and the Soviet occupation of Afghanistan, Carter was heavily defeated by Republican Ronald Reagan in 1980.

## The Helsinki Accords

One of the most significant moments during the period of détente came at the 1975 Helsinki Conference on Security and Co-operation. Here, the USA, Canada, the USSR and most of Europe finally and permanently accepted the boundaries for Germany and Eastern Europe that had been created at the end of the Second World War. The Helsinki Accords also endorsed human rights for all. This led to the formation of the independent trade union Solidarity in Poland, and to the establishment of Charter 77 in Czechoslovakia. Charter 77 was an informal document signed by writers, artists, architects and intellectuals, calling for greater human rights and artistic freedom. Solidarity and Charter 77 later played a key role in the fall of communism in Poland and Czechoslovakia.

# Why was Jimmy Carter an 'outsider' in foreign policy 1977–81?

Before his election in 1976, Jimmy Carter had been a one-term governor of Georgia with little national and no international political experience. After becoming president, he found himself something of an outsider – distrusted as too liberal by southern Democrats and too conservative by the northern Democrats who controlled Congress. Carter had his own foreign policy goals, believing in the rule of law in international affairs and in the principle of self-determination for all people. He demanded that 'we replace the balance of power politics with world order politics', adding that 'an inordinate fear of communism has led us to embrace any dictator who joined in our fear'.

In line with this belief in world order politics and interdependence, Carter sought a solution with Panama over control of the Panama Canal. He also had a major success in the Middle East, creating a framework for peace between Israel and Egypt at Camp David, the presidential retreat in Maryland. The Camp David Accords triggered a series of events that eventually led to a formal peace treaty in March 1979. This was Carter's greatest success, and his supporters hoped it would revive his declining popularity. However, although Israeli premier Menachem Begin and Egyptian president Anwar Sadat were awarded the 1979 Nobel Peace Prize for this agreement, Carter received no significant reward or political gain for his efforts.

Alongside these developments, Carter also wanted the USA to promote universal human rights. He had strong opinions about repressive regimes in the Americas, as well as those in countries such as South Korea and the Philippines. Carter felt that US power should be used sparingly and military intervention avoided if possible. He wanted to improve relations with the USSR. Despite these noble aims, however, Carter's foreign policy faced many problems.

# Mixed messages from the White House

US foreign policy during the late 1970s gave out mixed messages. Carter appointed Zbigniew Brzezinski as his national security advisor and recruited a former Defense Department official, Cyrus Vance, as his secretary of state. Brzezinski and Vance were both experienced in foreign policy, but had different world views. The clash of ideals and strategies between these two men caused Carter many problems.

Brzezinski was an anti-communist Polish immigrant, with a deep suspicion of Soviet motives and actions and little faith in détente. He believed that strengthening the power of NATO was more important than pursuing the SALT II agreement. As a result of these beliefs, Brzezinski steered Carter into several confrontations with the USSR. For example, he encouraged the president to launch a five-year defence programme that the USSR found provocative.

Vance adopted a more patient, intellectual form of diplomacy. He supported détente and viewed SALT II as the key diplomatic issue of the age, buying time until a new generation of Soviet leaders emerged. Vance was also instrumental in Carter's decision to return the Canal Zone to Panama, and in the Camp David Accords between Israel and Egypt.

The contradictions that arose from the different approaches of Vance and Brzezinski fed the public perception of indecisiveness, and ultimately ended Carter's presidency.

## SOURCE F

Only a president with deep experience in foreign affairs and a grasp of the issues equal or superior to that of such contending advisors could have prevented crippling contradictions. Carter lacked such experience and grasp.

*Smith, G. 1986. Morality, Reason and Power: American Diplomacy in the Carter Years. New York, USA. Hill and Wang.*

## SOURCE G

The advice [Carter] received on foreign affairs was often contradictory as Vance and Brzezinski were like horses pulling in different directions. They both agreed on one thing – that the Soviet Union was the key country – but they differed fundamentally on how to modify Russian behaviour.

*McCauley, Martin. 2004. Russia, America and the Cold War. Edinburgh, UK. Pearson Longman. p. 70.*

What do Sources F and G on page 73 suggest about Carter's difficulties with foreign policy? Do they help us to pass judgement on his qualities as a president? How useful or limiting are these sources when evaluating Carter's presidency in relation to the Cold War?

### Activity

Use the internet to find out more about the careers of Cyrus Vance and Zbigniew Brzezinksi. Who was most influential in policy-making? On what issues might they have clashed most? Where might they have agreed?

## Human rights as a focal point of foreign policy

During his 1976 election campaign, Carter promised to make human rights a key part of US foreign policy. He explained that US support for human rights involved promoting 'human freedom' worldwide and protecting 'the individual from the arbitrary power of the state'. This belief came from the United Nations' Universal Declaration of Human Rights, which was issued in 1948.

### Discussion point

To what extent should the driving force of foreign policy be respect for human rights at all times? Is the search for a truly humanitarian and ethical foreign policy realistic? What obstacles might prevent such a policy being achieved successfully?

Carter held both allies and enemies accountable for human-rights failings – an approach that risked straining relations with friends and widening rifts with foes. However, Carter's actions were not always consistent. He denounced violations by the Soviet Union and its Eastern European allies, implying his support for organisations such as Charter 77 and Solidarity (see page 71). He suspended military and economic aid in protest about the human-rights practices in Chile, El Salvador and Nicaragua. He also criticised US allies such as Argentina and South Africa. However, when Brezhnev threatened to end arms-control talks, Carter toned down his criticism of the USSR. By pushing for a foreign policy in which human rights played a central role, Carter was accused by conservative Republicans of attacking the USA's allies, damaging both the president's image and that of the USA.

# The 'Arc of Crisis' 1978–79

In 1978, Brzezinski spoke of an 'Arc of Crisis' running from Indochina to southern Africa. By this, he meant the regional powers that did not have direct connections to the main Cold War rivalries, but whose political, terrorist or religious groups could gain influence and cause conflict beyond their national boundaries. In particular, Brzezinski was concerned about the nations that lay along the southern borders of the Soviet Union. In the centre of this arc were Iran – the world's fourth-largest oil producer – and Afghanistan, a nation struggling with fragile social and political structures. Brzezinski believed that global dominance depended upon control of this area, and was afraid that Islamic fundamentalism might destabilise the USSR.

> Why were the countries that lay within the 'Arc of Crisis' of such concern to the USA in the late 1970s?

# The Iran hostage crisis

Iran's importance was based on its role as a major oil producer and on its proximity to the USSR. Mohamed Reza Pahlavi became shah of Iran in 1953, with support from the CIA. Pahlavi was a harsh leader, who repressed rival political parties and established a much-feared secret police force that violated human rights.

In 1978, the Shiite Muslims (an Islamic group to which the majority of the population of Iran belonged) began campaigning for a more Islamic government. Their religious leader, Ayatollah Khomeini, had been in exile for 15 years. By January 1979, the Shiite movement was so strong that the shah was forced to flee Iran. Khomeini returned as Iran's unchallenged spiritual and moral leader; he immediately imposed strict Islamic rule and denounced the USA. Iran was now an Islamic fundamentalist state.

In November 1979, after Carter allowed the shah to be treated for cancer in the USA, students loyal to Khomeini took over the US embassy in Iran's capital, Tehran, and seized 66 hostages. They demanded that the shah be sent back to Iran to stand trial. They also wanted the rights to any money that he had accumulated outside Iran, and an apology from the USA. In response, Carter froze billions of dollars of Iranian assets and began secret negotiations to free the hostages. These negotiations failed.

*Anti-US demonstrators burn the US flag in the Iranian capital Tehran in November 1979*

Images of the frightened and blindfolded hostages appeared on Iranian television alongside footage of the US flag being burned. When these scenes reached the USA, there was a public outcry. In April 1980, Carter ordered a secret rescue mission to free the captives, but the helicopters carrying the assault force developed problems and eight soldiers were killed in the unsuccessful operation. The Iranians then dispersed the hostages throughout the country, making another rescue mission impossible. For 444 days there was a stalemate that seriously damaged Carter's administration. Vance, who had opposed the mission, resigned.

These events contributed to the rise of an organisation that had been slowly gaining favour in the USA – the New Right. This was a group of aggressive right-wing conservatives, strongly in favour of a hardline anti-Soviet policy. They were later referred to as New Conservatives or Neo-Cons. The New Right forcefully condemned Carter's failure to resolve the Iranian hostage situation. Eventually, the president reached an agreement to release Iranian funds and promised not to interfere in Iran's internal affairs. Khomeini released the hostages on the day Carter left office.

Why do you think Khomeini waited until the day Carter left office to release the hostages?

# Events in Afghanistan

Afghanistan was important to the USSR, which had grown concerned about the emergence of fundamentalism in Iran. Several Soviet Central Asian republics bordered Afghanistan, and these had large Muslim populations. Moscow therefore needed a pro-Soviet government in Afghanistan.

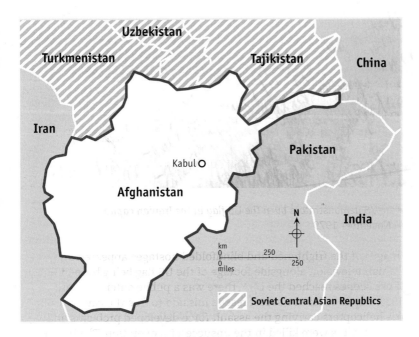

*A map of Afghanistan showing its proximity to Iran and its borders with three of the USSR's Central Asian republics: Turkmenistan, Uzbekistan and Tajikistan*

In April 1978, the pro-Soviet People's Democratic Party of Afghanistan (PDPA) seized power. However, there was serious opposition to the PDPA's policies, which many traditionalists believed were a betrayal of Islamic ideals. Within the PDPA, radical elements began to emerge under the leadership of Hafizullah Amin, who sought even greater reform. Due to the common borders of the Soviet republics with Afghanistan, the USA accepted that the country fell within the USSR's sphere of influence. As a result of this, the West took no immediate action against this coup.

Later, however, in an apparent reversal of Carter's ethical foreign policy, US intelligence services began to provide financial aid to the rebels in Afghanistan. On 3 July 1979, Carter authorised the CIA to conduct secret propaganda operations against the communist regime.

Amin took control of the government in September 1979, and began establishing a series of reform programmes. These included equal rights for women and secular (non-religious) education for both sexes. However, such changes were resented by an Afghan population immersed in Islamic tradition. Amin tolerated no opposition, and thousands were executed.

Civil war spread, and fundamentalist Muslims set up a group called the Mujahideen ('holy warriors'), which declared a holy war – *jihad* – against Amin. The KGB (the USSR's national security agency, including its secret police) warned that Amin's leadership might lead to active Islamic opposition within certain republics of the USSR. Brezhnev grew increasingly concerned about Amin's anti-Soviet statements, and by his relationship with the US government and CIA agents. The Soviet leader therefore decided to remove Amin, and ordered an invasion of Afghanistan. This began on 24 December 1979.

In response to this Soviet intervention, Carter cut off grain sales and other exports to the USSR, angering US farmers and businessmen. He also ordered a US boycott of the 1980 Olympic Games, which were being held in Moscow. Many felt that this punished US athletes rather than Soviet leaders, and Carter's decision reinforced his poor image. After the Vietnam War Carter was not prepared to risk another conflict. The establishment of Marxist governments in Grenada and Nicaragua in 1979 only added to the sense of the US being beaten by its opponents.

All these events contributed to Carter's fall. In the 1980 presidential election he was defeated by Ronald Reagan – who built his campaign around the promise of ridding the USA of its 'malaise' and restoring its status as a world leader.

Throughout most of the 1980s, the USA secretly sent billions of dollars of military aid to Afghanistan, supporting Amin's former enemies the Mujahideen against the Soviet Union (in fact, the US began helping to arm and train the Mujahideen before the Soviet intervention). This US support eventually succeeded in driving out the Soviets. However, out of radical Mujahideen elements, groups such as the oppressive Taliban and Osama bin Laden's al-Qaeda later emerged – the effects of which rebounded so tragically on the USA and the West on 11 September 2001.

## Discussion point

Do you think Carter was a weak president? Or was he a strong president trying to bring a new dimension to foreign policy? Was he a politician outside the mainstream and unable/unwilling to govern like some of his predecessors? Or was he the victim of wider international circumstances?

# What were the implications of US foreign policy for the wider Americas between 1961 and 1981?

## Washington's relationship with the Americas

The Caribbean and Central and South America were generally regarded as the USA's 'back yard' – a belief emphasised by the Monroe Doctrine of 1823. In this, President James Monroe declared that the USA was the dominant regional power and would not tolerate interference in the Americas by any European nation. By 1945, several governments in the region were greatly dependent on Washington for their economic stability. These nations included Cuba (before Castro's revolution), the Dominican Republic, Panama and Guatemala. Many governments in the Americas therefore defined their foreign policies by opposition to or agreement with the will of the USA.

The Rio Treaty of 1947 bound the Americas to accept that an attack on any American country was an attack on them all. The creation of the Organization of American States (OAS) in March 1948 took this relationship further. Although member states had different ideas about the ideals and purpose of the OAS, its charter stated that 'OAS member states committed themselves to continental solidarity [which the USA wanted] and total non-intervention [which the Latin Americans wanted], along with the principles of democracy, economic co-operation, social justice and human rights'. The charter also declared that communism was incompatible with freedom. The OAS therefore represented a key part of the USA's main objectives in the Americas: fighting communism and promoting free enterprise.

> What might have prompted states in the Americas to join the OAS?

## Kennedy's Alliance for Progress

The Alliance for Progress (Alianza para el Progreso) was endorsed by John F. Kennedy in August 1961, at a conference in Uruguay. This was intended to be a 'club of the Americas', to fight the spread of communism in Latin America by promoting economic co-operation with the USA. Washington would provide $20 billion in aid (over ten years) to other countries in the region to support the terms of the Alliance's charter. These included increases in per capita income, democratic governments, improvements in adult literacy, price stability, more equal income distribution and land reform, as well as greater economic and social planning. In providing this support, Kennedy hoped to draw American nations away from communism.

Between 1962 and 1967, the US supplied $1.4 billion a year to Latin America. However, several economists criticised the programme for fulfilling US aspirations rather than promoting genuine improvement. For example, five times more money left Brazil in the form of earnings and dividends paid to US companies than entered the country as direct investments. In addition, economic aid dropped sharply when the cost of the Vietnam War rose.

> What were the aims of the Alliance for Progress? Were there any weakness in these intentions?

The Alliance had a military and diplomatic branch in the newly formed US Peace Corps. This was made up of idealistic young people, who volunteered to work in Africa and in Latin American countries. They taught in schools or worked in factories, in agriculture, or for non-profit organisations, charities and the environment. The Pentagon and the CIA secretly trained police and paramilitary groups from several Latin American states to deal with guerrilla wars; in addition, 500 policemen from Central America also met in the Panama Canal Zone to learn about espionage (spying) and counterinsurgency (suppressing rebellions).

The Latin American military increasingly saw itself as the dominant force in stopping the 'communist cancer', and during the 1960s, 13 constitutional governments were replaced by military dictatorships. Kennedy's concerns about Castro led to a focus on security and counterinsurgency measures in Latin America. These encouraged the military to promote repression rather than freedom and democracy. As autocratic men in military uniforms took control, left-wing rebels and paramilitary groups resisted. Thus, instead of promoting and consolidating civilian rule, the old system and its inequalities were continued as a result of the Alliance for Progress.

> Was the Alliance for Progress an economic policy or more of a political plan?

# The frequency of US intervention

In reaction to the unrest that began to spread in nations under military control, Kennedy occasionally suspended relations with these dictatorships. However, the suspensions were only temporary. The crisis in Cuba forced the US to rethink its policies and, by 1964, discrimination against dictatorial regimes had ceased. US interventions still took place, though, to remind Latin American states that the USA still had power over them. There are several examples of how a Cold War mentality and a fear of revolution led the US to mistake nationalism for communism in Latin America.

## Brazil 1964

When President João Goulart took office in Brazil in 1961, he called for social reconciliation and economic freedom for the working classes. He restored diplomatic relations with the USSR, which resulted in a decline in relations with the USA. In March 1964, the CIA assisted a coup to overthrow Goulart and replace him with the right-wing military leader Humberto Castelo Branco.

## Ecuador 1964

The CIA infiltrated the Ecuadorian government, setting up news agencies and radio stations, bombing right-wing agencies and churches, and placing the blame for these actions on left-wing groups. Eventually these events forced the democratically elected Velasco Ibarra from office. When his replacement, Carlos Arosemara, refused to break off relations with Cuba, the CIA-funded military took over Ecuador and cancelled the 1964 elections.

## The Dominican Republic 1965

In 1965, Lyndon B. Johnson sent 33,000 troops to the Dominican Republic to stop a possible left-wing coup. Johnson's show of force prompted the comment that this was 'a democratic revolution smashed by the leading democracy of the world'.

## Bolivia 1964–78

The US became the major backer of right-wing Bolivian regimes. The CIA and US special forces helped suppress a leftist peasant uprising, which included the capture and execution of Ernesto 'Che' Guevara, a key leader in the movement. When General Hugo Bánzer seized power, he was supported by Washington, yet during Banzer's rule (1971–78) 2000 opponents were arrested and tortured, hundreds were killed and many others simply 'disappeared'.

### Activity

Brazil and other Latin American states were all affected by the USA during the period 1961 to 1981. Make a list of the ways in which each state was affected, using this book and your own research. Are there common features that link these states? Did US tactics differ greatly between countries, or were there common tendencies?

# Panama and the Canal Zone

One controversial aspect of Jimmy Carter's policy in the Americas was the signing of the Panama Canal Treaty in 1978. This treaty transferred control of the US-built Panama Canal to the republic of Panama. A 1904 treaty had permitted the US to occupy the Canal Zone – a strip of land next to the Panama Canal – which had opened in 1914.

In 1964, anti-US riots broke out in Panama City, as students demanded the return of the Canal Zone to Panama. The USA believed that the rioters were communist-trained extremists, yet it agreed to negotiate on the future of the Canal Zone and to transfer operation of the canal to Panama by 1999. Many in the USA resented this, arguing that as the US had funded the construction of the canal, it should retain rights over this important waterway. There was also the question of security – what would happen if a Soviet ally eventually seized control of the canal? The agreement was only approved by the US Senate after amendments had been made that allowed the US to take action in the region if problems arose. The Panamanian leader, Omar Torrijos, reluctantly agreed.

The Panama Canal Treaty might have been a great success for Carter. Despite Republican opposition, there were also many people who felt that as the canal was in Panama it should fall under Panamanian administration. Certainly Carter showed courage in following through with the agreement when opinion showed that 75% of Americans opposed it. However, the president was accused of weakness in 'giving away' the canal, and this added to his other perceived failures.

SOURCE A

Although these agreements protected US security interests, conservatives attacked them as proof of America's post-Vietnam loss of nerve, and recalled Teddy Roosevelt's boldness in bringing the canal into existence. But in a rare success for Carter, the Senate ratified the treaties.

Boyer, P., Clark, C. et al. 2008. The Enduring Vision: A History of the American People Vol. II. Boston, USA. Houghton Mifflin. p. 931.

A map of Panama, showing the Canal Zone, established in 1914

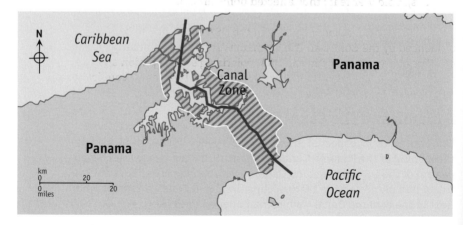

What does Source H tell us about the impact of the Panama Canal Treaty in the USA? How did an apparent diplomatic success by Carter turn into a failure?

 **Theory of knowledge**

### History, ethics and bias

The US government faced accusations of supporting repressive regimes in the Americas because they were anti-communist, and that in doing so, the US caused problems for millions of people in these countries. Are historians who choose to write about such topics bound to present biased accounts? For example, will the influence of current values and preoccupations result in them asking – or failing to ask – certain questions? Will such problems result in the writing or presentation of distorted explanations of policies and actions?

# How did the Cold War further influence domestic policy in the USA between 1961 and 1981?

As we have seen, heightened fears about communism and Soviet espionage, as well as the war in Korea, contributed to the rise of McCarthyism and the Red Scare in the USA throughout the 1950s. As America entered the 1960s, schools, colleges and universities were still monitored for signs of communist propaganda and other subversive activities.

Key social reforms in the late 1950s and 1960s were either blocked by Congress or limited by government. Many felt that welfare programmes requiring state-directed insurance contributions were too socialist. The reintroduction of a national health insurance act in 1958 failed, partly because it was considered 'too pink' (that is, having communist leanings). Cold War fears thus affected home affairs.

From 1961 to 1981, domestic policy in the USA continued to be influenced by the Cold War. The Vietnam War had a particularly significant impact on life in the USA, polarising social opinion and making it impossible for the US to commit to another major conflict for 30 years. Throughout the 1960s, traditions of subservience were broken, culture was redefined, and racism in US society was challenged. Domestic and foreign policy became connected. All these developments are discussed in the following sections.

Which areas of US domestic policy were most widely criticised in the Cold War climate?

# The New Frontier

When Kennedy came to power in 1961, there was a growing belief within the USA that issues such as health care, the environment and race relations should be key features of domestic policy. As a result, the new president launched a domestic strategy known as the 'New Frontier'. However, implementing domestic reform proved difficult, as Congress rejected many of Kennedy's policies. Increased federal aid for education was defeated, as was medical care for the elderly. The minimum wage was increased, but no defining legislation on poverty was passed. Nor were significant acts passed that addressed the issue of civil rights – Kennedy was too afraid of losing the support of Democrats in the South. Despite this, the New Frontier enjoyed some successes, most notably an increase in defence spending and investment in the space programme.

# The Great Society

The 'Great Society' was the name given to the domestic policies introduced by President Johnson. He aimed to eliminate poverty and racial injustice by introducing spending programmes that dealt with education, medical care, urban problems and rural development. After his election victory in November 1964, Johnson enacted more than 60 pieces of groundbreaking legislation.

## Health care

Millions of elderly people were helped by the Medicare Act, which provided free health care, paid for by social-security taxes. Johnson later passed the Medicaid Act, providing free health care for the unemployed, the disabled, and certain low-income groups who were under the age of 65 and therefore did not qualify for Medicare. Nearly $7 billion was spent on providing health-care access to those previously denied it. Johnson's opponents on the right called such legislation the 'advent of Soviet socialism in America', but the acts were widely popular.

## Employment

Johnson reduced taxes and increased consumer spending – policies that were aided by overall international economic growth and, in the USA itself, by Johnson's work programmes. The war in Vietnam created jobs in munitions, boosted employment and enlarged the army. Johnson also built 250,000 new homes, stimulating the construction industry and providing employment. The Appalachian Regional Development Act of 1965 continued support to depressed rural areas. With an expanding economy, unemployment dropped by 5%, and more African-Americans and women entered the workforce.

## Education

Johnson brought education under federal control for the first time. The 1965 Elementary and Secondary Education Act (ESEA) allocated large amounts of federal money – over $1 billion – to state schools. Head Start, a preschool programme for young children, was established. The Higher Education Act of 1965 funded lower-income students, offering assistance in the form of grants, work-study money and government loans. This ultimately benefited 25% of all US students.

The National Endowment for the Humanities and the Arts supported writers and artists and, in 1967, the Public Broadcasting Act created educational television programmes to supplement the existing broadcast networks.

> What benefits did Johnson's healthcare and education measures bring to US citizens? Why do you think his domestic reforms were regarded as 'Soviet' by his opponents?

By 1967, Johnson boasted that wages were the highest in history and unemployment was at a 13-year low. Historians Levine and Papasotiriou speak of Johnson's Great Society reforms as 'the most impressive legislative feats in American history [which have] lastingly shaped the American welfare state'. However, in the longer term Johnson underestimated the scale and cost of these health and education reforms, and the USA could not afford the social changes at the same time as meeting the costs of the war in Vietnam.

## The draft riots

For over 50 years, the draft system – by which young men were required to serve in the armed forces if called up – had provided reserve personnel. As US troop strength increased in Vietnam, more and more men were drafted to serve in the conflict. The increasing number of casualties from the war, and the widening of the draft, fuelled national resentment. In 1964, only 16% of those drafted had been killed; by 1968 this had risen to 60%.

The draft also drew unfairly on the population – wealthier young men were able to join the National Guard or reserve units, or could put off their military service until they had completed their university education. The draft hit African-Americans and white working-class men hardest – 80% of conscripted men came from such backgrounds. Many questioned why they should fight in Vietnam when they faced discrimination and lack of opportunity at home. Some escaped to Canada or Mexico in order to avoid being called up.

Student protests against the draft began to break out, during which rioters publicly burned their draft cards. These demonstrations grew after November 1965, when 40,000 protesters surrounded the White House and called for an end to the war. On the same day, Johnson announced a Vietnam troop increase from 120,000 to 400,000.

Johnson had a great deal of support from the teachers' unions, but none of his education reforms appeased professors and students. Increasingly unhappy with the situation in Vietnam, student protests in 1967–68 angered Johnson, who was disappointed by the 'ingratitude' shown by those he felt he had done so much to help.

## The end of the Great Society

Vietnam now seriously affected domestic policy. Black civil rights, anti-war protests and student movements challenged the government and radicalised a generation. The Free Speech Movement at the University of Berkeley, California, objected to bans on student meetings and occupied the administration building. The students were evicted by state troops and arrested, but this only fuelled student resentment nationwide. During the 1968 election campaign, the Youth International Party (Yippies) and the Radical Students for a Democratic Society (SDS) began calling for fundamental social change, battling with Chicago police at the Democratic Party Convention.

Amidst this serious unrest – and in the aftermath of the 1968 Tet Offensive (see page 66) – liberals finally spoke out against Johnson. They were angry that social reforms were being set aside in favour of a war costing $150 million and being fought by unwilling soldiers. Johnson stepped down from the presidential race when challenged for the nomination by candidates in his own party, who wanted an end to the war. He is now remembered for being politically destroyed by Vietnam – an event that overshadows his considerable advances in social reform.

*A political cartoon of Lyndon B. Johnson from the 1960s*

SOURCE 1

I tried to make it possible for every child of every color to grow up in a nice house, eat a solid breakfast, attend a decent school, and to get a good and lasting job. I asked so little in return, just a little thanks. Just a little appreciation. That's all. But look at what I got instead! Riots in 175 cities. Looting. Burning. Shooting … Young people by the thousand leaving the university, marching in the streets, chanting that horrible song about how many kids I had killed that day … it ruined everything.

*Lyndon Johnson, speaking to an advisor in 1968. Quoted in Chafe, W. H. 2003. The Unfinished Journey: America Since World War II. New York, USA. Oxford University Press. pp. 338–39.*

## Nixon's inheritance

Richard Nixon's election coincided with the onset of inflation and the end of a period of unprecedented prosperity in the USA. Nixon also inherited the task of overseeing US withdrawal from Vietnam, but soon found himself approving the secret and illegal bombing of Cambodia to destroy the Ho Chi Minh Trail (see page 65). When the New York Times printed the story, major protests broke out. Demonstrations took a tragic turn when a peaceful anti-war protest at Kent State University in Ohio resulted in four students being shot and killed by the National Guard. There was widespread anger when Nixon was reported as referring to the victims as 'bums'.

*A student who was shot and wounded during an anti-war protest against US escalation in Vietnam and Cambodia, at Kent State University, Ohio, May 1970*

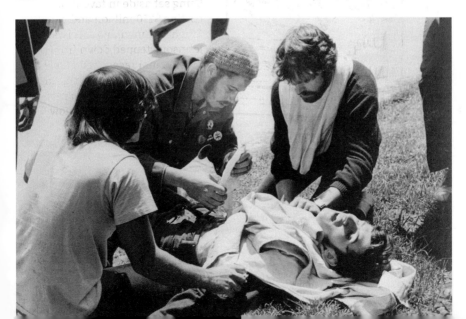

The protests at Kent State caused a conservative outcry, calling for moderation and traditional values, but radical students had drawn attention to deep-rooted problems in US society. Criticism of the war's planning and conduct led to debates in Congress about the way in which military action was authorised. One result of this was the War Powers Resolution, passed in 1973 (see page 69). Nixon was angered by this, but was soon distracted by the unfolding Watergate crisis.

Levine and Papasotiriou view the USA's withdrawal from Vietnam and Nixon's political downfall as reversing the trend towards a strong presidency that originated in the 1930s: 'The shift in power from the presidency to Congress coincided with an intense questioning ... of the foreign policy of Nixon and Kissinger.' Many hoped to replace power politics with world co-operation, opposing the idea of *realpolitik* – the practice of government politics or diplomacy based on practical considerations rather than on ideals or ethical considerations.

## The consequences of Vietnam for the USA

The Vietnam War had a powerful domestic impact, leaving 55,000 US soldiers dead and more than 300,000 wounded. Events in Vietnam encouraged the belief that protest could influence foreign policy. After North Vietnam won the war, there was mass emigration from the region, with 1 million refugees arriving in America, including Cambodians, Vietnamese and Amerasians (the children of Vietnamese and US citizens). Other effects included the increased use of drugs in 1970s America, which grew out of the near-epidemic level of heroin use among troops in Vietnam. There were also health problems among veterans who had been exposed to the chemical agent orange, which had a significant impact on welfare payments and employment.

### SOURCE J

Ultimately the 1970s became a microcosm of the unresolved conflicts within American society ... Americans faced a frightening array of prospects ... and bitter division over fundamental cultural values.

Chafe, W. H. 2003. The Unfinished Journey: America Since World War II. New York, USA. Oxford University Press. p. 432.

How did Nixon's handling of Vietnam change the US public's perception of the president? What was Vietnam's legacy to the USA?

# The energy crisis

Middle Eastern politics began to affect the USA directly when Israel was attacked by Egypt and Syria in October 1973. The Soviets offered assistance to Egypt, and the USA backed Israel. The superpowers persuaded Egypt and Israel to accept a ceasefire, but Saudi Arabia imposed an embargo on oil shipped to Israel's allies. Soon, other members of the Organization of Petroleum Exporting Countries (OPEC) quadrupled their oil prices. The embargo ended in 1974, but prices remained high. US gasoline edged towards the then-unheard-of level of $1 a gallon. This situation dramatically highlighted the degree to which the USA was dependent on Arab oil.

During this period, Carter introduced rationing of petroleum products, as the stock market shrank. A number of government agencies – including the Department of Energy – were founded in an attempt to change the way in which Americans used energy, and a national speed limit of 90 km/h (55 mph) was introduced. The New Right (see page 76) attacked Carter, blaming him for the USA's domestic stagnation. However, growing awareness of energy needs later led America to involve itself in Middle Eastern politics, as energy became a key issue.

Look back at this section and the information on Carter's foreign policy. Why might Americans have felt a general sense of frustration and a lack of confidence by 1980?

# Retrospective

For over 40 years, US–Soviet relations affected US domestic politics, as the Cold War influenced attitudes at home. However, by 1981 the USA had generally become a more tolerant, diverse and permissive society – although it had taken defeat in Vietnam, presidential humiliation and a major energy crisis to make them self-critical.

Many in the USA decided that Ronald Reagan's wholehearted belief in the country was the answer to the problems it had faced since the early 1960s. His uncomplicated patriotism, populism and anti-communism resonated with many in 1980. As a result, Carter lost heavily to Reagan in the November 1980 election.

Entering the White House in January 1981, Reagan championed conservative economic policies and cultural values. In addition, he endorsed a foreign policy that sought to move beyond détente by undermining the USSR and its communist satellites. A new era had dawned in Washington.

# End of chapter activities

## Paper 3 exam practice

### Question

To what extent was the Cuban Missile Crisis in 1962 proof of the failure of the policy of containment?
[20 marks]

### Skill focus

Planning an essay

### Examiner's tips

As discussed in Chapter 2, the first stage of planning an answer to a question is to think carefully about the wording of the question, so that you know what is required and what you need to focus on. Once you have done this, you can move on to the other important considerations:

* Decide your **main argument/theme/approach before** you start to write. This will help you identify the key points you want to make. For example, this question invites you to make a judgement about the USA's strategy of containment, and **to what extent** the Soviet placing of missiles on Cuba was proof of its failure. You might consider other factors, such as issues over Berlin or Vietnam, to be more important. Perhaps you believe that containment did not fail – after all, war was averted. Or was ideological advance of greater importance in this issue? Deciding on an approach will help you produce an argument that is clear, coherent and logical.
* Plan **the structure of your argument** – i.e. the introduction, the main body of the essay (in which you present precise evidence to support your arguments), and your concluding paragraph.

For this question, whatever view you have about containment, you should try to make a **balanced** argument. You will need to decide whether you think that, overall, it was or was not successful. As a rough guide for this type of question, you need to deal with both the 'yes' and 'no' arguments – for example, on the basis of 60% for your view and 40% for the opposing view.

Whatever the question, try to **link** the points you make in your paragraphs, so that there is a clear thread that follows through to your conclusion. This will ensure that your essay is not just a series of unconnected paragraphs.

You may well find that drawing a spider diagram or mind map helps you with your essay planning. For this question, your spider diagram might look this:

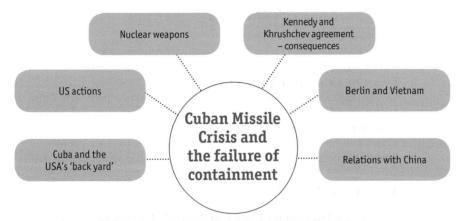

When writing your essay, include **linking phrases** to ensure that each 'bubble' (factor) paragraph is linked to the 'main bubble' (the question). An example is shown below.

## Sample linking phrases

**While** Castro's revolution had convinced Washington that communism had reached its back yard, US actions – in particular, the series of military manoeuvres in the Caribbean known as Operation Quick Kick – were significant in provoking Khrushchev …

**Although** the crisis saw Kennedy using superior military power to pressure Khrushchev into removing the missiles, Soviets regarded this as a humiliation. Some historians argue that forcing Moscow to respond to the threat of offensive power – rather than being deterred from taking action – was in itself was a form of containment. It was also a factor in Khrushchev's downfall in 1964. In relation to the US–Soviet agreement over Cuba, we must consider US missiles in Turkey, which …

**Also** significant was Kennedy's handling of the Berlin crisis, which has given rise to arguments both for and against the failure of containment. For example …

> As opposed to Cuba being the proof for containment's failure, it is also worth considering the USA's role in Vietnam and the final outcome of that conflict. Given that Vietnam was seen as the cornerstone of containment ...

There are clearly many factors to consider, which will be difficult under the time constraints of the exam. Producing a plan with brief details (such as dates, main events/features) under each heading will ensure you cover the main issues in the time available. It will also help you if you run out of time and can only jot down the main points of your last paragraph(s). The examiner will give you some credit for this.

## Common mistake

Once the exam time has started, one common mistake is for candidates to begin writing **straight away**, without being sure whether they know enough about the questions they have selected. Once they have written several paragraphs, they run out of things to say – and then panic because of the time they have wasted. Remember to produce a brief plan at the start of each of your Paper 3 questions, before writing up your answer. It will help you gather your thoughts, arguments and ideas.

## Activity

In this chapter, the focus is on planning answers. Using the information here, and in other sources available to you, produce essay plans – using spider diagrams or mind maps – with all the necessary headings (and brief details) for well-focused, clearly structured responses to **at least two** of the following Paper 3 practice questions.

Remember to refer to the simplified Paper 3 markscheme on page 219.

# Paper 3 practice questions

1   To what extent was the US policy of containment successful in the years 1961–81?

2   Assess the impact of the Cuban Missile Crisis on US foreign policy after 1962.

3   Analyse the impact of the Vietnam War on domestic policy in the USA between 1965 and 1974.

4   'Lyndon Johnson's Great Society was overwhelmed by Vietnam.' How far do you agree with this assertion?

5   Did Kennedy's Alliance for Progress subsequently fail Latin America in the 1960s and 1970s?

# 4 Canada and the Cold War 1945–63

## Timeline

**1945** **Jul:** Canada becomes founder member of United Nations

**Sep:** defection of Igor Gouzenko; Soviet spy ring discovered in Canada

**1949** Canada becomes founder member of NATO

**1950** **Jun:** Korean War begins; Canadian soldiers contribute to UN force

**1952** **Jan:** Old Age Security Act introduced

**Sep:** Canadian television (CBC) goes on air

**1953** **Jul:** Korean War ends; 314 Canadians have been killed and 1211 injured

**1954** Canada contributes to peacekeeping force in Indochina

**1956** **Oct:** Suez Crisis; Pearson proposes UN-sponsored force to supervise ceasefire; UN General Assembly accepts proposal

**1957** **Jan:** first Canadian peacekeepers arrive in Egypt after Suez Crisis

**Dec:** Pearson awarded Nobel Peace Prize

**1958** **Oct:** Diefenbaker agrees to take 56 Bomarc missiles from USA, but hesitates when pressed to accept them immediately

**1961** **Oct:** Saskatchewan passes bill creating Canada's first government-run health system

**1962** **Jul:** Medicare plan launched in Saskatchewan

**Oct:** Cuban Missile Crisis; Diefenbaker refuses to put Canadian forces on alert, angering USA

**1963** **Apr:** Diefenbaker government collapses after acceptance of Bomarc nuclear missiles from USA

## Key questions

- How are the government and political system in Canada structured?
- What were the long-term implications of the Cold War on foreign policy in Canada between 1945 and 1963?
- To what extent did the Cold War influence different areas of Canadian domestic policy?

This chapter examines the impact of the Cold War on Canadian foreign and domestic policy from 1945 to 1963. After a brief outline of the structure of Canada's government, the chapter investigates Canada's role on the world stage in the early years of the Cold War. It also discusses how the Cold War contributed to the establishment of domestic policies concerning health, women and ethnicity. The role of Quebec, with its linguistic and cultural divide, is also examined. References will be made to scholars such as Franca Iacovetta, Robert Bothwell, Reg Whitaker and Steve Hewitt, who fill important gaps in Canadian Cold War historiography where emphasis has usually been on the USA.

# Overview

- Canada emerged from the Second World War as a *minor great power* – richer and more politically stable than before, and seeking an influential international role in political and economic affairs.
- Canadians were drawn into the USA's political and cultural sphere of influence, as the ideological stand-off between Soviet communism and Western capitalism intensified.
- French-speaking provinces resented what they saw as the surrender of their identity to British culture, but strong anti-communist feeling kept the country united until the 1960s.
- Fears about communist infiltration heightened with an espionage scandal in 1946, while suspicion about the worldwide aims of the 'Reds' seemed justified due to events such as the Berlin Blockade and China's fall to communism.
- When the Korean War broke out in 1950, proof of the communists' desire for global domination seemed confirmed, and fears of communist expansion affected Canadian domestic and foreign policy for the next 30 years.
- In the 1950s, Canada became a founder member of NATO, which provided Europe with large quantities of military equipment and made up the single largest component of European air defence. Largely as a result of NATO membership, Canada emerged as a key player on the world stage.
- The actions of foreign minister Lester Pearson during the 1956 Suez Crisis marked a high point of Canadian political influence.
- Early in the Cold War, Canada supported the USA. However, by 1963 the relationship had changed and differences emerged – most notably over the placement of nuclear missiles on Canadian soil.

# How are the government and political system in Canada structured?

## The Canadian Constitution

The Constitution of Canada is the supreme law that outlines the country's system of government and its citizens' civil rights. In 1867, Britain passed the British North America Act. This document established Canada as an independent nation, but stated: 'The Executive Government and Authority of and over Canada is hereby declared to continue and be vested in The Queen.'

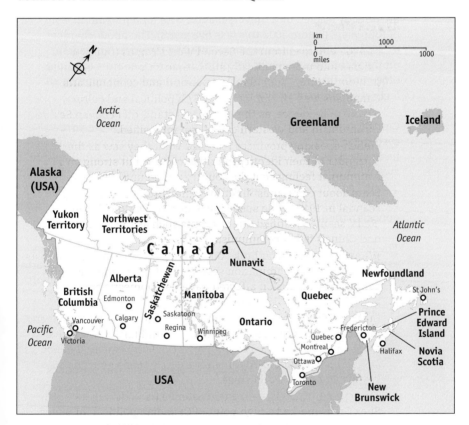

A map of Canada showing its provinces and main cities

Canada is a constitutional monarchy within the British Commonwealth, governed by its own parliament and with a prime minister as head of government. The head of state is the British monarch, who is represented in Canada by a governor-general. The governor-general acts only on the advice of the Canadian prime minister, but remains Canada's official figurehead in the monarch's absence.

Canada is a federation of 13 areas: ten provinces and three territories. Each of these has its own government, law-making body and lieutenant-governor. There is also a federal (or national) government based in Ottawa, which is made up of the House of Commons (elected), the Senate (appointed), and the governor-general as the monarch's representative. Provinces can make laws on some matters, while other laws are made by the federal government.

## The Canadian electoral system

The Canadian electoral system is modelled on that of the United Kingdom. Members of the lower chamber, or House of Commons, are directly elected by a universal adult vote for a maximum term of four years (before 2007 this was five years). The upper chamber, or Senate, contains members appointed by the governor-general on the recommendation of the prime minister. Senators can hold office until they are 75 years old. Both chambers must approve all legislative bills before they can become law.

Canada's electoral system is referred to as a 'first past the post' system. This means that the candidate with the most votes wins – he or she does not need to gain an absolute majority. Candidates are awarded a seat in the House of Commons to represent their district (or 'riding') as a member of parliament. Here, they influence government policy by voting on draft legislation (called bills) – either supporting or opposing them.

The leader of the party with the most representatives in parliament usually governs as prime minister. The Commons is the most powerful branch of parliament, and the prime minister must keep the support of the majority of members of the House of Commons in order to remain in office.

### Activity

Explain the key features of the structure of government and the electoral system in Canada. Compare this to the government of another country with a different political system.

## Political parties

Before 2007, national elections had to be called at least every five years (now it is every four years) and those elections were contested by a number of political parties. The Canadian Liberal Party and the Canadian Conservative Party were the main parties.

The oldest political party in Canada is the Liberal Party (known as the Grits), which lies between the centre and the centre-left. After the Second World War, the Grits campaigned for progressive social reform, and Lester Pearson later established Canada's welfare state. The Conservative Party arose out of a series of right-of-centre parties, and were backed by the Liberals at one time. The first conservative group was the Liberal-Conservative Party, which was founded in 1854. Conservatives were strong supporters of the British Empire and believed in one nation, one flag and one leader. Liberals felt that Canadians should acknowledge the two cultural groups within Canada – English Canadians and French Canadians.

## Activity

| William Lyon Mackenzie King | Liberal | 1935–48 |
|---|---|---|
| Louis St Laurent | Liberal | 1948–57 |
| John Diefenbaker | Conservative | 1957–63 |
| Lester Pearson | Liberal | 1963–68 |

Working in pairs, research the lives of these prime ministers and outline them in no more than 100 words each. Share your findings with other students.

Over time, differences developed within the centre-right and this proved damaging to conservative groups. The fact that the conservatives had no unified political party allowed the Liberal Party a succession of election victories. This historical pattern earned the Liberals the unofficial title of Canada's natural governing party. In the May 2011 general election, however, the Liberals (under the leadership of Michael Ignatieff) lost 18% of their vote and won the fewest seats in their history. As a result, this title has been called into question.

# The language divide

Canada is a multicultural, bilingual country with both English and French as official languages. Many Canadians believe that this linguistic relationship is the defining aspect of the Canadian experience. English is the native language of around 59% of Canadians and French is the first language of 23%. The majority of French Canadians live in the province of Quebec and refer to themselves as Québécois. The French were the first Europeans to permanently colonise the area that is now Quebec, as well as parts of Ontario and western Canada. Until the 1960s, religion was a key part of the French-Canadian national identity, and the Catholic Church was the focus of daily life. Religious orders ran French-Canadian schools, hospitals and orphanages. French-Canadian society was much more conservative than English-speaking Canada.

# What were the long-term implications of the Cold War on foreign policy in Canada between 1945 and 1963?

In 1945, the USA and the USSR became the key players in what quickly developed into the Cold War. Their rivalry set the tone for life in Canada for the next 20 years. Canadians knew that their country's prosperity depended on continued peace, domestic reform and a developing economy in a post-war world where collective security was vital. However, international co-operation was soon threatened by the spread of Soviet influence in Europe, Africa, the Middle East and Asia. The Canadian government realised that the freedom of Western Europe in particular was essential in preventing another global conflict, and in securing a peaceful future for Canada.

*Canadian political leaders William Mackenzie King (left) and Louis St Laurent (right) at the Canadian Liberal Party Convention, 1948*

Many Canadians were also concerned about their country's relationship with the USA. As neighbours, accord between the two countries was important. However, in the immediate post-war years, many Canadians feared that they might be bullied by the USA or pushed into military action based on the USA's fears of communism.

The Canadian government believed that forming wider international relationships was the best way to prevent it becoming too influenced by the will of the USA. Any alliance between Canada and the USA should therefore be made in partnership with Western European democracies. The establishment of NATO in 1949 was a significant success in this respect, as Canadians felt that the organisation would help restrain US Cold War activities. As international tensions grew, however, Canada and the USA drew closer – and in fact Canada began to feel the effects of the Cold War almost immediately.

# The Gouzenko spy scandal

By the end of the Second World War, deep differences had developed between the USSR and the Western Allies. The relationship between Soviet leader Joseph Stalin and his British and US counterparts grew increasingly strained. Canada was drawn into this East–West conflict when, in September 1945, Igor Gouzenko – a Russian clerk at the Soviet embassy in Ottawa – walked into the newsroom of the *Ottawa Citizen* and declared that he had proof of a widespread Soviet spy ring operating in Canada. The information he provided showed that Canadian, British and US citizens were involved in espionage.

The Liberal prime minister, William Mackenzie King, was shocked by this discovery and, despite Gouzenko's demands for asylum, initially considered turning him over to Stalin. However, as historian Robert Bothwell explains, 'in the end he shared him with his senior allies, American president Harry Truman and British prime minister Clement Attlee'. Mackenzie King met Truman and Attlee to inform them of the situation.

When news of the spy scandal was leaked to the media in early 1946, it made international headlines. The Canadian government arrested several people they suspected of espionage. For Canadians, the affair was proof of long-term Soviet intentions and a wake-up call to the West.

**SOURCE A**

Igor Gouzenko being interviewed in 1954.

## Discussion point

Look at Source A on page 99. Why do you think Gouzenko still chose to appear masked nearly ten years after he defected?

# The pursuit of collective security

Throughout the late 1940s and the 1950s, the Liberal governments of Mackenzie King and Louis St Laurent tried to achieve collective security by forming alliances with Western powers. Key features of this policy included support of the Marshall Plan, involvement in defence talks after the Brussels Treaty, and the formation of NATO.

## The Marshall Plan

The Marshall Plan (see page 23) was a reconstruction package that provided $18 billion in aid to European states whose economies had been destroyed by the war. Canada supported the Marshall Plan and gave practical help by supplying goods to Europe. However, Stalin regarded the plan as an attempt by the US to win over states that he believed to be in the Soviet sphere of influence, and he refused to allow Poland, Hungary and Czechoslovakia to accept Marshall aid.

Tensions mounted throughout 1947–48. When the Soviets blockaded the Allied sectors of Berlin in 1948, the USA, Canada and Britain launched a massive airlift of food and fuel to the inhabitants of the city. Although the Berlin Blockade was eventually lifted, it made the Western powers realise the need to form a military alliance that could operate beyond the responsibilities of the more global United Nations.

## The Brussels Treaty

As a result of this, several nations – including Britain and France – established a defensive alliance under the Brussels Treaty in March 1948. Later, Canada, Britain and the USA held further defence talks, and the alliance was eventually expanded to include all the nations that had signed the Brussels Treaty. The ultimate aim of these talks and treaties was to establish an organisation that would unite Western Europe and North America in the cause of common defence.

## NATO

Mackenzie King considered membership of NATO to be a way of boosting Canada's economic and trade position. While the organisation was being formed and its purpose agreed, the Canadian prime minister fought hard to include a clause that would require members to co-operate economically rather than just in a military alliance. He believed this would strengthen member nations and encourage genuine social, economic, political and military internationalism. The clause was accepted – despite British and US reservations – but in reality NATO became a military alliance.

By the time discussions about NATO were concluded, Louis St Laurent had taken over as Canadian prime minister, and his foreign minister Lester Pearson signed the treaty in Washington on 1 April 1949. Both the government and the press emphasised how important NATO membership was to the Canadian people. Acceptance or disapproval almost became a test of loyalty, and people who criticised it were accused of having communist sympathies. NATO membership gave Canada a more significant role in world politics, allowing it to influence international policy and to deal with events in its own sphere of the wider Americas. It also provided safety in numbers when standing against the potentially overwhelming power of the USA.

## SOURCE B

In government, in political parties, in the press, in business, in trade unions, in churches and other associations across the land, and in the minds of ordinary Canadians, it was decided that Canada had come out of one war only to enter an even stranger peacetime conflict. This conflict could not be allowed to become another shooting war, for the consequences in the atomic age were too dire to contemplate. Yet the war would be waged on all other fronts.

*Whitaker, R. and Hewitt, S. 2003. Canada and the Cold War. Toronto, Canada. James Lorimer & Co. p. 9.*

## Discussion point

According to Source B, almost all Canadians believed that they had exchanged one type of conflict for another. To what particular events might a Canadian in 1949 refer when justifying these feelings? What do the writers mean by 'the war would be waged on all other fronts'?

## Activity

Create a mind map outlining the reasons why Canadians were enthusiastic about involvement in NATO. When you have completed the mind map, list the reasons you have given in order of priority. Then use them to debate the assertion that Canadians embraced NATO chiefly as a means of gaining greater influence on the world stage.

## Canadian world presence in the 1950s

### The Korean War

The Korean War was the first large-scale military confrontation of the Cold War in which Canada was involved, and 400 Canadians were killed in the conflict. Canada had already played a small part in Korean affairs when it served on a UN commission to supervise elections in the country in 1947. This was one of the reasons why Canada came under pressure to contribute to the US-led UN coalition to defend South Korea after the North Koreans invaded in June 1950.

In July 1950, three Canadian destroyers were placed under UN command. However, Canada's foreign minister Lester Pearson was concerned that North Korea's actions might be a prelude to a communist offensive in Western Europe, and initially he hesitated to send troops to Korea in case they were needed for a defence of Europe.

Canada wanted Western involvement to take the form of a UN police action rather than an anti-communist crusade that could launch a wider conflict. Pearson also had his own concerns, believing that US strategy in Korea was based on brinkmanship (see page 30) and a show of military strength rather than on seeking a long-term solution to the problem. The aggressive actions of US commander-in-chief General Douglas MacArthur (see pages 26–27) only heightened these concerns. Even the British prime minister, Clement Attlee, had flown to Washington in 1950, fearful that MacArthur might persuade President Truman to use atomic weapons against North Korea.

Despite his hesitation about becoming too involved in the Korean conflict, Pearson had long been a vocal supporter of the struggle against communism. In the late 1940s, he had declared that the communist frontier was 'wherever free men are struggling against totalitarian tyranny ... it may run through the middle of our own cities, or it may be on the crest of the remotest mountain'. He could not, therefore, be seen to turn his back on a communist threat, and he eventually allowed a Canadian brigade to be sent to Korea.

Throughout the Korean War, Pearson tried to be a restraining influence. He opposed the US plan to advance into North Korea, afraid that this would provoke the Chinese into joining the conflict. Against Pearson's advice, UN forces moved into North Korea, and almost reached the Chinese border. In response, over 300,000 Chinese troops poured into North Korea and forced the UN into retreat.

After this, Pearson began to encourage ceasefire negotiations. He objected to the US demand that the UN General Assembly condemn China as an aggressor, because doing so would make peace efforts more difficult. However, when Pearson realised he was fighting a losing battle, he gave in to the US – afraid that Canada would lose influence in Washington if he continued to stand against the USA.

The USA resented Pearson's 'moralising'. US secretary of state Dean Acheson described Canada as 'the stern daughter of the voice of God' and Pearson as an 'empty glass'. Pearson later said that after Korea, he knew that the age of easy relations with Washington was over.

This was proven in 1952, when differences emerged over the UN prisoner-of-war camp on Koje Island, South Korea. The US claimed that North Korean and Chinese prisoners being held there were demanding political asylum in South Korea. Canadian troops were sent to control the unrest, but when they arrived they discovered that this was a piece of US propaganda to draw attention away from real events in the camp, where the prisoners had staged a violent uprising. A stern exchange between Ottawa and Washington was played down in public, but Canada distanced itself from future US intervention, focusing on developing its own international role through the UN.

## Discussion point

How might Canada's experience of the Korean War highlight the problems facing a so-called 'middle power' when attempting to establish its own diplomatic and political place in a world divided into 'us' and 'them'?

## The Suez Crisis

In 1956, the Egyptian president Gamal Abdul Nasser nationalised the Suez Canal Zone, which was run by British and French investors. British prime minister Anthony Eden was angered by this move, and secretly conspired with France to regain control of the canal. Canadian prime minister St Laurent was concerned that a British and French attack on Egypt would revive fears of Western imperialism in the Middle East. This could compromise Canada's position as a member of the Commonwealth, as well as undermining NATO.

Both Canada and the US advised Eden not to pursue matters, but he secretly continued with his plans for Israel to invade Egypt as a prelude to an Anglo–French landing to 'restore peace'. When these plans became known, there was international condemnation for the conspiracy. Canadian opinion was divided between those who supported the 'mother country' and those who opposed what they saw as Anglo–French hastiness. St Laurent publicly expressed 'some regret' for the situation, but privately rebuked Eden for deceiving him. Despite a sense of betrayal, Canadian diplomats protected their British and French allies from international humiliation.

Pearson suggested the creation of a UN force that would enter Egypt and separate the fighting parties while peace terms were negotiated. In November 1956, the UN General Assembly unanimously adopted this proposal, and Pearson was awarded the 1957 Nobel Peace Prize for his part in resolving the crisis.

*UN peacekeeping troops unload supplies in the Suez region, November 1956*

This was a great international triumph, but the Liberal government paid a high price. The Conservative opposition, led by John Diefenbaker, accused St Laurent of betraying Britain. There was anger when the prime minister described both Britain and France as 'declining European supermen' and when Pearson commented that Canada would not act as Britain's 'colonial chore-boy'.

Many Canadians clearly agreed that Britain and France had been betrayed over the Suez Crisis, and the Liberal Party lost the 1957 election. Foreign policy – and especially Pearson's internationalism – had affected internal affairs. The new Conservative prime minister emphasised the ties between Canada, Britain and empire, but as the 1960s approached Canada's foreign policy came under close scrutiny in light of Cold War tensions.

# The premiership of John Diefenbaker

Diefenbaker was a complex, suspicious man, wary of the media and of potential rivals. He had little experience of foreign affairs, but showed a great loyalty to Britain and a dislike of anything American. However, Diefenbaker was a strong anti-communist and he therefore supported US Cold War policy. His own foreign policy followed an inconsistent path, as can be seen in his attitude towards Britain and the European Economic Community (EEC), towards the USA over nuclear weapons, and in relation to Castro's Cuba, as discussed in the sections below.

## Diefenbaker's relationship with Britain

When Diefenbaker attended his first Commonwealth conference in London, his criticism of the previous government's 'betrayal of Britain' over Suez was naturally welcomed. He earned even greater favour by announcing that his government would move 15% of Canada's trade from the USA to Britain. Canadian ministers had not been consulted about this, and were shocked when they heard – Diefenbaker's promise was impossible to keep, because quotas had already been agreed with the USA, and treaties had been signed to enforce these quotas. Diefenbaker's announcement also irritated US officials.

Despite his support for Britain, Diefenbaker did criticise the country for attempting to join the EEC in 1960, accusing Britain of turning its back on Canada. The crisis was resolved when France vetoed Britain's application in 1962, but Diefenbaker's relationship with British prime minister **Harold Macmillan** was strained.

**Harold Macmillan (1894–1986)** Macmillan was the British Conservative prime minister from 1957 to 1963. He changed the world map by decolonising sub-Saharan Africa. He pioneered the Nuclear Test Ban Treaty with the USA and the USSR, and searched for a new British role in Europe. When Macmillan tried to gain membership of the EEC, Diefenbaker told him to place the Commonwealth first; Macmillan was annoyed at Canadian interference. However, Macmillan's refusal to share US atomic secrets with France led the French to veto British entry into the EEC in 1962.

## Defence co-operation with the USA

Relations between Canada and the USA were harmonious at first, and Diefenbaker had a great respect for Eisenhower. One of the Canadian prime minister's first acts was to sign the North American Air Defense Agreement (NORAD) with the US in August 1957, establishing an integrated air defence system under the joint control of both nations. A Canadian was appointed as deputy commander, and NORAD command posts were set up in both countries.

The Royal Canadian Air Force (RCAF) began working with the US air force headquarters in Colorado, and the US was permitted to intercept hostile Soviet aircraft in Canadian airspace. Radar lines had already been built across northern Canada, from Vancouver Island to Newfoundland, and these now came under NORAD's control, monitoring aircraft activity and warning of potential Soviet threats.

The USA saw Canada as the transit route for Soviet bombers, so in 1958 Diefenbaker gave the US permission to place two squadrons of 'Bomarc' anti-aircraft missiles in Canada. Some argued that the surface-to-air guided missiles would be an effective replacement for the Canadian Avro Arrow fighter plane, so production of the Arrow was cancelled. However, this caused controversy, as it meant that Canadian air defence relied exclusively on the Bomarc.

Many people believed that Diefenbaker had made a hasty decision that compromised Canadian sovereignty. They were further outraged when it was discovered that the Bomarcs would eventually be fitted with nuclear warheads. The level of public debate increased over whether Canada should adopt nuclear weapons and, under political pressure, Diefenbaker hesitated over accepting the warheads.

Within Canada, there was a feeling that Diefenbaker was indulging US paranoia about the USSR. Such paranoia appeared to be symbolised by the construction of what was nicknamed the 'Diefenbunker' – a large underground complex built outside Ottawa. This was intended as a post-nuclear shelter for the government and military, and contained a radio studio, a bank vault and a hospital. It could provide four weeks' protection from a five megaton nuclear detonation up to a mile away.

## Complications: Diefenbaker, Kennedy and Cuba

Diefenbaker's relationship with the USA really began to decline when John F. Kennedy became US president in 1961. The two men had little in common. Kennedy was young, energetic and active in the pursuit of US interests, and Diefenbaker much preferred the more considered approach that Eisenhower had taken. When Diefenbaker gave in to public pressure and suggested that the Bomarc warheads should only be transported on to Canadian soil during a time of crisis, Kennedy accused him of weakening defence plans in North America.

Although Diefenbaker wanted Canada to find its own voice in international affairs, he also recognised that the country would inevitably be drawn into the US sphere of influence in Cold War affairs. Despite this, after the Bomarc affair Diefenbaker increasingly viewed Kennedy as an irritant. In particular, he resented Kennedy urging Canada to join the OAS (see page 79) during a presidential visit to Ottawa in 1961, particularly as Kennedy referred to it in his address to the Canadian parliament *after* Diefenbaker had refused.

At the end of the visit, the US delegation mistakenly left behind a briefing memo that spoke of 'pushing Canada' in certain areas. This angered Diefenbaker, who kept the memo to use against Kennedy if the situation arose in the future. Although Diefenbaker never used it, Washington was furious at this breach of etiquette.

Canada's response to the Cuban Missile Crisis (see pages 58–61) further annoyed the USA. Diefenbaker had previously expressed concern about Cuba's relationship with the USSR, referring to the island as a 'bridgehead of international communism'. However, during the crisis, Diefenbaker's dislike of Kennedy seemed even to outweigh the Canadian prime minister's anti-communist beliefs.

When Kennedy discovered the Cuban missile sites in early October 1962, he notified Diefenbaker through the US ambassador in Ottawa, who showed Diefenbaker Kennedy's photographic evidence. Diefenbaker knew that Kennedy had personally telephoned British prime minister Harold Macmillan to brief him on the situation in Cuba, and felt snubbed.

Diefenbaker proposed an unbiased international commission to investigate the USA's claims about the missile sites and to resolve the tension with the USSR. He also hesitated over Kennedy's request to increase the alert level for Canadian forces. Although Canada ultimately supported the US in public, Kennedy felt that Diefenbaker had delayed unnecessarily in the middle of an international crisis. An opinion poll later revealed that 80% of Canadians agreed with Kennedy's view of Diefenbaker.

*John F. Kennedy (left) and John Diefenbaker (right) in May 1961*

**Discussion point**

Diefenbaker's personality has been studied closely in attempts to account for inconsistencies in Canada's foreign policy from 1957 to 1963. Robert Bothwell explains how Diefenbaker's own party members believed that 'he had a long and vindictive memory for slights, real and imagined'. Denis Smith looks at his personality through his rootless childhood and his 'dour, intimidating, prejudiced, ignorant, and wilful' mother, suggesting that Diefenbaker was 'resentful, paranoid, a cultivator of enemies'. Yet he was 'not naturally anti-American and as a staunch anti-communist accepted American leadership of the Western alliances', although Kennedy thought he was ignorant, petulant and a 'boring son of a bitch'.

Do you think there were inconsistencies in Diefenbaker's foreign policy? Do personality defects still apply in a modern political context? Can they be applied to any current or recent leaders?

What emerged from this difficult period in the Cold War was the realisation by ordinary Canadians that their government was relatively powerless compared to the USA and the USSR. Canadians were neither suddenly anti-American nor pro-Soviet, but the world *had* come to the brink of nuclear war, and many people believed that the superpowers needed to compromise. Countries like Canada felt marginalised and exposed to danger. Such fears increased after 1964, as events such as the Vietnam War began to cause a rise in youth protest and heightened activism in Canada.

# To what extent did the Cold War influence different areas of Canadian domestic policy?

## Canadian post-war domestic concerns

Canada emerged from the Second World War with a relatively strong economy. Having developed and refined its manufacturing sector during the war and avoided bombing at home, Canada was able to export key materials and food to Europe. Scientists and geologists had a major oil find in Alberta in February 1947. A total of 1278 wells later yielded 200,000 barrels of oil, and by 1950 there was more oil exploration and development in Canada than anywhere in the world. A housing boom encouraged consumer buying, and homes had all the latest electrical conveniences. In 1952, the Canadian Broadcasting Corporation (CBC) introduced television, which brought US culture to the forefront of Canadian life. This caused concern in some sections of society, most significantly amongst conservative Catholic elements in French-speaking Quebec. Historian Peter Dobell comments that divisions between English-speaking and French-speaking parts of Canada became increasingly apparent, and eventually drew the focus away from questions of 'freedom versus communism'.

At the same time, Canadian citizens began demanding more from their government. They believed that social reform was needed, and that governments owed their people a reasonable standard of living and access to basic services. Along with this desire for change, however, a fear of communism remained, and this influenced domestic policy and legislation. For example, in the name of national security, the Royal Canadian Mounted Police (RCMP) carried out secret surveillance, investigating groups and individuals they considered 'threats' to Canadian security (see pages 110–11).

## Ensuring domestic security

Gouzenko's revelations of an espionage ring in Canada (see page 99) had an immediate impact on domestic policy. MP **Fred Rose** and fellow communist **Sam Carr** were both imprisoned for espionage. Fears of communist infiltration were heightened by international events such as the Berlin Blockade, Soviet nuclear capability, the Korean War, and the trial and subsequent execution of Julius and Ethel Rosenberg in the USA (see page 41).

**Fred Rose (1907–83)** Rose was a Polish-born Jew. He moved to Canada, where he became a communist and a trade union organiser. Elected in a 1943 by-election for the Labour Progressive Party (LPP), he was re-elected with 40% of the vote in 1945. When the USSR then became 'the enemy', Rose was targeted. Charges against him were non-specific, but he was imprisoned and expelled from parliament. Released in 1951, he returned to Poland.

**Sam Carr (1906–89)** Carr was a Ukrainian-born immigrant who settled in Canada. Together with Fred Rose, he established the Young Communist League. Later a communist party newspaper editor, Carr was imprisoned several times. After the Communist Party was declared illegal in 1940, he formed the LLP in 1942 as a legal front for the communists. Carr became its national organiser, and was one of the main recruiters of spies for the USSR in Canada.

McCarthy's actions in the US gave even more weight to Canadian concerns. However, Lester Pearson warned against this, saying: 'Let us by all means remove the traitors from positions of trust, but in doing so, I hope we may never succumb to the black madness of the witch-hunt.'

## The role of the RCMP

Although Canada responded to the communist threat in a more controlled way than the USA did, Canadian actions were still undemocratic at times. The government set up a system of security checks on individuals – 70,000 in one year alone. It investigated civil servants, media personalities, scientists, university professors and trade unionists, and regarded anyone who was felt to be politically, socially or sexually non-conformist as a potential threat.

These investigations were overseen by the Royal Canadian Mounted Police and its political division, the RCMP Security Service. Gay men and lesbians working with confidential documents were thought to present a risk to national security due to the possibility of blackmail or coercion. The RCMP therefore urged public workers to report fellow employees they suspected of living 'alternative lifestyles', in order to identify them and thereby evaluate their threat potential.

Before 1939, the RCMP had conducted political surveillance on labour unions and the left through its Criminal Investigation Department. However, in general it was seen as a prestigious organisation – a symbol for Canada. Certainly its uniform of red jackets, distinctive hats and superbly groomed horses projected a romanticised image of reliability, which reassured Canadians.

*Members of the Royal Canadian Mounted Police during an inspection in the 1940s*

It was precisely this 'safe' image that allowed the RCMP to play such an important part in Canadian security during the Cold War – putting down strikes, installing telephone taps, and keeping files on 'enemies of the state'. Members of the RCMP – both uniformed and plain-clothes – acted with no specific legal authority, simply a moral duty to protect Canada. Sharing and receiving intelligence with the FBI in the USA and with MI5 in Britain, the RCMP was accountable only to its commissioner, Stuart Taylor Wood.

## Profunc

Wood devised a top-secret plan for dealing with subversives in the event of either a war with the USSR or a national state of emergency. The RCMP was instructed to draw up lists of individuals who could immediately be identified and imprisoned. This operation – Profunc (Prominent Communist Functionaries) – planned to send men to prisons across the country and women to Niagara in Ontario or Kelowna in British Columbia. Children (referred to as 'red diaper babies') would accompany their parents to prison or be sent to relatives.

### Activity

Was the RCMP the right organisation to lead the defence of Canadian society against communist infiltration? Split into two groups. One group should plan an argument to support that idea that it was the right organisation. The other group should plan an argument that it wasn't. Prepare a presentation for your fellow students, or set up a debate. Consider such factors as how far Canadian society was being infiltrated, the role of the media, and how dangerous the communist threat really was.

Profunc enabled the RCMP to extend its surveillance far beyond monitoring pro-Soviets. In the climate of the 1950s, such work naturally focused on communist sympathisers and on union members, but investigations developed a much broader scope. A number of charities, debating clubs and human-rights organisations realised that they were also being investigated as communists.

## Historical perspectives on the actions of the RCMP

Few people queried the moral and legal foundations of the RCMP's increased power. Most Canadians believed that people had nothing to fear unless they really were communist sympathisers. Some historians claim that Canada's campaign against potential subversives was more discreet and less hysterical than that in the USA. However, the fact that it was conducted mostly out of the public eye does not make it any less an infringement of civil liberties.

Richard Cavell argues that if one of the aims of the Cold War was to preserve a national identity in the face of a foreign threat, then 'for Canada that threat was coming from south of the border rather than from the Soviet Union'. Franca Iacovetta discusses Canada's inheritance from the USA, stating that the Canadians 'did not have a monopoly on the hypocrisy and corrupted democracy of this era'.

## SOURCE C

The only reason why Canada did not produce the level of anti-communism that reigned to the south ... was because the British style parliamentary system of government, with its greater executive dominance and deference to crown authority, choked off would-be McCarthys ... from taking anti-communism out of the control of the state sector and making it a divisive and destructive partisan issue. But on the fundamental question of the Cold War enemy, Canada was at one with the United States.

Whitaker, R. 'We Know They're There'. Quoted in Cavell, R. (ed). 2004. Love, Hate and Fear in Canada's Cold War. Toronto, Canada. University of Toronto Press. p. 39.

### Activity

Historians have compared and contrasted the nature of the Red Scare in Canada to what happened in the McCarthy era in the USA. Consider the following questions:

- How does Source C account for the difference between the two countries? Explain your answer carefully.
- From the information in this section, including the views of historians, can we understand why many Canadians thought that they had dealt with left-wing subversion more effectively than the USA?
- Can there ever be any justification for such intensive scrutiny by the state on the lives of its citizens?

The government gave vocal support to the RCMP's internal security operations, but never funded them directly. The Security Service was a special section that evolved from the core RCMP, with extraordinary powers but no specific legal mandate. In fact, operations were made more difficult by the lack of expertise among members of the RCMP.

Traditional roles such as general policing and criminal investigation did not equip them with the skills required for security intelligence. Several embarrassing incidents highlighted the fact that the Security Service was often unable to distinguish between subversion and legitimate dissent. However, in the Cold War climate of the 1950s and 1960s, it was inevitable that the RCMP would find a place. A magazine columnist described the paranoid atmosphere of the time with the words: 'If a housewife in Ottawa hears a knock on her door, it can be one of only two people: the milkman or the RCMP.'

## Discussion point

Look back at the actions of both the RCMP and the government outlined in the section above. How far does the state have the right to interfere in the lives of individuals for the benefit of the majority? Is it morally right to engage in bugging and other forms of electronic surveillance?

# Women and the Cold War

In 1945, the Canadian government declared that ensuring a stable family life was both a patriotic duty for all citizens and essential in the development of the country's post-war society. All political parties and religious groups urged women to give up the jobs they had taken on during the Second World War and return to traditional domestic roles. However, many women enjoyed the financial freedom that having employment offered them, and refused to leave their jobs. Some women who had not worked previously actually joined the labour force to express their objection to this policy. As with anyone who did not follow government ideas, these women came under suspicion of subversion.

During the war, the RCMP had secretly investigated women with connections to left-wing unions. They even reported on teas and Tupperware parties. Believing that fundraising activities could be a cover for subversive activity, the RCMP planted informants at these gatherings. After the war, such surveillance increased.

Many women wrote to the government complaining about the quality of housing, the rise in prices of goods, or asking for a national healthcare system. Such demands were considered destabilising, and so free-thinking women's organisations began to be regarded as disloyal. The RCMP particularly mistrusted the wave of feminism that began to emerge in the late 1950s, and carefully watched these women who were angered by social and employment inequality.

One significant example of RCMP monitoring concerned the Czech-born humanitarian Dr Lotta Hitschmanova. She settled in Canada in 1942 and began working with wartime refugees; she later formed the Canadian branch of the Unitarian Services Committee (USC). Receiving information from the US that the Boston branch of this organisation was under 'Red control', the RCMP opened a file on Hitschmanova and the Unitarian Church in Canada. Unitarianism regarded communism as 'objectively free from the antipathies which have characterised its reception by most other organised religions'. The Canadian government was concerned that Unitarianism might offer communism a way into Canadian society. The RCMP never arrested Hitschmanova, but continued to report on her until the 1970s.

Women were highly active in church groups, and Canada's largest Protestant denomination – the United Church of Canada – was also investigated after 1948, when it published a report that mentioned a 'synthesis between Western democracy and the Soviet Union'. In fact, the author of the report called this a 'delusion of sentimental liberalism', but the RCMP stated that 'the mere fact that Christian leaders are willing to associate with and/or discuss differences with Communists has given the Communist an appearance of respectability'. Despite this, the UCC remained untouched.

Balancing this was the strongly anti-communist Imperial Order of the Daughters of the Empire (IODE). This was a women's charitable organisation founded in 1900 to support the British Empire. Its areas of interest included child welfare, community health and social services. IODE wanted to play its role in the Cold War, and launched a Citizenship Department to help with 'Canadianisation'. This department targeted refugees fleeing Europe in 1945 and Hungary in 1956. As well as practical help, IODE members offered guidance in matters such as gaining English-language skills, and ensured that refugees read 'the truth' about the news in their native languages. Undoubtedly, IODE members also monitored people in the course of their charitable duties, reporting anything suspicious to the authorities. The government was keen to have such patriotic women on its side and encouraged IODE members to help with civil-defence preparations at the height of tensions in the 1950s.

## Health and welfare in a Cold War society

Canada introduced key social support systems such as old age pensions in 1927 and unemployment insurance in 1940. After 1945, the federal government looked cautiously at further expansion. It wanted to achieve full employment by providing assistance to private businesses, rather than interfering more widely in economic activity. In addition, the government wanted to avoid providing further support for existing social welfare measures, since in the Cold War climate many Canadians felt that state intervention was a Soviet-style policy.

Nonetheless, developments and improvements in health and welfare came about in several ways:

- In 1945, as part of the plan to return to traditional family values, the federal government introduced mothers' allowances (known as 'the baby bonus').
- Mackenzie King put forward proposals that included social assistance and hospital insurance measures, although the proposals were set aside for a decade.
- Under St Laurent, public housing, federal hospital grants and assistance programmes for disabled and blind people were initiated.
- A trade union campaign for changes in pensions led to significant progress by 1952 with the Old Age Security Act. This established universal old-age pensions for those over 70 and means-tested old-age security for those between 65 and 70.
- The government then extended provincial social welfare legislation to the native or 'First Nation' people of Canada, who were previously excluded because of cultural differences, cost, or by lack of access to healthcare centres.
- In 1946, near-universal health coverage was introduced in the province of Saskatchewan, where it was criticised by many conservatives. This was a significant moment in social reform. In 1948, Alberta established Medical Services (Alberta), which eventually provided medical coverage to over 90% of the population and later set up hospital programmes like the one in Saskatchewan.
- The first permanent programme for social funding, the Unemployment Assistance Act of 1956, was established after private charities stated that they could no longer support relief costs.
- In 1957, the federal government passed the Hospital Insurance and Diagnostic Services Act (HIDS), which remains the basis of the Canada Health Act today. By 1961, all ten provinces had agreed to start HIDS Act programmes.
- During Diefenbaker's government, funding of hospitals, higher education and job rehabilitation was introduced or extended.

## Cold War immigration in Canada

After the Second World War, the Canadian government attempted to aid population growth by encouraging immigration. However, immigration policies favoured those whom the government believed would best fit in with the existing population, and demonstrated a clear racial and ethnic bias. People from Britain, the USA, Western Europe and Scandinavia were considered 'preferred' immigrants, as they shared a common language or similar culture with many Canadians. The Netherlands Farm Families Movement – an initiative to encourage farmers from the Netherlands to move to Canada – brought thousands of Dutch immigrants to the country. By 1952, Germans had also made it on to the list of 'preferred' immigrants.

People from other countries found it more difficult to gain entry to Canada (and find acceptance once there), particularly those from East Asia and the Mediterranean. Although naturalised Chinese-Canadians and East Indians – as British subjects – could sponsor relatives from 1947, Asians were discouraged from entering Canada until the 1960s, and only small numbers settled there between 1947 and 1963.

The RCMP immigration bureau in London also showed an ethnic bias. Here, Canada blocked entry to suspected communists, those with 'questionable' political tendencies, and even people with 'inappropriate' physical characteristics or handicaps. In general, though, in the post-war years Canada welcomed anyone fleeing from communist repression. For example, after the Hungarian uprising of 1956 (see page 32), Canada accepted 37,000 refugees. However, Canadians remained wary of Eastern European immigrants, afraid that they might be used for communist infiltration.

> ## SOURCE D
>
> It is clear that Cold War immigration security imposed double standards ... those from countries with large communist movements such as Italy, France, and Greece, were screened more closely and more often barred from entry than were those from countries with few communists. In the case of France, an official policy that placed French immigrants on the same favoured basis as British applicants was secretly undermined by the application of security guidelines.
>
> Whitaker, R. and Hewitt, S. 2003. Canada and the Cold War. Toronto, Canada. James Lorimer & Co. p. 27.

 ## Theory of knowledge

### History and emotion

The content of the section above about immigration undoubtedly creates strong emotions in the reader – disgust, indignation, cynicism. What is your reaction to the information on Canadian immigration policy? Would a visual source have more emotive impact?

## Quebec under Duplessis

Today, Canada's language divide is also a cultural divide. From 1945 to 1963, however, both sections of Canadian society were united in their desire to stop communism reaching Canada. Throughout the 1950s and 1960s, Cold War politics particularly affected French Canadians. In Quebec especially, strong anti-communist feeling was encouraged by the premier, **Maurice Duplessis**.

**Maurice Duplessis (1890–1959)** Duplessis was a devout Roman Catholic and strongly anti-communist. As premier of Quebec (1936–39 and 1944–59), Duplessis presided over a period of great prosperity. He introduced a generous minimum wage and home-ownership assistance acts, as well as initiating road, hospital, school and university construction projects. However, his authoritarian regime was suspected of corruption, and his premiership is sometimes referred to as *la grande noirceur* ('the great darkness').

In the post-war years, the Catholic Church had a significant influence in Quebec. Anti-communist sentiments in the province were mainly fuelled by the persecution of Catholic clergy in the Soviet bloc, as well as the rising threat of communism in Catholic countries like Italy and France. Duplessis himself took a hard line against any group he considered to have communist or even socialist sympathies, including labour organisers and trade unions.

## The Asbestos Strike

In February 1949, asbestos miners in Quebec went on strike after the companies they worked for refused to meet their demands for safer working conditions and better pay and benefits. Duplessis sided with the companies, but the strikers earned sympathy from the public and, significantly, support from the Catholic Church, which had previously enjoyed a close relationship with Duplessis' government.

On 23 February, Duplessis declared the strike illegal and sent in the police to monitor the situation. As the weeks passed and the asbestos companies brought in replacement workers, violence broke out between the strikers and the police, and acts of brutality were carried out by both sides. The strike eventually came to an end in July 1949, after mediation by the archbishop of Quebec.

After the strike, Duplessis passed laws making it illegal for companies in Quebec to hire communists, Marxists or anyone associated with organisations that might have members with communist sympathies. Pierre Trudeau (see page 127), who was working as a journalist at the time and was sympathetic to the miners, later wrote that the strike was 'a violent announcement that a new era had begun'.

Many historians also believe that the Asbestos Strike marked the start of a change in attitude among the people of Quebec, questioning Duplessis' authoritarian regime. By the time Duplessis died in 1959, Quebec was ready for the 'Quiet Revolution' – a period in which the province experienced social and political changes, most significantly drawing away from Church control. By 1963, Quebec was progressing more independently and, crucially for Canada as a whole, it began debating whether or not to break from the country entirely.

*Maurice Duplessis (left) with Pierre Mendes-France during the French premier's trip to Quebec in 1954*

## What next for Canada?

Bothwell comments that the peaceful resolution of the Cuban Missile Crisis and the signing of the 1963 Test Ban Treaty allowed the government of Canada to turn its attention to domestic issues. These included health care and pensions for those too old or too sick to 'share fully in the good times and high incomes of the 1960s ... and problems that prosperity had ignored or by itself couldn't solve'. In Quebec, the Quiet Revolution and the emergence of Pierre Trudeau affected Canadian feeling about the Cold War. These factors also led Canada down a more radical path, as opposition to the Vietnam War intensified and Canada developed an increasingly independent approach to foreign policy.

# End of chapter activities

## Paper 3 exam practice

### Question

To what extent did Canadian foreign policy adopt an independent stance during the period 1945–63?
[20 marks]

### Skill focus

Writing an introductory paragraph

### Examiner's tips

Once you have planned your answer to a question (as described in Chapter 3), you should be able to begin writing a clear introductory paragraph. This needs to set out your main line of argument and to outline **briefly** the key points you intend to make (and support with relevant and precise own knowledge) in the main body of your essay. Remember – 'To what extent ...?' and 'How far...?' questions clearly require analysis of opposing arguments – and a judgement. If, after writing your plan, you think you will be able to make a clear final judgement, it is a good idea to state in your introductory paragraph what overall line of argument/judgement you intend to make.

Depending on the wording of the question, you may also find it useful to define in your introductory paragraph what you understand by any key terms – such as 'independent stance', 'middle power' or 'Cold War'. For example, for 'independent stance' you could define the term and give a brief summary of its main features.

For this question, you should:

- establish Canada's foreign policy aims
- consider its successes and failures
- write a concluding paragraph that sets out your judgement.

You need to cover the following aspects of Canadian foreign policy:

- Canadian policies that were influenced by the early Cold War
- Canada's interpretation of the Marshall Plan and NATO
- problems of establishing/maintaining a relationship with the USA
- problems facing a so-called 'middle power' in attempting to create its own independent diplomatic and political niche in a world divided into 'us' and 'them'

- Canada and Korea – relations with the USA and Britain
- Lester Pearson and his mediation during the Suez Crisis
- clashes between Canada and the USA over the tone of policy
- Diefenbaker's relationship with the USA and Britain
- North American defence.

Setting out this approach in your introductory paragraph will help you keep the demands of the question in mind. Remember to refer back to your introduction after every couple of paragraphs in your main answer.

## Common mistake

A common mistake (one that might suggest to an examiner a candidate who has not thought deeply about what is required) is to fail to write an introductory paragraph at all. This is often done by candidates who rush into writing **before** analysing the question and doing a plan. The result may well be that they focus entirely on the words 'foreign policy' and on the dates – an approach that may result in a **narrative** of Canadian Cold War foreign policy. Even if the answer is full of detailed and accurate own knowledge, this will **not** answer the question, and so will not score highly.

## Sample student introductory paragraph

From 1945 to 1963, Canada was at the centre of the ideological stand-off between Soviet communism and Western capitalism, being drawn into a US military, economic and cultural sphere of influence. Fears about communist infiltration were quickly realised with the 1946 Gouzenko spy scandal, while suspicions grew with the Berlin Blockade and the Soviet atomic bomb in 1948–49. These events influenced foreign policy for 20 years. But Canadian leaders were also anxious to play a significant role in world affairs: an independent Canadian role. Indeed, some historians have stated that Canada became a 'middle power', with a distinctive 'independent stance' from the USA on certain international issues.

In order to validate this opinion, we must define what is meant by an 'independent stance'. Then Canadian foreign policy aims must be established, considering where they matched those of the USA and where they diverged. Finally, we must examine and analyse how far these were or were not achieved. Areas such as NATO, Korea, the UN and shared US-Canadian defence of North America will be examined in turn. Despite some success in keeping Canadian foreign policy independent, it was not to the extent that many in Ottawa would have wished.

This is a good introduction, as it shows a clear grasp of the topic and sets out a logical plan, clearly focused on the demands of the question. It demonstrates a sound appreciation of the fact that to assess success, it is necessary to identify aims. It also explicitly demonstrates to the examiner which aspects the candidate intends to address. This indicates that the answer – if it remains analytical and is well-supported – is likely to be a high-scoring one.

## Activity

In this chapter, the focus is on writing a useful introductory paragraph. Using the information from this chapter and any other sources available to you, write introductory paragraphs for **at least two** of the following Paper 3 practice questions.

Remember to refer to the simplified Paper 3 markscheme on page 219.

# Paper 3 practice questions

1   Define and account for the main fears of Canadians in the decade after 1945.

2   To what extent did Canada and the USA disagree about foreign policy during the period 1945–63?

3   'The Royal Canadian Mounted Police defended Canada against the infiltration of communism.' To what extent do you agree with this statement?

4   Why were there tensions between Canada and the USA in the period 1961–63?

5   Assess the impact of the Cold War on Canadian domestic life in the period 1945–63.

# 5 Canada and the Cold War 1964–81

## Key questions

- What were the long-term implications of the Cold War on foreign policy in Canada between 1964 and 1981?
- How did the Cold War in the 1960s and 1970s influence different areas of Canadian domestic policy?
- Did the Cold War change Canada?

Canada experienced a time of upheaval between 1964 and 1981. As youth movements grew increasingly aware of international issues, university students became politicised, vocal and determined to change society. Quebec's Quiet Revolution altered the status quo, and Lester Pearson gave Canada its modern welfare state. Canada appeared in the world spotlight with Expo 67 and the 1976 Montreal Olympics. However, the oil crisis of the mid 1970s brought economic problems. Pierre Trudeau became prime minister and 'Trudeaumania' altered Canadian politics, as calls for Quebec's independence developed into the October Crisis of 1970. Unease over US policy in Vietnam was followed by Cold War détente, as international relations between West and East improved.

## Overview

- By 1964, Canada was playing a significant role in world peacekeeping; it was a key member of NATO and seemingly well qualified to mediate and exert influence. Pierre Trudeau became premier in 1968, claiming that Canada was 'probably the largest of the small powers' and re-evaluating Canadian foreign policy.
- The USA's involvement in Vietnam, and US president Richard Nixon's improved relationship with China and the USSR, highlighted Canada's need for a more independent voice.
- In October 1970, radical Quebec nationalist and Marxist militants of the Front de libération du Québec (FLQ) kidnapped Quebec labour minister Pierre Laporte and British trade commissioner James Cross. Laporte was murdered, and Trudeau declared martial law in Canada under the War Measures Act.
- The election of the Parti Québécois brought to power the first political party committed to full Quebec independence. However, a 1980 referendum rejected this.
- By 1980, Canadians recognised the economic benefits of having access to US markets and supported Cold War collective security. However, many still sought greater Canadian independence.
- The government became concerned with 'patriation' – the extent to which the British parliament determined Canada's constitution. This was resolved by the Constitution Act of 1982 – the last piece of British legislation to have force in Canada.

## What were the long-term implications of the Cold War on foreign policy in Canada between 1964 and 1981?

Early in the Cold War, Canada was undoubtedly – although not always unconditionally – supportive of the USA. However, this relationship changed after the Diefenbaker–Kennedy era.

In part, the changing relationship between the two countries was determined by the shifts in Cold War tensions.

- From 1964 to 1973, the USA was involved in the escalating and increasingly embarrassing war in Vietnam.
- In 1968, the USSR occupied Czechoslovakia to suppress growing opposition to Soviet control.
- By 1972, evidence was emerging of a three-way relationship between the USA, China and the USSR.
- The 1970s witnessed a growing desire for greater co-operation, or détente, between the superpowers. The most obvious signs of this were the two Strategic Arms Limitation Treaties (SALT I and II).
- The Soviet invasion of Afghanistan in 1979 seriously damaged the process of détente.
- A second Cold War began in 1981, with US president Ronald Reagan and British prime minister Margaret Thatcher taking a hard line against the USSR.

In 1964, the effects of the Cold War were still being felt in Canada, although many Canadians no longer believed that communism should be actively opposed by foreign intervention. However, Canada was officially bound to assist in resisting acts of international aggression (as it had during the Korean War). Vietnam may have been 'America's war', but Canada played its part. Around 30,000 Canadians volunteered to fight in Southeast Asia. The country was involved in secret missions in the region, as well as weapons testing and arms production. It also provided a home for draft dodgers from the USA (see page 128).

## Canadian peacekeeping in the 1960s and 1970s: an overview

Throughout the 1960s, Canada developed an increasingly independent approach to foreign policy – especially in light of the Vietnam War. However, the foundations for this change had been laid in the 1950s. As foreign minister, Lester Pearson disagreed with his US counterpart Dean Acheson over Korea, and was accused of 'moralising'. Later, Pearson's suggestion of a Suez peacekeeping force was unanimously backed by the UN General Assembly, which placed Canada at the forefront of peacekeeping in the region. In the face of British and French disapproval, this move earned Canada a reputation for non-partisanship (not being biased towards any one group).

One longer-term consequence of the Suez Crisis was that Canada remained involved in international peacekeeping efforts throughout the 1960s and 1970s. This role had a tragic chapter when, in August 1974, a Canadian military plane making a scheduled supply flight from Egypt to Syria was shot down by surface-to-air missiles. Nine Canadians were killed – the worst peacekeeping loss in a single day.

**Discussion point**

Why might Britain and France have felt uncomfortable about Pearson's peacekeeping proposals during the Suez Crisis? From the events described in the preceding pages, can we assume that peacekeeping is something inherently Canadian and central to the country's foreign policy?

# The Vietnam War and its impact on Canada

By 1964, Cold War anxieties in Canada were not as severe as they had been in the 1950s. The successful resolution of the Cuban Missile Crisis and the establishment of a 'hotline', providing direct communication between Washington and Moscow to resolve future crises, comforted many people. Robert Bothwell believes that emerging from this period of reduced threat there was 'a tinge of nationalism', and suggests that 'the Americans' tendency to … equate Canadian life with their own offended some, perhaps many, in Canada.'

At the same time, however, the disagreements between John Diefenbaker and John F. Kennedy over how to deal with the situation in Cuba (see page 107) had caused many Americans to question whether Canada was really a reliable ally in terms of foreign policy. This feeling was heightened when Canada proved reluctant to support the USA in Vietnam.

Lester Pearson was elected Canadian prime minister in 1963, and he and US president Lyndon B. Johnson met for the first time at John F. Kennedy's state funeral. Over the next year or so, their contrasting world visions became apparent. Johnson was determined to prevent an invasion of capitalist South Vietnam by the communist North, and committed the first US ground troops in 1965. By 1968, when he abandoned his campaign for re-election, 500,000 US soldiers were fighting a losing battle in Vietnam. Pearson believed that Johnson had dragged the US into a conflict that could not be won.

**SOURCE A**

Lester Pearson (left) and Lyndon B. Johnson (right), after John F. Kennedy's funeral in Washington, 25 November 1963.

**Activity**

Study Source A on page 125. Using your knowledge of the relationship between Pearson and Johnson, and considering the occasion of the meeting, what do you think they might have been discussing? Does this photograph reveal anything about their respective personalities?

US–Canadian differences became more evident after Pearson gave a speech at Temple University, Philadelphia, in April 1965. Whilst encouraging firm support for US policy, Pearson called for a halt to the US bombing of North Vietnam. Johnson considered this a betrayal. The following day, Johnson and Pearson met and there was allegedly an angry exchange between the two men. After this incident, Pearson returned to Ottawa and wrote what Bothwell describes as 'a cringing letter to Johnson which didn't help'.

However, it later emerged that in 1964 Pearson actually gave Johnson his approval for a limited bombing campaign against the communists in Korea, on condition that the US did not use nuclear weapons. This came to light in the Pentagon Papers – a top-secret US Defense Department history of the USA's involvement in Vietnam. The content of these papers was leaked to the *New York Times* in 1971, and the information they contained proved very damaging to the US government. In addition to the Pentagon Papers, other aspects of the Vietnam War reveal an even deeper secret Canadian involvement.

## Behind-the-scenes involvement

Canada was not officially a participant in the Vietnam War, but it was a major supplier of equipment and provisions to US forces. Because of its formal neutrality, Canada could not send these supplies directly to South Vietnam, but instead sold them to the USA. Indeed, throughout the war Canadian manufacturers profited from such items as army boots and Canadian whiskey. However, both napalm and the chemical agent orange (now classified as weapons of mass destruction) were made in Canada and transported over the border to be sent to Southeast Asia. Pearson's government also allowed the US to use Canadian facilities for training exercises and weapons testing.

Also crucial was Canada's membership of two international truce commissions, which provided medical supplies and technical assistance to all sides involved in conflicts between 1954 and 1975. Historian Victor Levant states that Canadian diplomats used their country's role as peacekeeper to encourage positive negotiations between the US and North Korea. However, US documents about the truce commissions reveal that Canada actively supported US counter-insurgency operations during the Vietnam War.

In addition, some Canadians engaged in espionage for the CIA and were involved in secretly introducing US arms and personnel into South Vietnam. They also shielded the US chemical weapons programme from public inquiry – most importantly, the fact that these weapons were produced in Canada.

On the surface, though, Canada seemed to be impartial in the conflict: an independently minded peacekeeping nation. The Canadian government later argued that its behind-the-scenes involvement was intended to balance the activities of some Eastern bloc countries – also members of the truce commissions – which were being used as information channels by the USSR and China and, by extension, North Vietnam.

During a 1950 Commonwealth Conference in Colombo, Sri Lanka, it was agreed that efforts should be made to improve living standards in the Asia-Pacific region. The Colombo Plan was established as a regional organisation responsible for constructing factories, dams, hospitals, universities and steel mills. People were trained and educated to manage this infrastructure. Originally, this plan was scheduled to last for six years, but it was later extended indefinitely.

By the time the Vietnam War broke out, therefore, Canada was already a presence in Southeast Asia. Direct Canadian aid during the war went only to South Vietnam, but Canadian aid to the whole region, both before and during the war, totalled $29 million between 1950 and 1975.

## Pierre Trudeau, public reaction and the draft dodgers

By 1966, US involvement in Vietnam had intensified, and Canada became increasingly drawn into aspects of the conflict. There was growing concern about the war across the whole of North America, mainly due to the introduction of the draft.

**Pierre Trudeau** succeeded Lester Pearson in 1968. He immediately began a major review of foreign policy, designed to keep Canada active in international affairs – but in more modest ways and not necessarily tied to the USA.

**Pierre Trudeau (1919–2000)** Trudeau entered politics in the 1960s. He was appointed as Lester Pearson's parliamentary secretary, and later served as minister of justice. Apart from a brief period in 1979–80, Trudeau was prime minister of Canada for more than 16 years between 1968 and 1984. He was a charismatic liberal leader and inspired a following that came to be known as 'Trudeaumania'. He dominated the Canadian political scene, preserving national unity against Quebec separatists and aiming to make Canada a 'just society'.

With the introduction of conscription in the USA, Canada faced a new problem. Draft dodgers – young American men trying to avoid being sent to Vietnam – sought refuge in Canada. While those in both Canada and the US who supported the war called these men cowards, the draft dodgers themselves believed that they were making an ethical protest against US actions. No separate records were kept of draft dodgers fleeing to Canada, but their numbers are estimated at between 20,000 and 90,000. Controversially, Trudeau welcomed them.

The inclusion of these young Americans into Canadian society created the basis for an anti-war movement that eventually reached Canadian university campuses, centred in Toronto and Vancouver. The draft dodgers were mostly white graduates, and many found work at Canadian universities and schools, boosting Canada's academic institutions. Organisations were formed to assist them, including the Toronto Anti-Draft Programme, which created and distributed a pamphlet to aid the war resistors.

*Anti-Vietnam War protestors march on Parliament Hill in Ottawa in 1967*

Many draft dodgers also published material encouraging those who had been drafted to desert from the army. These pamphlets were smuggled into the US at the height of anti-war feeling between 1967 and 1970. As Canada had no draft, *evasion* was not a criminal offence. However, *desertion* from the armed services was a crime in Canada. When some US deserters crossed into Canada, Johnson (and later his successor, Richard Nixon) pressured the Canadian government to arrest them and send them back to the US. However, Trudeau allowed the deserters to remain in Canada, arguing that they could be prosecuted there instead of the USA. In reality, the Canadian government left them alone.

Many draft dodgers and deserters from the US army remained in Canada permanently. The RCMP monitored both both groups carefully, as well as any organisations considered sympathetic to their cause. However, this surveillance was not entirely driven by Canadian concern over their actions. The FBI and the CIA wanted the activities of the protestors to be carefully watched, and the RCMP provided these intelligence organisations with information.

The anti-Vietnam War movement was particularly strong in Quebec, where it was encouraged by the anti-American separatist group the Front de libération du Québec (FLQ). One notable incident at this time occurred during Expo 67 in Montreal – a world fair celebrating Canada's centenary year. President Johnson attended the opening of the American pavilion, during which a large US flag was to be unfurled. The FLQ informed the Canadian government that whoever tried to raise the flag would be shot. Although this threat was not carried out, when the flag was raised it was discovered that a protestor had cut out all the stars.

## Discussion point

Re-read the text above on public reaction to the war. How far might the US government feel betrayed by Canada? To what extent were the draft dodgers both a positive and a negative presence in Canadian society at the end of the 1960s?

# Foreign policy under Trudeau

In foreign affairs, Trudeau kept Canada firmly in NATO but followed an independent path in international relations. He established diplomatic links with the communist People's Republic of China, and went on an official visit to Beijing. Trudeau was also known to be a friend of Fidel Castro in Cuba. As a result, in the 1970s, Canadian policy often conflicted with that of the USA, and sometimes even caused concern within the British Commonwealth.

US–Canadian relations grew more strained over the question of nuclear weapons. The issue of the Bomarc anti-aircraft missiles and the nuclear warheads under Diefenbaker's government set off a fierce debate (see page 106). Under political pressure, Diefenbaker hesitated over accepting the warheads, but Lester Pearson eventually allowed them on to Canadian soil in late 1963. Trudeau felt that this was one of several US attempts to dominate Canada, and he decided to remove nuclear weapons and reduce the number of Canadian NATO troops stationed in Europe.

As Cold War tensions relaxed during the 1970s, Trudeau found he had more independence and flexibility, without coming under the type of pressure the USA often exerted on unfriendly or unco-operative governments. Although he was sometimes criticised by the US government, Trudeau's commitment to NATO went some way towards appeasing his detractors. During this period of renewed optimism in North America and beyond, cultural exchanges and arms-reduction talks took place between East and West. In fact, Canada's greatest post-war threat emerged from within, as nationalist groups openly questioned the USA's political and cultural influence. All these issues are discussed in more detail in the sections that follow.

*Pierre Trudeau in 1969; his great popularity among the Canadian people has been called 'Trudeaumania'*

## Divergence and the Third Option

Historians Gordon Mace and Jean-Philippe Thérien state that a Canadian foreign policy document made public by Trudeau in 1970 contained six key features to guide Canadian policy into the 1980s:

- foster economic growth
- preserve sovereignty and independence
- contribute to peace and security
- promote social justice
- improve Canadians' quality of life
- maintain environmental harmony.

Surprisingly, nothing in this document addressed the relationship between Canada and the USA. Canadian divergence became even more evident in 1972, when the country adopted a policy called the Third Option. Through this, Trudeau tried to increase Canada's foreign partners and hoped to establish economic and commercial relationships with Latin America, Japan and the EEC. As a starting point for this, Canada doubled its aid to Latin America. However, the private sector in Canada was cautious, and the country still needed to maintain a good economic relationship with the USA. These factors, combined with the oil crisis of 1973 (see page 89), meant that the Third Option policy was never fully implemented.

Personal relationships between Trudeau and a succession of US presidents – Nixon, Ford and Carter – were not always easy. In particular, the US disapproved of Trudeau's relations with Cuba. Ford eventually acknowledged that Canada (and many others states) had grown immune to US feelings about Cuba. As a result, Ford began moves to resume normal relations with Castro, but stopped when Castro sent troops to Angola (see page 169). In June 1976, Trudeau met Ford in Washington and confirmed Canada's commitment to NATO. Carter recognised Canada's importance and respected the country's growing sense of nationalism. He thus established annual meetings between the heads of government of the two countries, alongside interim meetings between other officials, to maintain good relations.

## Discussion point

Historian Peter Dobell has suggested that Canadians had a problem of national identity and needed to demonstrate how they differed from the USA; at the same time, however, they knew that in terms of US security they would 'never be dispensable'. How far might this observation account for both Trudeau's foreign policy intentions and Canada's desire to balance co-operation with independence?

## Trudeau and Cuba

The Canada–Cuba relationship was central to US–Canadian tensions, and dated back to the disagreements between Diefenbaker and Kennedy in the 1960s. Trudeau visited Cuba in 1976, and Castro proudly showed him the developing country. The Canadian prime minister shouted 'Viva Castro!' to a crowd of 25,000 cheering Cubans.

While Washington considered this diplomatic trip to be ill-advised, Trudeau disagreed, and again argued that Canada had to maintain an independent foreign policy. Castro and Trudeau later developed a personal friendship that continued until Trudeau's death in 2000.

Trudeau's relationship with Castro led to economic ties between Canada and Cuba. Canadian businesses gained access to markets that were free from US competition, and Cuba benefited from the rise in numbers of Canadian tourists visiting the island. Although Cuba was no longer a Cold War threat, the Cuban–Canadian friendship still caused problems between Washington and Ottawa.

## Trudeau and China

Canada's relationship with the communist People's Republic of China also marked a significant move away from US influence. In 1960, Diefenbaker had spotted the opportunity to trade with China, a large country free from US involvement. Canada sold $60 million worth of wheat to China and, when combined with sales to the communist USSR, Canadian wheat exports increased by over 200% in the 1960s. This provided a lifeline for Canadian farmers, as well as confirming Canada's international trade presence. Under Diefenbaker, Pearson and Trudeau, foreign policy and economic policy gradually merged.

Out of respect for US foreign policy throughout the 1960s, neither Diefenbaker nor Pearson officially recognised Communist China. However, in 1970, Trudeau formalised the relationship with China, making Canada the first Western power to establish diplomatic relations with the communist country. Canadian security services and the US government were deeply concerned by this, and Nixon despised Trudeau for associating with a communist nation.

### Discussion point

Re-read the text about Canada's relationship with Cuba and China and the benefits of commerce. Working in pairs, discuss whether a government (or state) is right to trade with an autocratic or undemocratic regime and, if so, why? Can you think of any examples today? Does economic recognition give respectability to dictators?

## Nuclear weapons

In the late 1970s, Trudeau addressed the United Nations Assembly and unveiled what he called his 'strategy of suffocation' for the international arms race. This included:

- a comprehensive test ban
- a ban on the flight testing of new strategic missiles

- a halt to the production of fissile material (used to fuel a thermal reactor or a nuclear explosive)
- reductions in defence spending.

Trudeau's fissile material proposal was significant, and it led to a resolution in the UN General Assembly, which asked the Committee on Disarmament to consider banning the production of such material. The USA and Britain were less enthusiastic than in previous years, but remained in favour of the proposal. However, the USSR opposed Trudeau's resolution because it did not go as far as stopping the production of nuclear weapons.

In his later years, Trudeau openly criticised US foreign and defence policies, and this breach widened when Ronald Reagan became president in 1980. Reagan took a particularly hard line with the USSR and Central America, and many of his policies were damaging to Canadian economic interests.

By 1981, Trudeau had begun fostering what he called 'North–South dialogue' between wealthy industrial nations and developing countries. He was increasingly involved in personal peace initiatives, visiting leaders in several countries in both the Eastern and Western blocs to persuade them to negotiate the reduction of nuclear weapons and to lower the level of Cold War tensions. Trudeau was later awarded the Albert Einstein Peace Prize for these endeavours.

However, Trudeau's government was also responsible for agreeing to Reagan's request to test cruise missiles over Canadian territory in April 1981. This was widely opposed by Canadians, who were not only concerned about the heightened nuclear arms race, but also confused by this contradiction in Trudeau's actions.

> Why was Trudeau critical of US foreign and defence policies? What were the key elements of his 'strategy of suffocation'?

## Trudeau's foreign policy: a summary

Canada annoyed the US by its relationship with Cuba and China, by discussing nuclear disarmament, and by courting countries in Latin America that the USA distrusted. However, given Canada's peacekeeping history, perhaps it is not really surprising that Trudeau sought to ease Cold War tensions. Trudeau inherited and continued a strong Canadian role in the Commonwealth (see the section on domestic policy in the following pages). For these reasons, many historians argue that despite his desire to 'put Canada first', Trudeau also sought to implement policies that were in accord with both the USA and other Western powers.

SOURCE B

We shall do more good by doing well what we know to be within our resources to do, than to pretend either to ourselves or to others that we can do things clearly beyond our national capacity.

Extract from a press release issued by Trudeau's office, 1968. Quoted in Dobell, P. C. 1972. Canada's Search for New Roles. Oxford, UK. Oxford University Press. p. 5.

As Whitaker and Hewitt explain, in Canada 'there was a dogged insistence on retaining at least some semblance of sovereignty ... [but] the Americans were our best friends, whether we liked it or not'.

What do you think Whitaker and Hewitt meant by the statement that the USA was Canada's best friend, 'whether we liked it or not'?

## Historical debate

It has been suggested that politicians and historians have exaggerated the strength of Trudeau's disagreement with the USA, and that instead of being anti-American, his policies simply reflected his desire to pursue independence in foreign affairs. What do you think? Was Trudeau ahead of his time by being an internationalist in a world still divided by Cold War ideology? Or might the necessities and realities of Canada's proximity to a powerful neighbour have restrained Trudeau?

Using any resources available to you, see if you can find further examples of Trudeau disagreeing with Washington. Use your information and ideas to come to a conclusion about this Canadian leader.

# How did the Cold War in the 1960s and 1970s influence different areas of Canadian domestic policy?

## Social reforms under Lester Pearson

When Lester Pearson's Liberal Party defeated Diefenbaker's Conservatives in the 1963 election, Pearson was determined to introduce the type of reform he considered essential for Canada to move forward as a modern democracy. Pearson operated without an overall majority, but as he wanted to wage a war on poverty, his minority government was supported in the House of Commons by the New Democratic Party.

Pearson's enthusiasm resulted in significant domestic achievements. These included the Canada Pension Plan, the Canada Assistance Plan (by which Ottawa shared social assistance costs with the provinces), the Guaranteed Income Supplement, universal healthcare through the 1966 Medical Care Act, and the introduction of the Canada Student Loan Programme.

In addition, Pearson introduced a federal labour code, which outlined a 40-hour work week and two weeks' holiday a year. It also established a minimum wage, created new regulatory agencies, funded universities, expanded crop insurance for farmers, and substantially increased arts funding.

Pearson signed the Canada–United States Automotive Agreement (or Auto Pact) in January 1965, and unemployment dropped to its lowest level in over a decade. He also instigated the 'great flag debate', which resulted in Canada adopting the red and white maple leaf flag. Increasingly, the Canadian government intervened in the economic life of businesses and individuals.

As well as this, Pearson established a number of Royal Commissions, which introduced changes that helped create legal equality for women and brought the question of Canada's official language to the fore. Pearson hoped to be the last prime minister of Canada to speak only one of the two recognised national languages, and after this, fluency in both English and French became an unofficial requirement for prime ministers.

To many people, these successes linked Pearson with the former US president Franklin D. Roosevelt, whose New Deal had so greatly influenced American life in the 1930s. Pearson also pointed out that his contemporary, Lyndon B. Johnson, was a similar reforming character, introducing legislation for his Great Society (see page 84). However, Pearson still had his critics who, in the Cold War climate, pointed to similarities between the Canadian welfare state and Soviet-style state control.

Some historians credit Pearson with being more instrumental in Canada's transformation than Pierre Trudeau. Certainly his government introduced many of the social programmes now well-established in Canada, which are often credited to Trudeau.

## Separatism and the consequences of the October Crisis of 1970

One of the most significant issues that arose in Canada in the 1960s was that of Quebec separatism. After Maurice Duplessis' authoritarian rule (see page 117), the province began to move away from its strongly Catholic, agricultural past, and became increasingly middle class and urban centred. These changes, under the Liberal premier Jean Lesage, became known as the Quiet Revolution. However, further changes in leadership resulted in demands for greater provincial power, and the separatist movement gained momentum.

*Police restrain a demonstrator at a separatist march in Montreal, Quebec, in 1965*

### Quebec under Lesage

When he came to power in 1960, Lesage promised to rid the provincial government of corruption, introduce educational reform and improve the social infrastructure. He also nationalised energy services and introduced laws designed to reduce the Catholic Church's political influence in the region. As the 1960s progressed, however, nationalists in Quebec began demanding even greater autonomy, seeking constitutional change and challenging the basis of national unity.

In 1966, Lesage was defeated in the provincial elections, and the Union Nationale (the party Duplessis had previously led) returned to power. This provoked a serious split in Québécois politics. The Liberals believed that the reforms they had introduced should be followed through within the current federal system. However, the Union Nationale believed strongly in gaining more provincial control for Quebec, and leader Daniel Johnson called for 'equality or independence'. A leftist fringe movement emerged, which sought total independence from Canada. This led to the formation of the separatist Parti Québécois (PQ) under the leadership of **René Lévesque**. At Expo 67 in Montreal, French president Charles de Gaulle closed a speech with 'Vive le Québec libre!' ('Long live free Quebec!'), which became the rallying cry for the separatist movement.

**René Lévesque (1922–87)** Lévesque was a former television news reporter and a Liberal politician. He founded the Parti Québécois and was premier of Quebec from 1976 to 1985. During his period in office, Lévesque attempted to win separation from Canada for Quebec. A referendum was held in Quebec in 1980, which he lost with 60% opposed to separation (the turnout was 86%).

## The FLQ and the October Crisis

De Gaulle encouraged a fervour that played into the hands of the FLQ (see page 129), which was already conducting a bombing campaign across the province. Over the next few months, FLQ activities increased in scale and violence. In 1968, the organisation bombed a federal government book shop, McGill University, the residence of Jean Drapeau, mayor of Montreal, and finally the Montreal stock exchange, where 27 people were injured. The FLQ's campaign reached a climax in October 1970, when members of the group kidnapped Quebec's labour minister, Pierre Laporte, and the British trade commissioner, James Cross. Cross was released unharmed, but Laporte was later found murdered.

Trudeau's government and the RCMP were outraged by the FLQ's actions, and believed that the group was motivated by Marxist ideology and encouraged by the Cuban Revolution. Adding to the concerns of the federal government was the fact that, in the Cold War climate, it was essential that Canada maintained a sense of national unity, which the FLQ threatened to destroy.

After Laporte's murder, Trudeau declared martial law in Montreal and suspended some civil liberties under the War Measures Act. He authorised the arrest of nearly 500 people, including 150 suspected FLQ members, who were detained without legal representation. FLQ members Paul Rose and Francis Simard were eventually sentenced to life imprisonment for Laporte's murder, and others were convicted of his kidnap. James Cross's abductors fled to Cuba and then France; they returned to Canada many years later.

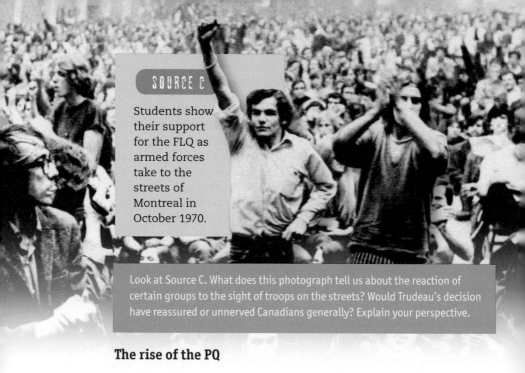

Look at Source C. What does this photograph tell us about the reaction of certain groups to the sight of troops on the streets? Would Trudeau's decision have reassured or unnerved Canadians generally? Explain your perspective.

## The rise of the PQ

Most Canadians – whether French or English – supported Trudeau's decision over the October Crisis, believing that members of the FLQ were communist-inspired extremists. Support for Trudeau reached 90% nationally, and even higher than this in Quebec itself. The FLQ ceased its activities in 1971, but the separatist movement continued.

By 1974, French had become the official language of Quebec. On 15 November 1976, the separatist Parti Québécois swept to victory in the provincial election. Lévesque passed measures to strengthen the separatist movement. Under a controversial law of 1977 (Bill 101), education in English-language schools was greatly restricted. All immigrants moving to Quebec had to enrol in French-language schools, regardless of their native language. The law also changed English place names and made French the language of business, government regulations and public institutions.

Although the PQ retained power, a referendum to make the province an independent country was rejected by the Quebec voters in 1980. The Quebec government opposed the new 1982 constitution, which included a provision for freedom of language in education.

## Historical perspectives on Quebec separatism

Whitaker and Hewitt argue that by debating the basis of national unity, the Quiet Revolution and provincial separatism actually undermined the Cold War consensus. It left behind 'the conservative Catholic anti-communism of an earlier generation', with the people of Quebec amongst the most supportive of moves towards nuclear disarmament and the most critical of US policy in Vietnam.

Bothwell regards the emergence of separatism in 1960s Canada as 'responding to international currents' running alongside the near collapse of European colonial empires between 1945 and 1970. He states: 'It didn't matter that Quebec had representative and democratic institutions, the separatists argued: Quebec politicians really served the English establishment.'

Most historians agree that the climax of the disagreements over separatism – the October Crisis – endangered Canada's very foundations. After a high point in 1970, admiration for Trudeau began to decline, and there were calls for a reappraisal of the national security services and the RCMP, whose surveillance continued in Cold War-era Canada.

 # Theory of knowledge

### History, change and explanations

The historian H. A. L. Fisher (1856–1940) said: 'The human universe is so enormously complicated that to speak of the cause of any event is an absurdity.' There has been some debate about what triggered separatism in Quebec. Some argue that it developed both in response to the end of colonialism in Africa and Indochina, and to unease about growing French dominance. How do historians decide which factors are more important than others? Are such developments usually the result of a combination of factors?

## State surveillance in the 1960s and 1970s

### The RCMP and the FLQ

Throughout the 1960s, the RCMP monitored several separatist groups, but focused on those in Quebec as they were the most forceful and outspoken. These groups were largely targeted because they were thought to be potential 'tools of Moscow', able to destabilise Canada from within. The RCMP underestimated the genuine strength of feeling about the more personal issues of cultural and linguistic freedom that motivated the separatist movement.

By 1970, the RCMP had gathered a great deal of information about radical FLQ members. After the October Crisis, Trudeau instructed the RCMP to prioritise destruction of the separatists over investigating espionage and monitoring communism. This order effectively gave the RCMP permission to use investigative techniques such as mail-opening, blackmail, bugging, intimidation and break-ins, even though such practices were illegal. PQ leader Lévesque was particularly angered by this. He protested that his party was legitimate – unlike the FLQ – and criticised the RCMP's 'cowboy cop' tactics. (In 1980, it was discovered that Lévesque's deputy, Claude Morin, was in fact a paid informant for the RCMP at the time.)

## Operation Feather Bed

The best example of the extent of state surveillance in Canada in the 1960s and 1970s is Operation Feather Bed. This operation actually began in the 1950s, and involved opening investigation files on 'suspect or known communist sympathisers employed by the federal government'. It was prompted by a belief that many communist spies had escaped the Gouzenko disclosures (see page 99).

After 1963, with tensions heightened by events in Cuba and Vietnam, as well as the exposure of the so-called 'Cambridge Traitors' spy-ring in Britain, the RCMP decided to review its operation. Feather Bed widened the organisation's scope to look beyond the civil service, and expanded its secret surveillance. It eventually produced a list of 262 alleged secret Communist Party members. These included doctors, lawyers, economists and academics – all suspected of indulging in activities that came dangerously close to espionage.

By 1968, Operation Feather Bed had developed into a special intelligence section. This differed from the FBI in the USA in that it remained more or less an attempt to hunt down Soviet spies and infiltrators, rather than targeting people such as politicians and officials for supicious business dealings.

News of the Feather Bed files later became public, and caused a scandal in 1979–80 when the Conservatives under Joe Clark were briefly in office. Clark criticised the RCMP for reporting 'gossip often of the most malicious kind, about virtually every senior public servant of prominence in Ottawa at a particular point in time'. Many people claim that there was a Feather Bed file on Trudeau, but this cannot be released until 20 years after his death – in 2020.

> How and why did the RCMP change its approach to surveillance in the mid 1960s?

## The Commission of Inquiry

In the late 1970s, it emerged that the RCMP Security Service had stolen documents from René Lévesque's Parti Québécois. The RCMP was also discovered to have used several illegal investigative techniques. Although many people had long suspected that such activities were taking place, there was public outrage when it was confirmed.

This discovery led to the Royal Commission of Inquiry into Certain Activities of the RCMP – more commonly known as the McDonald Commission after its presiding judge, David Cargill

McDonald. The commission recommended that the RCMP no longer carry out intelligence duties, and instead a separate intelligence agency be established – the Canadian Security Intelligence Service (CSIS). By 1984, intelligence work was separate from policing. Throughout the period 1964–81, though – during détente and beyond – the surveillance of Canadians continued.

It is tempting to regard Canada in this period as something of a police state, but in reality many countries – both East and West – adapted technology and espionage techniques in order to develop and refine surveillance on others. However, the effects of the Cold War were more pervasive than anyone imagined at the time – especially ordinary Canadians.

# Protest, gender and ethnicity

## Protest

In the 1970s, Canada realised the need to encourage a new generation of industrialists, scientists, educators and builders to ensure a prosperous future. The youth of this generation needed to remain in secondary education and then go on to study at universities and colleges. As such opportunities expanded, a restless, militant group of university students emerged. They were increasingly aware of international issues, and became particularly radicalised over the Vietnam War. Carleton University and the University of Manitoba were among the first to experience anti-war campus marches in 1965.

This generation of Canadians also involved itself with the peace movement generally. Throughout US involvement in Vietnam – up to 1973 – the RCMP monitored Canadians who organised campus protests or took leading roles in distributing literature, as well as watching groups that helped US draft dodgers.

## Gender

The women's movement grew significantly in post-war Canada. In 1961, the oral contraceptive pill was introduced; by 1963, 10,000 women were using it, and by 1967 this had risen to 0.75 million. The pill brought women control and self-determination, and introduced a culture of wider sexual liberation.

In 1963, American Betty Friedan's book *The Feminine Mystique* was published. In it, Friedan argued that women needed to break away from their roles as wives, lovers and mothers and instead seek new, more fulfilling identities. By 1968, women in many countries were seeking 'liberation' and women's groups sprang up across Canada.

The Vancouver Women's Caucus was established in 1968. Its magazine *The Pedestal* – published from 1969 to 1973 – triggered a great response, and women from Vancouver to Halifax began forming their own groups. Especially prominent amongst these were the Montreal Women's Liberation Movement, founded in 1969, and the Front de libération des femmes du Québec (FLF), which published a feminist manifesto in 1970. The Centre des Femmes edited the first French-language radical feminist periodical – *Québécoises Deboutte!* – and by the 1970s, women's liberation had become a major social movement that transcended the linguistic and cultural divide.

The government and the RCMP Security Service were alarmed by the sudden rise in these groups, particularly against the background of Quebec separatism and the ongoing Cold War. Most of the groups focused on raising the profile of women by distributing literature and similar forms of campaigning. However, some turned to action, providing abortion services, health centres, feminist magazines, militant theatre, day-care for children, shelters for battered women and rape crisis centres. They also campaigned for equal pay.

Lester Pearson had already responded to feminist pressure in 1967, announcing a Royal Commission on the Status of Women, headed by Ottawa journalist Florence Bird. The commission reported to the House of Commons in 1970, and its 167 recommendations included equal pay for work of equal value, a national day-care network and paid maternity leave. Two years later, the National Action Committee on the Status of Women was founded as a lobby group to monitor and press for action on these recommendations. It ensured that the political visibility of women's issues continued into the 1980s. Trudeau responded by creating new positions and procedures to deal with women's rights.

In 1978, the Canadian Human Rights Act came into effect, prohibiting discrimination on the basis of gender (among other things) in the case of employees under federal jurisdiction. A Women's Programme was established, which made money available for special projects, including women's centres, research programmes and professional associations, as well as refuges for physically abused women.

By the mid 1980s, however, women in Canada still did not have full equality. They made up just under 50% of the workforce, but full-time female employees still earned only 72% of the equivalent salary paid to men. Some 60% of the workers earning less than $10,000 a year were female. Women's groups fought to ensure that the Charter of Rights and Freedoms in Canada campaigned to strike down discriminatory laws, particularly Canada's abortion law.

Re-read the section about women in Canada. From the text, what can you learn about the development of women's movements in Canada and the changing role of Canadian women between the 1960s and 1980s? Does this information actually tell us the whole story?

## Ethnicity

Canada's native people also took advantage of the spirit of awakening and protest that characterised the 1960s and 1970s. The American Indian Movement and Red Power in the USA – organisations inspired by the Civil Rights Movement – persuaded many Native Canadians (or First Nations people) to push for reform of the Indian Act, which gave the federal government control over Indian affairs. They also aimed to reduce poverty on many of the Indian reservations.

Bothwell reports that the 1951 Canadian census recorded fewer than 10,000 Inuit and around 150,000 Indians. Throughout the 1960s, their numbers began to rise, but despite this Native Canadians were still governed by old-fashioned laws and practices, which resulted in rural slum conditions far below the standard of living enjoyed by most white Canadians.

The National Indian Council was created in 1961 to represent indigenous people, including Treaty/Status Indians (officially recorded Indians with additional rights), non-status people and the Metis people. However, this had collapsed by 1968, as the three groups failed to act collectively. The non-status and Metis groups formed the Native Council of Canada, and Treaty/Status groups formed the National Indian Brotherhood (NIB), an umbrella group for provincial and territorial First Nations organisations. Various other organisations were established, some more regional, others to address specific native grievances.

In 1969, Trudeau's government proposed to end previous treaties made with Canadian Indians and abolish reserves. By this, Trudeau aimed to end their special status and integrate them into the general community. This encouraged the Indian leadership, which had now emerged as active, informed and better-educated than before. The Native Canadians objected to what they feared would amount to a loss of their cultural identity through the assimilation of First Nations people into the Canadian population. They felt this gave them the same status of other ethnic minorities rather than being treated as a distinct group.

The following year, Alberta natives occupied a rural school, demanding the right to control their own education. The two-week sit-in marked the start of a new era in native activism.

The NIB grew in status, and in 1972 its policy paper 'Indian Control of Indian Education' was generally accepted by the federal government. By 1980, the NIB had become the Assembly of First Nations (AFN). Its aims were to protect the rights, treaty obligations, ceremonies and claims of First Nation citizens. The AFN was eventually recognised by Ottawa as a forum for certain issues. However, the federal government did this without acknowledging native sovereignty, as demanded by some of the more radical Indians.

### Activity

Carry out some additional research on the significance of the NIB for First Nations rights in Canada.

# Did the Cold War change Canada?

The Cold War undoubtedly left its mark on Canada. In particular, the country found itself at the forefront of international activities in its role as NATO and UN peacekeepers. In an attempt to distinguish itself from Britain and the USA by acting as a 'middle power', Canada developed its own international role in mediation. As time passed, however, Canadian influence changed.

## Canada, Europe and NATO

By the 1970s, the USSR felt reassured that West Germany would not challenge the borders established in 1945, and Trudeau realised that a Canadian garrison in Europe was no longer necessary. He therefore announced the withdrawal of half of Canada's forces from the region. Britain was concerned by this move, and in the early 1970s relations between NATO and Canada became more strained. However, Trudeau was simply responding to the changing nature of the Cold War and Canada's involvement in it.

As we have discussed, Canada's foreign affairs became much more internationalist throughout the Cold War. While few countries doubted that Canada was a loyal Western ally, some in the West were unhappy with what they regarded as its 'non-alignment'. Trudeau responded to suggestions of being 'soft on communism' by emphasising his desire to work for peace, thereby avoiding confrontation.

# Canada and the USA

The USA frequently put pressure on Canada, as we have seen in the events surrounding the Bomarc missiles, Cuba and the Vietnam draft dodgers. Canada's desire to retain its distinctive identity was made even more difficult by its reliance on the US nuclear shield, the need for Canadian policies to work within the broader security needs of North America as a whole and, above all, the proximity of the USA.

Canadian television offered overwhelmingly American programmes, while reception of US TV channels, especially news programmes along the border, made it impossible for Canadians to avoid being influenced by US interpretations of Cold War events.

## SOURCE D

In Canada, the Cold War had a distinctly cultural dimension because it raised issues of national self-representation that went beyond international political tensions related to capitalistic versus communistic regimes. The prevailing atmosphere of the Cold War in Canada was anti-communist, but it was also anti-American in many ways.

Cavell, R. (ed). 2004. Love, Hate and Fear in Canada's Cold War. Toronto, Canada. University of Toronto Press. p. 3.

Clearly, issues of self-representation influenced groups such as the separatists in Quebec, the Native Canadian people, and the generation of women exposed to the freedom of the pill and the writings of Betty Friedan. By the mid 1960s, several elements combined to challenge both the Cold War consensus in Canada, and the received wisdom from the USA about its role in Vietnam.

# Social changes

Throughout the 1960s and 1970s, Canada was still capitalist, still a member of NATO, still patriotic, but it was also more cynical, less innocent and less reverential towards Britain. It was conscious of the vulnerability of the West during a time of economic crisis.

Canadians exhibited two kinds of nationalism: one English-speaking, the other French-speaking. They had something in common, though – irritation with the USA. In addition, because of the Cold War, or perhaps in spite of it, all Canadians finally gained the welfare system they had long hoped for. Fears of adopting a Soviet-style state-planned medical and benefits system were overcome by the desire to live in a healthier and more secure country. By introducing such measures, the government hoped to win the support of the people.

*The new maple-leaf national flag of Canada is raised over the Canadian embassy in Washington, 1965*

## Attitudes towards communism

In 1979, following the revolution in Iran and the Soviet invasion of Afghanistan, tension between the USA and the USSR increased. Canada joined the USA in boycotting the 1980 Summer Olympic Games being held in Moscow. Shortly afterwards, the Soviets turned their intermediate-range nuclear missiles towards Western Europe, prompting a warning from NATO that it would use its own missiles unless the Soviet ones were withdrawn.

In April 1981, Trudeau's government received a request from the USA to test cruise missiles over Canadian territory. In the letter, Reagan claimed that these Tomahawk missiles needed to be tried out in conditions similar to the Arctic and the Russian steppes. He also explained that these were defensive weapons, and would not be used for a first strike. This request put Trudeau in a difficult position and he spent a long time deciding what to do. Eventually, in December 1981, he offered Reagan a qualified agreement to the testing. Legislation for the Canada–US Testing and Evaluation Programme (CANUSTP) was passed in early 1982. There was widespread opposition from the Canadian people, who were already concerned about worsening superpower relations and felt this put Canada back in the front line of the Cold War. Events such as this contributed to the revival of a peace movement both in Canada and abroad in the early 1980s.

This re-emergence of superpower grievances marked the start of the final showdown in the Cold War. Canada itself was a very different country from the one that was drawn into the Cold War by Gouzenko, and operated in a different world to a different set of criteria. Despite its comparatively moderate attitude towards communism, the Canadian state continued intensive surveillance of communists and sharing of intelligence with the US. It played a middle-power role in international affairs, and pursued diplomatic relations with communist countries that the US had cut ties with, such as Cuba and China after their respective revolutions. But Canada could never truly escape being part of the British Commonwealth, nor could it entirely distance itself from its powerful neighbour.

## SOURCE E

The federal government geared up for extensive protest in the 1970s. Instead, there was a noticeable decline in the discontent that had marked the previous decade. One factor in the shift, and an issue that plagued the Trudeau Liberals, was a major economic downturn in the early 1970s that left many with a sense of financial insecurity. Between 1971 and 1974, the rate of inflation more than tripled ... a $300m budgetary surplus in 1970 had turned to a $5billion deficit by 1976. The government responded with dramatic measures, in particular the introduction of wage and price controls. Despite the reduction in Cold War tensions in the 70s, they did not really disappear.

Whitaker, R. and Hewitt, S. 2003. Canada and the Cold War. Toronto, Canada. James Lorimer & Co. p. 186.

What does Source E suggest are the reasons for an absence of civil discontent in Canada in the 1970s?

## Activity

Re-read the text in the section 'Did the Cold War change Canada?' Make a list of the ways in which you think Canada changed. Put them in order of importance. Then swap lists with another student and discuss your findings.

# End of chapter activities

## Paper 3 exam practice

### Question

'Canada's attitude to the Vietnam War between 1964 and 1973 sometimes made the US feel betrayed by its neighbour.' To what extent do you agree with this statement?
[20 marks]

### Skill focus

Avoiding irrelevance

### Examiner's tips

Do not waste valuable writing time on irrelevant material. If it's irrelevant, it won't gain you **any** marks. Writing irrelevant information can happen because:

- the candidate does not look carefully enough at the wording of the question
- the candidate ignores the fact that the questions require selection of information, an analytical approach and a final judgement; instead, the candidate just writes down all that he or she knows about a topic (relevant or not), and hopes that the examiner will do the analysis and make the judgement
- the candidate has unwisely restricted his or her revision (for example, if a question comes up on Canada and the Korean War, rather than the expected one on Canada and the Vietnam War, the candidate might try to turn it into the question he or she wanted); whatever the reason, such responses rarely address any of the demands of the question.

For this question, you will need to:

- cover the various aspects and details of Canadian foreign policy with respect to both the USA and Vietnam
- outline the results of those various policies
- provide a judgement about whether Canada did 'betray' the USA, or whether Canada's desire to pursue an independent foreign policy was justified.

### Common mistakes

One common error with questions like this is for candidates to write about material they know well, rather than material directly related to the question.

Another mistake is to present too much general information, instead of material specific to the person, period and command terms.

Finally, candidates often elaborate too much on events outside the dates given in the question (see the guidance in Chapter 2, page 51).

## Sample paragraphs of irrelevant focus/material

A comment made in Washington at the height of the Vietnam War implied that Canada was 'betraying its neighbour and friend' by harbouring American draft dodgers and helping to supervise ceasefires. Yet simultaneously, about 40,000 Canadians volunteered to fight with US forces against the spread of communism in Southeast Asia. Before trying to decide whether either the statement or Canada's attitude to the war were justified, it will first be necessary to highlight US-Canadian relations prior to 1964, and to examine underlying tensions that had developed during the premiership of John Diefenbaker.

Canada had tried to develop an increasingly independent approach to foreign policy from 1945. This came to the fore after the Vietnam War escalated in 1965, particularly under Pierre Trudeau from 1968. But the problems were already there. In the 1950s, Lester Pearson had clashed with his US counterpart Dean Acheson over Korea, and was accused of 'moralising'. It has also been suggested that there was some US jealousy when Pearson won the Nobel Peace Prize for his mediation during the Suez Crisis.

When John Diefenbaker became prime minister in 1957, he had relatively little experience of foreign affairs. However, he also had a great loyalty towards Britain combined with an innate mistrust and dislike of things American. Yet by virtue of his anti-communist beliefs, Diefenbaker was a supporter of US Cold War policy. However, he clashed with the USA on several occasions and by the time he left office in 1963, Canada and the USA were not always seeing eye to eye.

[There then follows another paragraph on Canada's role within the UN and how it struck an independent note, before the candidate actually gets to full-scale US troop involvement in Vietnam in 1965.]

This is an example of a **weak answer**. Although a brief comment on the state of relations between Canada and the USA would be relevant and helpful, there is certainly no need to go into so much detail about the period under John Diefenbaker from 1957 to 1963 and even prior to that. Thus, virtually all of the underlined material is irrelevant, and will not score any marks. In addition, the candidate is using up valuable writing time, which should have been spent on providing relevant points and supporting knowledge.

## Activity

In this chapter, the focus is on avoiding writing answers that contain, to a greater or lesser extent, irrelevant material. Using the information from this chapter, and any other sources of information available to you, write an answer to **one** of the following Paper 3 practice questions, keeping your answer fully focused on the question asked. Remember – doing a plan **first** can help you maintain this focus.

Remember to refer to the simplified Paper 3 markscheme on page 219.

# Paper 3 practice questions

1   Analyse Canada's success in establishing an independent foreign policy between 1963 and 1981.

2   Compare and contrast the policies of the governments of Lester Pearson and Pierre Trudeau.

3   'The Cold War had changed Canada enormously by the end of the 1970s.' To what extent do you agree with this statement?

4   Evaluate the changes in attitude towards gender and ethnicity in Canada from 1963 to 1981.

5   Assess the impact of the 1970 October Crisis on Canadian attitudes to separatism and ethnicity.

# 6 Cuba and the Cold War 1945–81

## Timeline

**1952 Mar:** former president Batista seizes power

**1953 26 Jul:** Castro launches a rebellion, resulting in his imprisonment

**1954 Nov:** Batista dissolves parliament and is elected constitutional president without opposition

**1955 May:** Castro released from prison

**1956 Dec:** Castro's rebels land in Cuba; guerrilla war against Batista begins

**1959 Jan:** Castro's revolutionary government takes control; Batista flees to Dominican Republic

**Feb:** Castro becomes prime minister

**1960 Jul:** all US businesses and property in Cuba nationalised

**1961 Jan:** USA breaks off diplomatic relations with Cuba

**Apr:** US Bay of Pigs invasion fails; US trade embargo

**1962 Jan:** Cuba expelled from Organization of American States

**16–28 Oct:** Cuban Missile Crisis

**1967 9 Oct:** Guevara captured and executed in Bolivia

**1972** Cuba becomes full member of Soviet-based Council for Mutual Economic Assistance

**1975** Cuban forces airlifted by USSR to help MPLA in Angola

**Dec:** Cuban Communist Party approves new socialist constitution; Castro elected president

## Key questions

- Why were relations between Cuba and the USA historically important?
- Why was there a revolution against Batista?
- What impact did the Cuban Revolution have on the Cold War?
- Did the Cold War influence Castro's domestic policy?

This chapter examines the impact of the Cold War on Cuba from 1945 to 1981. It considers the relationship between Cuba and the USA before Castro's revolution, then looks at how this relationship changed under Castro. The effect of the Cuban Revolution on both regional and international relations is also discussed. Finally, this chapter explores the impact of the Cuban Missile Crisis – viewed by many historians as the most dangerous moment of the Cold War – and Castro's attempts to establish an independent role in world affairs while pursuing a socialist revolution in Cuba.

# Overview

- The Caribbean island of Cuba was ruled by Spain until it gained independence at the end of the Spanish–American War in 1898.
- In the first decades of the 20th century, Cuba increasingly came under the influence of the USA, and soon the Cuban economy was heavily dependent on US trade and investment.
- In 1933, the army general Fulgencio Batista overthrew the Cuban government in a military coup. From this time, he effectively ruled Cuba as a dictator through a series of 'puppet' presidents. Batista protected US interests in Cuba, and grew wealthy as a result.
- By 1945, Cuba was practically a US colony – an American holiday destination and a centre for organised crime, prostitution and drugs. While rich Americans and the Cuban élite enjoyed lavish lifestyles, most Cubans lived in poverty, with limited access to health care and education.
- In 1956, Fidel Castro organised a rebellion to overthrow Batista. This developed into a three-year guerrilla war, but in January 1959 Castro emerged victorious and Batista fled the country.
- US leaders were suspicious of Castro, and their attitude eventually caused him to turn to the USSR for support. Consequently, Cuba was drawn into Cold War politics.
- After a failed US attempt to overthrow Castro in 1961, he appealed to Soviet leader Nikita Khrushchev for help. In response, Khrushchev sent intermediate-range ballistic missiles to Cuba.
- This triggered the Cuban Missile Crisis of October 1962, which nearly brought the superpowers into open conflict. After several tense days, a compromise was reached and war was avoided.
- After the crisis, the USA remained hostile to Castro; as a result, Cuba moved towards the USSR, China and other communist states or non-aligned countries.
- Castro encouraged revolution by supporting any movements with anti-US sentiments in Africa and the Americas, including Nicaragua, Angola and Ethiopia.
- By the 1980s, however, the USSR could no longer provide support for Cuba's interventionist foreign policy. As Soviet aid was withdrawn, Cuba's influence on the world stage began to decline.

# Why were relations between Cuba and the USA historically important?

## Cuba and the USA 1898–1945

### Economic factors

The USA and Cuba share a complex, connected history. Cuba was part of the Spanish Empire until the US won the Spanish–American War of 1898. Cuba gained independence from Spain, but the USA ensured that the peace terms allowed significant US control of the island. The Cuban army was immediately disbanded, removing a potential source of opposition to US domination.

The Americans began an extensive building programme in Cuba, constructing badly needed schools, roads, sewers and telegraph lines. They believed it was their duty to 'civilise' Cubans and integrate them into the USA's sphere of influence. Between 1901 and 1921, the US military intervened on four occasions to help secure Cuban governments that would support the USA and help protect its growing interests. By the 1930s, the Cuban economy was supported by nearly $1500 million of US investment.

### SOURCE A

US government leaders saw these economic, moral and political responsibilities all going hand in hand. The Cubans were allowed, even encouraged, to choose a constitutional convention, which produced a charter in 1901. But the US government harboured doubts about the new country's ability to govern itself, so Washington forced the Cubans, under protest, to incorporate an amendment (the Platt Amendment) which gave the United States the right to intervene in domestic politics at will. This proviso remained in force until 1934, making Cuba an American protectorate.

*Skidmore, T. E. and Smith, P. H. 2001. Modern Latin America (5th Edition). New York, USA. Oxford University Press. p. 261.*

Sugar production was a major part of the Cuban economy. American companies owned the sugar mills and controlled large areas of rural land, which produced around 75% of Cuba's sugar. Almost all Cuban sugar was exported to the USA, and this made the island nation dependent on America, creating an unequal export economy in which foreign consumers (mainly the USA) determined the degree of prosperity or recession in Cuba. By 1959, the USA was Cuba's largest trading partner.

To what extent was Cuba really independent in the early years of the 20th century? What proved to be ironic about Cuba ridding itself of Spanish colonial rule?

## Geographical factors

At its nearest point, Cuba is only 145 km (90 miles) from the tip of Key West in Florida. This close proximity meant that the USA had long taken an interest in Cuban affairs. Historically, the US also viewed Cuba as a key part of a broader regional policy, and understood the strategic importance of states in the wider Americas. In 1823, US president James Monroe issued the Monroe Doctrine, which declared that the USA would not tolerate any European interference in the Americas.

In 1904, Theodore Roosevelt reinforced this policy with the Roosevelt Corollary. This addition to the Monroe Doctrine stated that the US would intervene anywhere in the Caribbean and Central America if such intervention was considered necessary to protect US lives, property or interests.

*A map of Cuba showing its position in relation to the USA and the Caribbean*

During the Second World War, Cuban president **Fulgencio Batista** formally supported the Allies. After 1945, Cuba increasingly came to be seen as a buffer against anti-US interests in the region, and its stability was of major importance to the USA. As the Cold War developed, president Harry Truman and his successors watched closely for signs of any communist or socialist state emerging in the Americas (the USA's 'back yard').

> **Fulgencio Batista (1901–73)** In 1933, Batista led the Sergeants' Revolt – an uprising that overthrew the Cuban government. By 1934, he had established himself as head of the armed forces, and from this time on he was the real power behind several civilian 'puppet' presidents. Batista served as the elected president in 1940–44, and enjoyed genuine popularity. However, after assuming leadership again in a 1952 coup he became a corrupt, right-wing dictator. Batista was overthrown by Fidel Castro in 1959, and died in exile in Portugal.

> Why was Cuba historically important to the USA? Was Cuba more important to the USA economically or politically? What can we learn about US attitudes in general towards the Americas by reading about its attitude towards Cuba?

## Theory of knowledge

### History and inevitability

Commentators have said it was 'inevitable' that Cubans would eventually challenge US dominance, particularly if a radical nationalist – like Castro – came along. Is 'inevitability' as a historical concept misleading, or even unacceptable? Rather than steering us towards understanding causation, does it merely lead us towards uncritical assumptions and away from alternative arguments by suggesting that 'things just happened that way'?

# Why was there a revolution against Batista?

## Batista's Cuba

In September 1933, Fulgencio Batista led an army uprising that overthrew the liberal Cuban government of President Gerardo Machado, marking the start of military influence in Cuban politics. Although Batista did not formally seize power for himself, for the next few years he effectively ruled the country through a series of 'puppet' presidents. During this period, Batista emerged as the USA's preferred ruler in the Caribbean.

## The new constitution and Batista's first presidency 1940–44

In 1940, a new Cuban constitution was agreed. This was one of the most progressive constitutions of its time, encouraging land reform, public education and a minimum wage. It introduced the eight-hour working day and was the first constitution in Latin America to approve (at least in principle) the right of women to vote and work, and equal rights for different sexes and races.

The 1940 Constitution also defined the responsibilities of each branch of the Cuban government, created the role of prime minister, and established clear rules about representation in Congress. Under this new constitution, general elections were held in July 1940, and Batista became president as the leader of the Democratic Socialist Coalition – a group that included both liberals and communists.

Although Batista did not enforce all the provisions of the 1940 Constitution during his four-year presidency, he did carry out widespread reforms, including improving the education system and launching an extensive programme of public works. Batista also reinforced ties with the USA by increasing trade between the two countries. Cuba joined the Second World War on the Allied side on the day after the Japanese bombing of the US naval base at Pearl Harbor in December 1941, further strengthening the bond with the USA.

As his presidential term came to an end, Batista supported Carlos Saladrigas Zayas as his successor. However, in the 1944 elections Zayas was defeated by Ramón Grau San Martín. Batista moved to the USA, but he remained head of the Cuban army and continued to influence Cuban politics.

## Batista's coup 1952

By the early 1950s, the Cuban government under President Carlos Prío Socarrás was suffering from accusations of corruption and fighting between political factions. Batista knew that Prío would lose the 1952 elections, so he decided to run for president again, this time at the head of his own party – the United Action Party. Batista's earlier popularity with the Cuban people made him believe he would be welcomed back. However, during the election campaign an opinion poll revealed that Batista was coming last in the presidential race.

Batista's two opponents, Roberto Agramonte and Aurelio Hevia, both stated their intention of making the widely respected Colonel Ramón Barquín head of the Cuban armed forces if they won the election. Unwilling to lose both the presidential election and his control of the army, Batista staged a coup before the elections could take place, removing Prío from power and establishing himself as provisional president, with backing from the army.

Despite Batista's illegal seizure of power (which he justified by claiming that Prío had intended to stage his own coup to retain the presidency), the USA formally recognised Batista's government. This encouraged the Cuban leader to fill government positions with people who he knew would do his bidding without question.

Shortly after Batista's coup, a radical young lawyer named Fidel Castro tried to have him prosecuted. When this attempt to bring Batista to justice failed, Castro reached the conclusion that the Cuban leader could not be removed from power by any legal means.

In 1954, Batista held an election in which he was the only legal candidate. Despite formalising his power in this way, the Cuban people no longer trusted Batista, and there were public calls for new – legitimate – elections. However, no moderate political group could challenge Batista's dictatorial regime, and there was no public forum for debate on the issue. The scene was set for armed opposition or civil war.

*A 10-m (32-ft) figure of Batista near the US embassy (the building on the right) in Havana; this was part of his 1954 election campaign – the words below the figure say, 'This is the man'*

On seizing power, Batista stated that he remained loyal to the 1940 Constitution, but he suspended parts of it almost immediately. This deeply angered the Cuban people. Although several of its provisions had never been implemented, the constitution was greatly respected. It was seen as an instrument of social and democratic change, and an ideal towards which Cubans should strive.

Historian Hugh Thomas writes that in April 1952, 'Batista proclaimed a new constitutional code of 275 articles, claiming that the "democratic and progressive essence" of the 1940 Constitution was preserved in the new law'. However, few people believed Batista's argument. Castro was furious, and became further convinced that Batista must be overthrown. Many Cuban professionals, intellectuals and members of the middle class shared Castro's view.

## Activity

Using books, the internet and other resources, find out more about the 1940 Constitution. What made it so important? Why was it never fully implemented? Which parts of the constitution might upset the USA in the post-1945 Cold War climate? Why?

## Castro's response to Batista's coup

On 26 July 1953, Castro and a group of 165 revolutionaries stormed the garrison at the Moncada army barracks in Santiago. The assault failed and Batista's forces killed, wounded or arrested half the attackers, although Castro and his brother Raúl escaped. Batista ordered the district military commander to kill ten rebels for every soldier that had died in the attack until the Castro brothers surrendered.

Fidel and Raúl duly turned themselves in. They were tried alongside over 100 other rebels, and were sentenced to long terms of imprisonment (15 years for Fidel, 13 for Raúl). Yet two years later, in 1955, both were released after Batista granted them amnesty in order to improve his image.

*Fidel Castro (left) gives his deposition after the failed coup of July 1953*

During his trial, lawyer Fidel gave a spirited defence of his actions. In his closing speech he declared, 'La historia me absolverá' ('history will absolve me'). Castro also spoke of his plans for Cuba, which included nationalising public utilities, restructuring education and controlling financial speculation. The content of his speech became the text for the Cuban Revolution, based in particular on five key laws that would have been enacted if the rebels had succeeded:

1   a reinstatement of the 1940 Constitution and the return of power to the Cuban people
2   a 55% share of profits for sugar planters
3   workers in mining and major industries to receive a 30% profit share
4   land rights for those holding less than 165 acres
5   people guilty of embezzlement (stealing money they had been entrusted with) or fraud to have their property seized and sold, with proceeds going to medical care, workers' pensions and charities.

With the rebellion's failure, however, none of this happened. After his release from prison, Castro went to Mexico to build a new revolutionary force, which became known as the 26 July Movement.

## Activity

To what extent were Castro's laws 'revolutionary'? List them and then discuss with a partner how acceptable these might or might not be in many countries today.

Castro's decision to leave Cuba was wise, as it distanced him from Cuban politics. By going to Mexico instead of the USA, he avoided detection by US authorities and becoming involved in the politics of the many Cuban exiles who had settled in Miami. While in Mexico, Castro met **Ernesto 'Che' Guevara**, who became an important and effective recruit to the revolutionary band.

**Ernesto 'Che' Guevara (1928–67)** Born in Argentina, Guevara trained as a doctor. In 1954, the socialist government of Guatemala was overthrown by a US-backed coup, planned by the CIA. Disgusted by such evidence of Washington's apparent hold over Central America, Guevara joined Fidel Castro in Mexico. In 1956, Guevara, Castro and 80 others arrived in Cuba to overthrow Batista's government. After two years of fighting, Castro became Cuba's premier in 1959. Guevara served as minister for industries (1961–65), but left Cuba to become a guerrilla leader in Bolivia. He was captured by Bolivian and US special forces, and executed in October 1967.

*Che Guevara in 1959*

Guevara was already angered by the USA's overthrow of Guatemalan president **Jacobo Árbenz** in 1954. He was inspired to join Castro after watching Cuba descend into corruption and repression, as US cultural and commercial influences grew on the island. Throughout the 1950s, Cuba was known as the 'whorehouse of America' – a playground for US businessmen and a centre for drugs, prostitution and the Mafia. Batista became the Mafia's Cuban ally through his business dealings with the gangster Meyer Lansky, who controlled gambling in Cuba (Batista allegedly received 30% of Lansky's takings).

## Activity

Use the internet to find out more about the Sicilian Mafia. How has this criminal gang achieved such influence in business and politics? Why do you think the Mafia was so keen to establish itself in Cuba in the 1950s? Why might Batista want friends in the Mafia?

**Jacobo Árbenz (1913–71)** Originally an army officer, Árbenz was Guatemala's defence minister (1944–51) and then president (1951–54). Árbenz alarmed Washington in 1951 when he promised to convert Guatemala from 'a backward country with a predominantly feudal economy into a modern capitalist state' by limiting the influence of foreign corporations over Guatemalan politics. He also stated that he would modernise Guatemala's infrastructure without foreign capital. Árbenz's relative tolerance of the Guatemalan Party of Labour (PGT) and other left-leaning groups unnerved the US government, and prompted the CIA to draw up a plan to remove Árbenz as a communist threat. This plan was implemented in June 1954. Árbenz fled Guatemala and died in Mexico in 1971.

## Castro's revolution 1956–59

In late 1956, student riots and anti-Batista demonstrations increased. Police reaction to these riots grew increasingly brutal, and protesting students were often viciously beaten. When a popular student leader was killed, his funeral became a focus for protest, and workers went on strike all over the country. Batista's response was to close Havana University and establish stricter media censorship. He ignored further calls for new elections to be held, believing that he could defeat any attempt to overthrow him by force.

Having trained their revolutionaries in Mexico, the Castro brothers and Che Guevara sailed for Cuba in late November 1956, ready to begin their rebellion. Their arrival was planned to coincide with an uprising in Havana led by Frank País, a Cuban revolutionary who co-ordinated urban underground resistance to Batista's regime for the 26 July Movement while Castro was in exile.

However, events did not go as Castro had planned. País' rebellion was rapidly crushed, and the revolutionaries landed in the wrong place. Many of them were killed or captured by Batista's forces. Only 16 of the 82 men escaped, including Guevara, Fidel and Raúl. They fled into the Sierra Maestra mountains in eastern Cuba, where they regrouped and began planning a guerrilla war against Batista.

## Guerrilla warfare

Immediately after the failed rebellion, Batista spread the word that Castro had been killed when the revolutionaries landed. However, a journalist for the *New York Times* discovered that Fidel was alive and living in the mountains. When this news was published, it alarmed both Batista and his supporters in the USA. Batista ordered bombing raids on the mountains, but these caused more casualties among the peasants who lived in the Sierra Maestra than among the rebels. The mountain peasants came to be strong supporters of Castro and his group. The revolutionaries helped local people on their farms, gave them medical aid and even established basic schools in rural villages.

*Fidel (centre) and Raúl (kneeling centre) Castro with Che Guevara (second from left) and other revolutionaries in the Sierra Maestra mountains, 1958*

Historians Thomas Skidmore and Peter Smith note that although Castro attracted peasant support, the rebel band itself was mainly middle class, and point out that 'most revolutions in history have been led by members of a counter-élite'. With the help of Frank País, Castro also established a strong following in urban areas, which he used to orchestrate a civil resistance movement to encourage uprisings by liberal, middle-class professionals and skilled workers.

Castro's guerrilla band was small – sometimes numbering less than 200 members – while Batista had 30–40,000 troops at his disposal. Although the revolutionaries were often successful in their fight against the Cuban military, Castro realised he needed to extend his support base. In July 1957, encouraged by Frank País, businessmen and politicians who were sympathetic to Castro's cause issued the Pact of the Sierra, which called for a 'civic revolutionary front' to drive Batista from office. Despite the pact's stated intention, this revolutionary front was never established and no civic uprising occurred.

As violence and unrest spread across the country, the USA realised that time was running out for Batista. However, the US disliked the idea of Castro assuming power, mainly because he was unlikely to be as supportive of US interests in Cuba as Batista had been. The US encouraged Batista to resign, hoping that a similarly US-friendly leader could be installed before Castro took power by force. Batista refused.

Under increasing public criticism for supplying weapons to Batista, the US placed an embargo on arms shipments in March 1958. This hit Batista badly, severely limiting his military capability. He knew that this withdrawal of US support undermined his legitimacy as president.

### SOURCE B

[Commerce, industry and capital] which have whole-heartedly supported President Batista since he took over the government in 1952, are growing impatient with the continued violence in the island.

*Comments made by the* New York Times *correspondent in Havana, 1957. Quoted in Bethell, L. (ed.) 1993.* Cuba: A Short History. *Cambridge, UK. Cambridge University Press. p. 90.*

> What does Source B tell us about the attitude of business interests towards Batista by the end of 1957? Why might there be a connection between these comments and the US government embargo of March 1958?

### Batista's overthrow

In April 1958, Castro's cause gained a significant boost when the communists pledged support for the revolutionaries. With forces now exceeding 5000, Castro increased his use of guerrilla tactics, carrying out bombings, sabotage and assassinations on government targets. Batista also resorted to guerrilla warfare, but the torture and executions carried out by the government made the Cuban people even more sympathetic to the rebels. In July 1958, Castro's position as leader of the anti-Batista movement was confirmed at a meeting in Venezuela. The Pact of Caracas, agreed at this meeting, formally recognised Castro's army as Cuba's 'liberation force'.

Throughout 1958, towns across Cuba fell to Castro as his guerrilla army grew to 50,000 men and Batista's offensive collapsed. By autumn of that year, all support for Batista had evaporated and Castro's gradual advance on Havana prompted spontaneous uprisings. On 1 January 1959, Batista fled and a ceasefire was agreed. Castro entered the capital on 8 January, announcing to crowds of cheering Cubans that 'the revolution begins now'.

## Why did Castro's revolution succeed?

There are several reasons for the success of the Cuban Revolution and Batista's downfall. Firstly, Batista's cruelty and disregard for human rights increased opposition and ultimately cost him US support. Many members of the middle classes who opposed Batista's regime had been arrested, tortured or killed. Batista also vastly underestimated Castro's revolutionaries, who were a determined and intelligent force.

By 1959, there was a genuine desire for change among the Cuban people. The rural poor and urban working classes had little power or influence. Trade links with the USA had stunted economic growth and caused a recession in Cuba's largely sugar-dependent economy. Unemployment stood at nearly 20%, and even some members of the middle classes and businessmen were moved by appeals for greater social justice. However, the main factor that contributed to the success of the revolution and unified Cubans in 1959 was a desire to be free from US influence and control.

### Discussion point

From 1956 to 1958, Fidel Castro fought to overthrow Batista. How justifiable is any armed struggle against a government? Does it make any difference if the government is retaining power illegally through rigged elections? If the government is causing suffering to the population, should the ideal of 'the greatest good/harm to the greatest number' be used to get rid of them? Or is it always morally questionable to attack a government in power?

What was the main turning point for Castro in his revolution against Batista? What was the turning point for Batista? Were these key moments the same?

# What impact did the Cuban Revolution have on the Cold War?

## What did Castro stand for?

US interests in Cuba were widespread, so there was no doubt in Washington that the Cuban Revolution would affect the USA. People in America began to question the new regime and to wonder where Castro's sympathies lay. Was he a communist or a nationalist? Was he anti-American or just pro-Cuban?

Castro's revolution was supported by diverse groups, ranging from communists and prominent businessmen to leaders of the Catholic Church. In the Cold War climate, the USA was naturally concerned about Castro's communist support. In addition, although the USA suspended arms shipments to Cuba, Washington refused to recall the military advisors it had sent to assist the Cuban air force in bombing Cuban rebels. As a result, the US government alienated both sides – it weakened Batista's forces and incited Castro's anger. These factors contributed to uncertainty in the USA about how Cuba's relationship with its near neighbour would now develop.

Castro's beliefs have been the subject of considerable historical debate. Some orthodox historians have argued that Castro was a communist with a long-term plan. However, others claim that he had no detailed ideology when he seized power. John Aldred notes that 'Castro's seizure of Cuba was the first time an apparent Marxist–Leninist revolt had succeeded in establishing control of a state since Mao Zedong's revolution in China in 1949'. This view is contested by Leslie Dewart, who argues that there is no evidence to suggest that Castro was a 'dedicated agent of international communism'.

Levine and Papasotiriou believe that Castro was 'without a sharp ideological orientation, though he was against American hegemony in Latin America'. They comment that early relations with Washington were not antagonistic and that within six months of the revolution, the USA officially recognised Castro's regime. Allan Todd notes that even when Castro began a general programme of nationalisation in 1960, he was still not a member of the Cuban Communist Party, although he 'came to rely increasingly on [the communists] to provide administrators for his reform programmes'.

To begin with at least, Castro was outwardly ambiguous about his own beliefs, and such caution suggests that he was very much a realist. Historians have spent many years trying to define his political beliefs. However, it seems that above all else Castro was a nationalist with socialist leanings and a tendency to adapt to a situation as the need arose – a politician who would work with anyone for Cuba's benefit.

What do *you* think Castro's intentions were? Split into groups of four and then into pairs. Using the information in this book and any other sources available, gather evidence both for and against Castro being a communist. Draw up a table with two columns headed 'Communist' and 'Nationalist', to highlight different points in the debate. In your groups of four, one pair should present an argument for Castro being a communist and one pair an argument against. As you gather evidence, consider the following:

- historiography
- a lack of/the presence of ideology
- US reactions
- responses of traditional supporters
- responses of people who might not be counted as allies (such as the business community and the Catholic Church).

# The aftermath of the Cuban Revolution

## Searching for friends

Castro visited the USA in April 1959 in the hope of securing US aid to improve the situation in Cuba. He was careful to emphasise his plans for radical land reform, which he felt the US would approve of. Addressing a meeting of the United Nations in New York, Castro stated that – like other developing states – Cuba remained neutral in the Cold War. Despite this, US president Eisenhower declined to meet Castro, and he was not warmly received by vice-president Nixon.

How might Castro have reacted to being shunned by Eisenhower? In what ways might this have influenced his future plans for Cuba?

On his return to Cuba, Castro introduced the radical Agrarian Reform Law, which limited *latifundia* (large estates) to 1000 acres. This broke the monopoly of land held by the wealthy few. Castro divided nearly half of all Cuban farmland into smaller plots for peasants and small farmers, or for plantation workers who had no land at all. The law also provided for the nationalisation of large ranches, to be run as farming co-operatives. These changes gave Cuban agricultural workers greater influence and a financial stake in the system. However, the USA was concerned that the law banned foreigners from owning agricultural land. Washington was also worried by the appointment of the communist Nuñez Jimenez as head of the reform programme. Despite these concerns, Eisenhower knew that the USSR was watching events in Cuba unfold, and realised that any aggressive US action against Cuba might force Castro to seek an alliance with Moscow.

A succession of events in 1960 increased tensions between Cuba and the USA. Firstly, Castro accused Cuban exiles in Florida of flying bombing missions against Cuba. He then nationalised all US-owned oil refineries in Cuba. In response, Eisenhower introduced economic sanctions and stopped buying sugar from Cuba. Castro turned to the USSR for economic assistance, and Nikita Khrushchev agreed to provide Cuba with $100 million in aid and a sugar contract.

Castro's dealings with the USSR heightened US fears of communist influence on its doorstep, and these fears seemed confirmed when Castro concluded a trade agreement with Communist China. Eisenhower could no longer ignore the risk of Cuba becoming a Soviet base. He authorised plans for Castro's overthrow, and training began for the Bay of Pigs invasion (see page 57).

## Castro turns to the USSR

The USA cut off diplomatic relations with Cuba in January 1961. Initially, the USSR's response to this was hesitant, but Moscow soon realised that this was an opportunity to gain a foothold less than 100 miles from the US and to alter the Cold War balance of power. The failure of the Bay of Pigs invasion in April 1961 gave both Castro and Khrushchev confidence that they could stand against the USA.

When Castro openly declared his communist sympathies in December 1961, the US felt its actions against Cuba had been entirely justified. The USSR regarded Castro's announcement as evidence of his development from bourgeois nationalist leader to revolutionary democrat. However, Castro's motives for declaring himself a communist may have been more practical – he needed Soviet support to consolidate his revolution and prevent a potential US invasion.

Soviet involvement in Cuban affairs led to the establishment of missile bases on the island to counteract the threat of the USA – a move that triggered the Cuban Missile Crisis (see page 58). In negotiating the removal of the missiles, the USA promised never to invade Cuba and to remove its own missiles from Turkey.

Some historians have argued that if the US government had not tried so hard to undermine Castro, the Cuban Missile Crisis might never have occurred. For example, John Aldred cites the USA's attitude as the main cause of the crisis, believing that the Soviets acted defensively and only intended the missiles to be a deterrent to US attack. However historians might choose to interpret events, the result was that Castro was able to develop his agenda without fear of US invasion.

What did the USSR stand to gain by supporting Cuba?

# Castro and the Cold War after 1962

After 1962, Castro's main foreign policy goal was to liberate poorer nations from the domination of wealthier ones. He voiced strong support for international revolution, based on his intense dislike of imperialism in general and the USA in particular.

The US government's tactic of weakening Cuba by applying a trade embargo won Castro sympathy from several nations already hostile to the USA. As a result, Cuba's prestige and influence on the international stage increased.

## Cuban influence in the Americas

The Cuban Revolution had significant influence in the Americas. It either provoked hatred and derision, or it won praise for representing the ideals and aspirations of many ordinary Latin Americans.

Che Guevara (see page 159) left Cuba in 1965 to help revolutionaries in Bolivia. In 1967, US-trained forces captured and executed him. In death, Guevara became a martyr to many idealistic, reforming young Latin Americans. Guevara's legend was linked with Castro's in encouraging revolution in the Americas. This concerned the USA, but the USSR also had misgivings about Castro's desire to export revolution.

Castro's victory marginalised Cuba from the Latin American mainstream, and the USA encouraged a right-wing reaction that introduced a number of military dictatorships across the Americas in the 1970s. Despite this, Castro maintained good relationships with several states in the region.

In Chile, President Salvador Allende's socialist beliefs led him to form a friendship with Castro. The Cuban leader made a month-long visit to Chile and offered Allende advice. The political right believed that the Chilean 'path to socialism' was an effort to recreate the Cuban Revolution in Chile, and this was of major concern to the USA. In 1973, Allende was killed during a CIA-backed coup, and a right-wing military dictatorship was established. You will learn more about the situation in Chile in Chapter 7.

In Peru, General Juan Velasco stated his aim of achieving justice for the poor. He nationalised industries and exerted greater government control over economic activity. The media became increasingly influenced by left-wing intellectuals, and Velasco also made major purchases of military hardware from the Soviet Union. Castro praised Peru as a 'new phenomenon' with 'a group of progressive military playing a revolutionary role'. Velasco and Castro became close associates, diplomatic relations were established between Cuba and Peru, and Castro sent advisors to assist Velasco.

Castro developed similar relations with Panama's General Omar Torrijos and Ecuador's autocratic Velasco Ibarra. Neither of these leaders took definite steps towards establishing socialist systems in their countries, such as nationalising industries, but both made it clear that they were prepared to act relatively independently of the USA, and this encouraged Castro's support.

However, during this period it was only in Nicaragua that a real revolution similar to that in Cuba took place. Here, a guerrilla band from the Sandinista National Liberation Front (FSLN) succeeded in overthrowing the right-wing dictatorship of Anastasio Somoza in 1979. The Sandinistas established a socialist government, aimed at achieving social and economic justice and pursuing an independent foreign policy.

### Activity

Using this book and other sources available to you, consider why the majority of Latin American states in the 1960s and 1970s were right-wing and militaristic. Write a paragraph explaining your views.

*Sandinista rebels celebrate the overthrow of the government in Nicaragua in June 1979*

In 1981, US president Ronald Reagan condemned the FSLN for supporting Cuba in encouraging Marxist revolutionary movements in other Latin American countries. The CIA began funding, arming and training Nicaraguan rebels, many of whom were former members of Somoza's National Guard. The Sandinistas were voted out after a decade, partly due to being undermined by the USA.

## Activity

Research the history of another country in the Americas during the 1970s, such as Bolivia, Argentina, El Salvador, Guyana or Venezuela. Did Castro have any impact on the political development of your chosen country? Did the Cuban Revolution inspire opposition groups? Did it influence governments either way? How did the superpowers react?

## Cuba and the Cold War in Africa

Throughout the 1970s, Castro grew increasingly willing to assist liberation struggles outside the Americas – most notably in post-colonial Africa. This brought another geographical dimension to the Cold War, as Castro involved Cuba in a series of revolutionary campaigns in the developing world from 1974 to 1981.

Relations between Cuba and the USSR had become strained after Castro declared his aim of encouraging international revolution. By 1970, however, the situation between the two countries had improved. In particular, Castro won back Soviet trust by speaking out in support of the invasion of Czechoslovakia by the USSR and its Warsaw Pact allies in August 1968. A downturn in Cuba's economy also meant that Castro was more in need of Soviet support than ever. He still hoped for revolution in the developing world, but expressed his commitment to liberation through internationalism.

An opportunity for Castro to prove this commitment came with the collapse of a dictatorial regime in Portugal in 1974. When the new Portuguese government announced plans to grant independence to Angola – an oil- and mineral-rich African colony – a power struggle began between various groups in Angola.

Civil war erupted in Angola between the Soviet-backed MPLA, the US-backed FNLA, and UNITA, which was supported by China, South Africa and Israel. Later, after China withdrew, the USA supported UNITA. By 1975, 12,000 Cuban troops were actively fighting for the MPLA, supplied with Soviet weapons. Cuban forces were a significant factor in the MPLA's victory in 1976 and in the creation of the People's Republic of Angola (PRA). Although Cuban troops left in 1977, Castro promised military aid if Angola faced threats from South Africa or the USA in the future.

In 1977, Castro also involved Cuba in a Cold War power struggle in the Horn of Africa, where a liberation movement in Eritrea was fighting against occupying forces from Ethiopia. To begin with, the USSR and Cuba gave aid to the liberation movement, but a coup in Ethiopia led to a new government that proclaimed allegiance to the USSR rather than the USA. As a result, Cuba and the USSR began providing military aid to the Ethiopian army in Eritrea. They also supported Ethiopia in its efforts to take the the Ogaden region from Somalia.

Between November 1977 and February 1978, Castro sent around 17,000 soldiers to Ethiopia. With Cuban support, Ethiopian units won several victories, and in March 1978 the Somali president announced the withdrawal of his army from the Ogaden region.

US president Jimmy Carter was alarmed by these events, believing that Castro was motivated purely by a desire to oppose the USA. However, Castro claimed that he was following through on his belief in internationalism, and consolidating Cuba's role on the world stage. Before 1959, the outside world – especially the USA – had influenced Cuba. Now Cuba was influencing other countries.

## SOURCE C

[This was] a source of pride and opportunity to so many Cubans with between 11,000 and 20,000 serving on 'internationalist duty' in up to 37 countries by the 1980s … an experience that impressed itself on thousands of mostly young Cubans … having their eyes opened by contact with countries that were mostly poorer than Cuba.

Kapcia, A. 2000. Cuba – Island of Dreams. New York, USA. Berg. p. 201.

How did the USA interpret Castro's policy of internationalism? How did Cuban people see their role on the world stage? What was the impact of the Cuban Revolution on the Cold War?

# Did the Cold War influence Castro's domestic policy?

## Background to domestic reforms

Castro's plans for domestic reform were intended to complement his international policies. He had lived among rural peasants and understood the difficulties they faced; this experience helped shape his social policy.

## The INRA

After seizing power, Castro's coalition of radicals and moderates established the National Institute of Agrarian Reform (INRA), with Castro himself as president. The INRA had broad responsibilities – dealing with both agrarian reform and industrial development – and the organisation effectively became the unofficial government of Cuba, embracing all domestic policy. However, when the Marxist Nuñez Jimenez was appointed as its chief executive, many moderate members of the programme resigned in protest against Jimenez's communist policies.

By 1960, almost all anti-communists or non-communists had left the government, and power lay with Castro and a few of his closest associates – known as *Fidelistas*. The cabinet now had full executive and legislative powers. Castro had the authority to sack existing judges and appoint new ones, and the press came under the control of communist-led trade unions.

## The CDRs

Despite the promise made by the USA at the end of the Cuban Missile Crisis that it would not invade Cuba, Castro still feared an attack. To help defend against this, he established groups known as Committees for the Defence of the Revolution (CDRs). By late 1961, every city, town, neighbourhood, factory and workplace in Cuba had a CDR. The purpose of these units was to identify opponents of the revolution, to stifle counter-revolutionary opinions and to spread government information. By the late 1970s, the CDRs were also involved in sporting and cultural initiatives and promoting health campaigns.

The CDRs were effective mass organisations for both surveillance and education, consolidating the revolution and enforcing domestic policy. They were also a vital link in the communications network, and a means by which the average Cuban could contribute to the aims of the revolution.

Why were the CDRs important to Castro in consolidating his regime? How did these committees fulfil an important social role within Cuba? What other examples in history are there where a government has introduced organisations like the CDRs?

Cuba's economy was transformed from a capitalist system, dominated by US investment, to a socialist one in which the state owned most enterprises and set plans for all sectors of the economy. In terms of economic development, Castro successfully addressed many issues, and advances were made in general living standards, health care, education, industry and agriculture.

## Health care

Before the revolution, health care in Cuba was better than in many developing countries. Cuban doctors were well-trained in modern (US-influenced) practices, and medicine was a widely respected profession. However, most doctors were based in and around the cities, and people in rural areas had limited access to healthcare facilities.

When Castro came to power and began his reform of the healthcare sector, more than half of the doctors in Cuba – unhappy with his socialist policies – left to find work in the USA. Soon there were fewer than 3500 doctors in Cuba, only 16 professors of medicine and a single medical school. In a country with a population of 6 million, the lack of doctors and other health professionals was a major problem. The US embargo on Cuba also hit medical supplies, which badly affected people who depended on imported medicine. This meant that Cuba urgently needed to produce its own pharmaceuticals.

Castro believed that good health care was the right of all citizens, and that providing it was the government's responsibility. He wanted a unified national healthcare system that would provide universal, accessible and free health services. In the 1960s, therefore, Castro began a recruitment drive for the new Rural Health Service, and set about establishing hospitals in rural areas. In addition, he opened 160 community clinics in urban areas, and began a national children's immunisation programme. Equally importantly, more health personnel were trained.

By the 1970s, the government had made significant investments in general hospitals and factories to produce pharmaceuticals. Community clinics took responsibility not just for providing primary health care, but also for health education, disease prevention and family planning.

As more young Cubans qualified in the health professions, many of them chose to take part in international service abroad, providing free medical care in Africa and Latin America. By the 1980s, the healthcare system in Cuba was so successful that it earned praise from the World Health Organization, and was regarded as an example of how a viable health service could be established in developing countries.

In addition to health care, Castro identified the need to raise general living standards in Cuba. Before 1959, less than 20% of the rural population had running water and only 10% had electricity. However, the hospital-building programme was given priority and, while 16,000 housing units a year were being built by the late 1970s, this was still 10,000 a year less than under Batista. Overall, though, the poor enjoyed a substantial rise in living standards under Castro's regime.

Why were Castro's healthcare policies so successful? How might Castro's health policy have overlapped with his foreign policy?

# Women's rights

In 1960, Castro's government established the the Federation of Cuban Women (FMC). The aim of this organisation was to promote women's welfare and education, and to guarantee them equal pay. The FMC was deeply involved in the 1961 Cuban literacy campaign (see the section on education below). It also recruited and supplied labourers when many trained workers left Cuba after the revolution.

Castro actively encouraged women to join the labour force, and thousands answered this call. However, many women left when the combination of family and work proved too difficult to maintain. During the 1970s, therefore, the government initiated reforms that would make it easier for women to return to work, including the establishment of day-care centres. By the mid 1970s, though, women still only made up 25% of the workforce. In 1975, the FMC began a national inquiry to find out why this was. The result was the Family Code of 1975, which gave men and women equal rights and equal responsibilities in the home. The government also subsidised family planning and offered free abortions. By 1981, the female labour force had almost doubled from what it had been in 1959.

## Activity

Using the internet and any other resources available to you, find out more about the FMC. Why was it so important to women in Cuba?

# Education

When Castro took power in 1959, 22% of Cubans over the age of 14 were illiterate and 60% of the country was classified as having 'poor literacy'. Initiating a successful education programme was therefore vital for the new government. Castro believed that for Cuba to prosper its citizens must be able to contribute to society. To do this, they must be educated. As a first step towards this, Castro nationalised all educational institutions – including church schools – and created a system operated entirely by the government.

Castro designated 1961 as the 'year of education', and launched a huge literacy campaign. 'Literacy brigades' were sent into the countryside to build schools, train new teachers and teach the largely illiterate peasant population to read and write.

Supporters of the revolution saw this as an opportunity to contribute to the success of the new government. However, Cold War politics were never far from Cuban life, and US-sponsored counter-revolutionaries began a wave of attacks to terrorise farming communities and reduce support for the literacy campaign. Teachers, students and peasants were tortured, and some were murdered. Despite this, literacy initiatives and education reforms continued throughout the 1960s. With financial assistance from the USSR, Cuba was able to develop a free education system from kindergarten through to university.

*Members of Castro's 'literacy brigades' wave books in the air during a parade in Havana in 1961; thousands of students spent time in the countryside, working to eradicate illiteracy*

There were differences in the standards available in rural education centres and those in urban areas, but overall there were great improvements after the revolution. Technical education, engineering and medicine were favoured over humanities and social sciences. This led Castro's opponents to accuse him of stifling the study of history, economics, politics and philosophy, in order to prevent analysis or discussion of non-communist theories or capitalist principles. Some people also criticised what they felt was an overly regimented approach to pre-university learning. The dismissal of staff believed to be 'politically unsuitable' added weight to this argument.

Nonetheless, by 1980, adult literacy in Cuba had dropped to less than 6%. This meant that Cubans had an education system and standard of literacy that was unequalled in Latin America.

Why do you think Castro's education policies between 1959 and 1981 were successful?

## Industry

Before the revolution, Cuban industry was almost exclusively based on sugar – a crop with a limited domestic market. Cuban industry and agriculture were interdependent, and unemployment and poverty were widespread. The US controlled Cuba's profitable national resources, and banks, electricity and other areas of industry were dominated by US capital – including 25% of the best agricultural land in the country. Castro considered unequal land distribution to be the greatest social evil in Cuba. When he came to power, he immediately began a system of reforms designed to reduce US control, broaden Cuban industry and improve the lives of the Cuban people.

### SOURCE D

The inequities ... and the injustices of land misuse were so great in Cuba, that land reform was the minimal measure that a genuine thorough and efficient social reform programme could have undertaken.

Dewart, L. 1964. Cuba, Church and Crisis. London, UK. Shed and Ward Ltd. p. 34.

What does Source D reveal about Castro and his 'diagnosis' of the situation in Cuba in 1959? What else does it suggest about the revolution?

### The sugar crisis

Before 1959, around 90% of Cuba's raw sugar and tobacco exports went to the USA. This changed dramatically after the revolution, when Washington introduced an embargo on Cuban goods. Castro resolved the problem in the short term by establishing a trade agreement with Khrushchev, by which the USSR purchased a substantial amount of Cuban sugar. By 1961, sugar production had increased by more than one-third. This allowed Castro to invest more in agriculture, and he also allowed farmers to sell any surplus. However, sugar made up 75% of all Cuban exports, which meant that the country was still overly reliant on this crop as its main industry. The US embargo continued to affect Cuba, and by 1963 sugar production had dropped to 3.8 million tonnes – the lowest since 1945. Castro found himself facing an economic crisis, and introduced food rationing to try and ensure a fair distribution of food among the people. The USSR expressed a willingness to provide further investment, but there were conditions attached.

## SOURCE E

The Russians seemed uneasy about underwriting a socialist utopia in the Caribbean. In mid-1963 they put their foot down. The Cubans must slow down the industrialisation drive and improve their planning. They must recognise Cuba's comparative advantage: sugar ... Fidel, ever on the initiative, now embraced sugar, which he had so recently spurned ... he announced that in 1970 Cuba would break all records of production: it would harvest 10 million tons.

Skidmore, T. E. and Smith, P. H. 2001. Modern Latin America (5th Edition). New York, USA. Oxford University Press. p. 279.

Over the next few years, Castro carried out a campaign to increase sugar production in Cuba. He built more sugar mills and aimed to produce 10 million tonnes of sugar a year by 1970. Although the eventual quota fell short of this (the 1970 harvest was 7.5 million tonnes), this still marked Cuba's highest ever production level. Despite this, Castro felt that his 'sugar quota battle' had failed, and he took personal responsibility for this in a long speech in Havana in July 1970. He even offered to resign, but the adoring crowds were dismayed by this suggestion.

### Nationalising industry

As part of the trade agreements made with the USSR shortly after the revolution, Cuba received 3000 tonnes of Soviet crude oil. However, many of the oil refineries in Cuba were US-owned, and these plants refused to process the oil. As a result, Castro nationalised the refineries and soon did the same with many other businesses. He took banks, sugar mills and large factories out of private – overwhelmingly US – ownership, and organised them into collectives or co-operatives.

By 1961, Castro had brought nearly all Cuban industry under state control. As industry minister, Che Guevara devised a four-year plan to stimulate industry and increase consumption, which would help to improve the diet and living standards of the Cuban people. Despite this plan, Cuba lacked the raw materials and expertise to rush into industrialisation.

## Ties to the USSR

By the early 1970s, Castro realised that he needed a new approach to industrial policy. He therefore restructured the sector in four key ways: he introduced new management systems, gave the private sector a greater role in both industry and agriculture, announced that pay would be linked to output, and pressed for greater economic interaction with the West. At the same time, Castro strengthened state control over both education and mass media, and gave communists and unions much more significant roles. In 1972, Cuba joined Comecon – the economic and trading union of communist states. Castro signed a 15-year deal with the USSR, which increased the Soviet subsidy to Cuba's economy.

It was evident to many that Cuban industry was heavily dependent on the USSR, and that the reorganisation was based on Soviet models of economic and political decision-making. There were some who wondered whether Cuba had simply exchanged dependency on one Cold War superpower for another, and whether Cuba was being exploited by the USSR in its Cold War rivalry with the USA. However, Cuban ties to the USSR never resulted in the level of direct foreign ownership that had caused so much anger under Batista. Between 1975 and 1981, the Cuban economy grew by just over 4% a year, compared to an average of 1.2% across Latin America.

> What evidence is there to suggest that Castro simply replaced US domination with Soviet domination?

Some historians believe that the Cuban economic success was purely the result of Soviet subsidies. However, the amount of Soviet aid was about the same as that received by US-backed regimes in other Latin American countries. Cuba's industrial dependency on the USSR had a political price, too, including the need to supply troops and social service personnel to Angola and Ethiopia in support of Soviet interests there. However, Cuba was also one of the few developing countries to provide foreign aid. Throughout the 1970s, Cubans built housing, roads, airports, schools and other facilities in Guinea, Tanzania and around 20 other Asian, African and Latin American countries.

In summary, the deterioration in US–Cuban relations led Castro to form an alliance with the USSR at a key moment in the Cold War. Whether or not he exchanged control by one foreign power for another is a matter for debate, but Cuba's significance in the outside world – and the significance of the outside world to Cuba – was changed forever by the Cuban Revolution. Once a strong US ally, Cuba eventually became the USA's enemy, taking steps towards the USSR from alliance to dependency.

# End of chapter activities

## Paper 3 exam practice

### Question

'Castro's triumph over Batista was inevitable.' To what extent do you agree with this statement?
[20 marks]

### Skill focus

Avoiding a narrative-based answer

### Examiner's tips

Even once you have read the question carefully (and so avoided the temptation of including irrelevant material), produced your plan and written your introductory paragraph, it is **still** possible to go wrong.

By 'writing a narrative answer', history examiners mean providing supporting knowledge that is relevant (and may be very precise and accurate) **but** which is not clearly linked to the question. Instead of answering the question, the answer merely **describes** what happened.

The main body of your essay/argument needs to be **analytical**. It must not simply be an 'answer' in which you just tell the story. Your essay **must address the demands/key words of the question**. Ideally, this should be done consistently throughout your essay, by linking each paragraph to the previous one, in order to produce a clear, 'joined-up' answer.

> You are especially likely to lapse into a narrative essay when answering your final question – and even more so if you are getting short of time. The error here is that, despite all your good work at the start of the exam, you will lose sight of question and just produce an account rather than an analysis. Even if you are short of time, try to write several *analytical* paragraphs that link to the key words of the question.

A question that asks you the extent to which you agree with a statement expects you to come to judgements about success/failure, the relative importance of a factor/individual, or the accuracy of a statement. You need to provide a judgement on the views expressed in the statement. Very often, such a question gives you the opportunity to refer to different historians' views.

A good way of avoiding a narrative approach is to continually refer back to the question, and even to mention it now and again in your answer. This should help you to produce an essay that is focused on the specific aspects of the question, rather than just giving information about the broad topic or period.

For this question, you will need to cover the following aspects of Castro's defeat of Batista:

- Castro's aims – or even his lack of aims/ideology. What might this say about Batista and his supporters? What do historians say about Castro and his revolution?
- Castro's tactics and their consequences (for example, leadership, leaving Cuba when he was released from prison, gathering forces, training, his 'hearts and minds' policy during his period in the mountains of Cuba, organisation of resistance to Batista in the towns and the countryside).
- Batista's actions and their results (for example, the 1953 rebellion and its consequences, Batista's domestic policies). Was there a point at which Batista could have saved himself? Would resigning have defeated Castro's plan? Should Batista have held elections as the public demanded? Comment on the living standards of the Cuban people, corruption in Batista's regime, contrast with Castro – and ask, were guerrilla actions lawful?
- US/foreign intervention – key moments of support and withdrawal for Batista and Castro.

Having considered both sides, you will then need to make a judgement in your concluding paragraph as to how 'inevitable' Castro's success in defeating Batista really was. Were there moments when Batista nearly/could have prevented Castro's triumph, making his ultimate victory anything but inevitable? If so, what secured Castro's success and set him apart from Batista?

## Common mistake

Every year, even candidates who have clearly revised well and have a good knowledge of the topic, and any historical debates surrounding it, still end up producing a mainly narrative-based or descriptive answer. Very often, this is the result of the candidate not having drawn up a proper plan.

The extracts of a student's answer on page 180 show an approach that essentially just describes Castro's campaign against Batista's government, without any analysis of his aims, his degree of success or failure, and without offering sufficient discussion of Batista's actions, decisions or policies.

## Sample paragraphs of narrative-based approach

This example shows what examiners mean by a narrative answer – it is **not** something you should copy!

Fidel Castro entered Havana in January 1959 after a three-year guerrilla campaign to oust President Batista, who had fled to the Dominican Republic on 31 December 1958. Batista was a corrupt, brutal dictator, dependent on the USA, having turned Cuba into an American colony.

But with Cuba being only 90 miles at its nearest point from the tip of Florida's Key West, the politics and economics of that island were crucial to Washington during the Cold War. Unrest in Cuba was a strategic worry for Washington, so it is little surprise that the USA initially supported Batista.

Castro's first attempt to overthrow Batista took place on 26 July 1953, when a group of revolutionaries led by him stormed the garrison at the Moncada army barracks in Santiago. The assault failed. Fidel and his brother Raúl escaped, but later gave themselves up to avoid a massacre of suspects. They were both jailed, but were released by Batista in 1955 as part of an amnesty designed to improve his image. Fidel left Cuba, and by doing so he distanced himself from further plots against Batista and discord between plotters. He went to Mexico to plan Batista's downfall and build a new revolutionary force, which became known as the 26 July Movement.

It was here that he met Che Guevara, whose input would be invaluable to Castro's revolution, as they trained and prepared their army to return to Cuba. Guevara joining up with Castro was important as they left Mexico for Cuba in November 1956 ...

The rest of the essay continues in the same way, with relevant facts about Castro's actions, as well as a comment on the significance of Guevara, hinting at some notion of 'inevitability'. However, there is no real attempt to balance the answer by analysing Batista's role during 1953–58, nor does the candidate address the concept of 'inevitability' in the opening. The answer begins as a narrative.

## Activity

In this chapter, the focus is on avoiding writing narrative-based answers. Using the information from this chapter, and any other sources of information available to you, try to answer **one** of the following Paper 3 practice questions in a way that avoids simply describing what happened.

Remember to refer to the simplified Paper 3 markscheme on page 219.

# Paper 3 practice questions

1   Analyse the reasons for Castro's victory in the power struggle with Batista from 1953 to 1959.

2   Why were Castro's industrial and agricultural reforms only partially successful?

3   To what extent was Batista's Cuba an American 'colony'?

4   Compare and contrast the influence over Cuba of both the USA and the USSR in the period 1945–81.

5   Assess the impact of the Cuban Revolution and its aftermath on superpower relations between 1956 and 1981.

# 7 Chile and the Cold War 1945–81

## Key questions

- How did the early years of the Cold War affect Chile?
- To what extent did the USA influence Chilean politics 1952–64?
- How did the left come to power in Chile?
- What was the impact of the Pinochet regime after 1973?
- How far has Chile's political history since 1945 been determined by the USA and the Cold War?

This chapter examines the impact of the Cold War on Chile from 1945 to 1981. It focuses on the relationship between Chile and the USA, against the background of superpower rivalry between the USA and the USSR. The chapter discusses the presidencies of González Videla and Eduardo Frei, and the 1964 'Revolution in Liberty'. The 1970 election of the Marxist Salvador Allende is considered, as is his overthrow in 1973 by Augusto Pinochet, who established a military dictatorship in Chile.

# Overview

- After 1932, Chile changed governments regularly without serious upheaval, and was considered more politically stable than its South American neighbours. Chile did not have a parliamentary system of government, but was instead ruled by a president, a congress and a judiciary.
- The Cold War reached Chile in 1947, when the Communist Party faced criticism from many parts of Chilean society as fears about increasing Soviet power and the spread of communism grew throughout the Americas.
- The Chilean Anti-Communist Action (AChA) began a campaign of persecution; hundreds of communist leaders were detained and, eventually, the Communist Party was banned.
- Throughout the 1950s and 1960s, Chile was strongly influenced by the USA, both politically and economically.
- In the 1964 election, Eduardo Frei narrowly defeated Salvador Allende, a Marxist candidate with support from Chile's revived Communist Party.
- In September 1970, Allende was elected president, heading the Popular Unity (Unidad Popular, UP) coalition of leftist parties.
- From 1970 to 1973, Allende pursued a course of progressive economic measures, such as nationalising Chile's extremely profitable copper industry.
- Allende introduced government-subsidised services, and a land-reform programme that mainly benefited poor families. The USA and politicians on the Chilean right were alarmed by these steps.
- On 11 September 1973, military forces led by General Augusto Pinochet succeeded in overthrowing Allende's government. Pinochet ruled Chile as dictator and head of state until 1990.

# How did the early years of the Cold War affect Chile?

By the 1930s, Chile had established a reputation for political stability in Latin America. Its president was elected for a six-year term and Chile also had a congress, a judiciary and several political parties that were allowed to express themselves freely.

*A map showing Chile in relation to South America during the Cold War*

In 1938, a liberal government was formed under the leadership of Pedro Aguirre Cerda. This government was a coalition of centre-left democratic groups united as the Popular Front. Cerda adopted an ambitious reform programme similar to Roosevelt's New Deal in the USA (see page 29). When the Second World War broke out in 1939, Chile initially remained neutral. However, wartime tensions developed as pro-US and pro-German groups encouraged the government to join the war, which it eventually did – on the side of the Allies – in December 1941.

Chile escaped the physical destruction of the conflict, and during the war its mineral exports increased. In 1945, Chile became a founder member of the United Nations. With the election of Gabriel González Videla in 1946, Chileans hoped for peacetime stability and access to new markets for trade.

SOURCE A

In Chile there is a highly developed sense of decency and fair play ... the respect for freedom of expression and exchange of ideas seems at times more fundamental than in the United States ... it is revealing that the populace continues to feel a sense of national guilt over the 1938 cold-blooded assassination of 62 youths who spearheaded an attempted Nazi revolution. Bloodier and less excusable acts have readily been forgotten elsewhere in the American hemisphere, including the United States.

Pike. F. B. and Bray, D. 'A Vista of Catastrophe: the Future of United States-Chilean Relations' in The Review of Politics XXII, No. 3 (July 1960). pp. 394–95. Quoted in Pike, F. B. 1963. Chile and the United States 1880–1962. Notre Dame, USA. University of Notre Dame Press.

### Activity

Look at Source A. What is the author's impression of Chileans and their country? Look carefully at the origin of the source. Is there anything in the source to suggest that the author had cause for concern at the time of writing?

## The AChA

In 1946, the USA began a campaign to isolate left-leaning political parties in Latin America. This led to a split in the main Chilean trade union, the Confederación de Trabajadores de Chile (CTCh), with opposing communist and socialist branches. During the Second World War, the socialists had developed ties to US labour interests, and there were now aligned with the American Federation of Labor. The communists wanted more Soviet-style labour policies in Chile.

In November 1946, González Videla appointed several communists to his cabinet as a reward for having backed him in the election. However, a series of communist-led strikes and riots in Chile prompted the US to pressure González Videla to 'sort out' the communists in his country.

Various groups, including anti-communists and nationalists, joined together to form the Chilean Anti-Communist Action (AChA). This developed into a powerful organisation, and gained followers throughout Chile. These were mainly people sympathetic to the dictatorships being established in Spain and Portugal under Francisco Franco and Antonio Salazar respectively. The AChA warned about growing Soviet dominance, pointing to spying in countries such as

Canada, the USA and Britain as evidence of the spreading 'communist cancer'. The AChA challenged the existing government, demanding a structured society headed by a strong leader and administered by an upper-class élite.

In the elections held in May 1947, the communists won 18% of the vote – an increase of 6% from 1941. This success encouraged the AChA to publish a manifesto entitled 'AChA, In Defence of Chile and its Democratic Institutions'. The manifesto was military in tone, and indeed the AChA was set up like a military unit. Its few thousand members were organised in regiments that were led by retired army officers, and they freely used terrorist tactics in their fight against communism. After the manifesto was published, the AChA gained increasing popularity in Chile, aided by socialist dissidents who feared a communist government takeover. Such dissidents became an important support base for the AChA, and the inclusion of socialists in its ranks made the organisation appear more widely representative.

Neither González Videla nor his government had much tolerance for the AChA, and after 1949 the group's influence declined significantly. This was partly because some members were accused of being involved in an unsuccessful coup in 1948. Despite this, most AChA leaders remained in politics, and some were involved in Carlos Ibáñez's election campaign in 1952 (see pages 188–89).

## The Ley Maldita

By 1948, González Videla had turned against his communist allies and dismissed them from the cabinet. The same year, an act of Congress – the Law for the Defence of Democracy – banned the Chilean Communist Party (it remained illegal until 1958). The Act stopped communists holding official posts or even running for office. Videla then cut off diplomatic relations with the communist USSR, Yugoslavia and Czechoslovakia.

A witch-hunt followed, in which communists in academia, the arts and public service were all persecuted. This destroyed careers, causing many communists to leave Chile. Many of those who remained were arrested. The real effect of the 1948 law – nicknamed the 'Evil Law' or 'Ley Maldita' – was to make the communists change their name to the Proletarian Party. In this way, they remained active without attracting widespread attention.

Many Chileans felt that the Ley Maldita had been imposed as a result of outside (mainly US) influences, and this led to a change in the political leaning of the Chilean working class. Socialists and communists put aside their rivalries, and over the next 20 years a socialist–communist alliance developed.

The Communist Party was officially allowed to re-form in 1958, but by this time a coalition of leftist parties called the Frente de Acción Popular (Popular Action Front, FRAP) was already gaining popularity. In the September 1958 elections, FRAP candidate Salvador Allende came within 35,000 votes of the presidency.

What effect did the 1948 Law for the Defence of Democracy have on communists in Chile?

Some historians believe that in cutting ties with communism, González Videla acted under pressure from US president Harry Truman to forge a closer economic and military relationship with the USA. Ian Roxborough, Philip O'Brien and Jacqueline Roddick comment that 'Videla was looking for an excuse to break with the Communist Party, in order to satisfy the demands of American businessmen, and the pressures of the Cold War'. They point to the fact that, in appreciation of González Videla's actions, the USA later widened the scope of its loans to, and investments in, Chile. González Videla also agreed to a military assistance pact with the US, but there is no conclusive evidence that the USA directly pushed him towards this.

*US president Harry S. Truman (left) sits with González Videla (centre) at a dinner Truman hosted in Washington for the Chilean president in 1950*

Other historians believe that González Videla had different motives for his actions against the communists. For example, Rex Hudson argues that although González Videla feared communist intentions and was anxious to avoid US disapproval, he mainly turned his back on communism in an effort to appease centre-right critics of his government – especially landowners. He also wanted to weaken the labour movement during this time of economic uncertainty, and to remove any incentive for a coup against him.

González Videla's purge of the communists coincided with a new policy that abandoned social reform in favour of promoting industrial growth. US investments in Chile increased from $414 million to $540 million in five years, largely in copper production. Mining, rather than agriculture, became the most important industrial sector. By 1952, the USA had loaned Chile over $300 million, and in doing so it had bought itself a reliable and stable ally in the Americas.

### Activity

Re-read the information about the possible motives for González Videla turning against the communists. In pairs, draw up a list of the reasons given. Which interpretation do you think is the most convincing? Rank them in order, and then compare your findings with another group.

## To what extent did the USA influence Chilean politics 1952–64?

US influence in Chile grew significantly in the 1950s and early 1960s, during the governments of Carlos Ibáñez and Jorge Alessandri. Economic involvement in Chile helped the USA increase its political influence there. Under Carlos Ibáñez, Chile received assistance from the International Monetary Fund (IMF), which strengthened US influence. Later, Jorge Alessandri's reduction of import tariffs – on US recommendation – flooded the domestic market with cheap American products. This allowed US companies to tighten control over different sectors of the Chilean economy. These moves were largely driven by the USA's desire to restrict the political left in Chile, most notably Salvador Allende, whose popularity and close relations with Cuba concerned Washington. As time passed, therefore, Chile's destiny became closely tied to the US government's agenda.

### The return of Carlos Ibáñez 1952–58

In 1952, former president Carlos Ibáñez was re-elected. He was over 70 years old, and many people viewed him with scepticism. During his previous government (1927–31), Ibáñez had based his administration on army support and loans from private US lenders. He created the national police (*Carabineros*) and expanded central government. The economy initially prospered under his leadership, but the Great Depression that began in 1929 left 25% of Chile's workforce unemployed, and Ibáñez lost popularity. He began to face unrest due to his autocratic rule, and he eventually fled into exile in Argentina rather than risking a civil war.

By 1952, however, the old president had reinvented himself as a unifying candidate. His popular appeal was aimed at the centre-right, since many were fearful of the left. Despite a deeply divided vote, several factors – including the Berlin Blockade, the ongoing Korean War and the Red Scare in the USA – helped persuade the Chileans to return Ibáñez to office.

## Discussion point

Discuss why Chileans in 1952 might have elected a 70-year-old ex-president who had previously fled office.

Ibáñez believed himself to be the spokesman for Latin America, and promoted himself as a nationalist and a reformer. He invited the Argentinean president, **Juan Perón**, to visit Chile. Perón was extremely popular, and Ibáñez hoped that aligning himself with the Argentinean leader would reflect well on his own presidency and enhance his status amongst ordinary Chileans.

**Juan Perón (1895–1974)** A skilled politician, Argentinean leader Perón had millions of supporters even during his years of exile (1955–73). His policies were mostly populist and favoured the working class; this made him immensely popular. Perón was the most influential leader in Latin America, having maintained a greater independence from outside influence than many other countries in the Americas. His second wife, Eva, was also a formidable figure who contributed greatly to his success.

In the first few years of Ibáñez's presidency, price increases averaged 38% per annum; as a result he stopped wage increases. Even the benefits of rising copper prices were offset by a large fall in production. This badly affected Ibáñez's key supporters – rural workers – even though he introduced a minimum wage for agricultural labourers.

Ibáñez approached the International Monetary Fund for help in tackling these financial problems, but the IMF insisted on overseeing all Chile's future economic policies. To many Chileans, this meant a humiliating dependency on other countries.

SOURCE B

As a result, the IMF came to be seen by most Chileans – and by most other Latin Americans – as an extension of US economic and political power ... his government soon paid the price ... An early target was the public utilities ... riots began in Santiago and spread to other cities. Given the strength of labour and the leftist parties, Chile was a difficult place for anti-inflation policies. Ibáñez ... had proved to be a tired old general who had little political base and even fewer political ideas.

*Skidmore, T. and Smith, P. 2001. Modern Latin America (5th Edition). Oxford, UK. Oxford University Press. pp. 120–21.*

### Activity

Read Source B and the text on Ibáñez above. Chile's economy was stagnating and inflation was a problem, so approaching the IMF would seem a logical step. Why do you think Chileans were cynical about this?

## The presidency of Jorge Alessandri 1958–64

When Jorge Alessandri was elected president in 1958, Chile's middle class effectively installed one of their own in the presidential palace. Alessandri was a leading industrialist, the son of a former president, and the right wing's preferred candidate. However, during the election the USA was shocked by how close Salvador Allende came to winning. As the left's nominee for the second time, Allende polled almost 29% of the vote, while Alessandri won 31.6%. The USA no longer took Chilean stability for granted.

One of the first challenges Alessandri faced was the Great Chilean Earthquake in May 1960. Measuring 9.5 on the Richter Scale, the earthquake's epicentre was just 570 km (355 miles) south of the capital, Santiago. The city of Valdivia suffered the worst devastation: 40% of houses were destroyed and 20,000 people were left homeless. The earthquake triggered localised tsunamis that severely battered the Chilean coast. Up to 5000 people were killed.

Thousands of volunteers helped rebuild local infrastructures, and the USA, Brazil, France, Britain, Italy and Cuba all sent aid. Total damage and losses to agriculture and industry were estimated to be over half a billion dollars. Despite this trauma, Chile went ahead with hosting the 1962 soccer World Cup, and this event gave Alessandri's government a boost.

*Residents of Valdivia examine the effects of the earthquake that struck Chile in May 1960*

 ## Theory of knowledge

### History and emotion

Photographs such as this one of the 1960 earthquake can create a powerful emotional response in the viewer. Why does a visual source often have a stronger impact than a written source? What limitations do photographs have as historical evidence?

Adding to Chile's problems in the early 1960s was the fact that so many of the rural poor were moving to cities such as Santiago and Valparaiso. Thomas Skidmore and Peter Smith observe that 'they were, ill-housed, ill-fed and ill-educated. Furthermore there was little work.'

Despite this, Alessandri maintained a certain stability, and temporarily reduced inflation by placing a limit on wages. However, this caused union protests so Alessandri launched a programme of public works, financed mainly by the USA. The economy grew and unemployment dropped. In 1962, after prompting by John F. Kennedy, Alessandri also introduced a modest agrarian reform law. In part, Kennedy's encouragement in this matter was driven by his desire to distract Chile from the increasing influence of Castro's revolution in Cuba – a US policy that was embodied in the Alliance for Progress.

### Activity

Review the information about Kennedy's Alliance for Progress on pages 79–80. How do you think this might have affected Chile? Why was the US so concerned about events in Chile?

During the local elections in Chile in 1963, Alessandri's liberal-conservative coalition lost many seats. The Christian Democrats and the socialist–communist alliance FRAP (see page 186) both made gains. Those on the left felt that Alessandri had made Chile completely dependent on the USA. They accused him of compromising their country's independence, making Chilean industry part of 'the planned global strategy of American corporations ... walking off with all the economic gains'.

*US president Kennedy (left) and Chilean president Alessandri (right) inspect an honour guard in Washington, 1962*

What evidence is there of increased US influence in Chile during Alessandri's presidency from 1958 to 1964? Why was there growing support for left-wing political parties, despite a strong US presence in Chile?

## Chile in 1964

By 1964, Chile's foreign debt had reached $1.9 billion. Most of this was owed to the USA, and this allowed the US to exert some control over decisions made by the Chilean government. The left wing resented this, and as the 1964 presidential elections approached, the communist–socialist alliance gathered strength.

Four groups initially fought for power in the election: the right (including conservatives and liberals); the centrist Radicals; the Marxist left (the communist and socialist FRAP); and the centrist, reforming Christian Democrats (PDC), under the leadership of Eduardo Frei. The PDC rapidly won over voters from the moderate left and right, and it soon became clear that the election battle was really going to be fought between Frei and Allende.

# How did the left come to power in Chile?

## The Revolution in Liberty 1964–70

The USA feared that if Allende won the Chilean election, it would give the USSR a new foothold in the Americas. Washington therefore contributed over half of Frei's campaign expenses. The USA used radio and print to spread a 'Red Scare', warning Chileans about the dangers of communism. The CIA also spent $1 million on establishing a peasant union to rival the left-wing organisation that already existed. As well as support from the USA, Frei enjoyed the backing of the Catholic Church. He was also popular among certain social groups, including women, the middle classes, peasants, and residents of the shanty towns (*callampas*) that existed on the outskirts of many Chilean cities. Allende was most popular with men and the working classes.

Despite their opposing policies and ideologies, Frei and Allende did agree on certain national issues. These included greater Chilean control over US-owned copper mines, improvements in education, fairer income distribution and a more independent foreign policy. However, when Allende declared that capitalism was the cause of the poverty that affected many Chileans, Frei responded by promising a 'Revolution in Liberty'. His centre-right alliance polled 56% to Allende's 39%.

### Activity

Find out more about the plans and policies of Frei and Allende during the 1964 election campaign in Chile. In what ways were they similar? How did they differ?

## Frei's 'Chileanisation'

Despite calling his campaign a revolution, the USA knew that Frei posed no threat in the Americas, and his reform programme was favoured by the Alliance for Progress. Many Americans realised that change was necessary to avoid a future communist victory in Chile. The 'Chileanisation' of copper became a key feature of Frei's policy, and it was carried out both successfully and moderately. Frei's government gained 51% ownership of US-controlled mines. Critics complained that the terms US companies received were too generous, pointing out that these companies had invested little in Chile. Nonetheless, copper production rose and Chile made a higher profit from these enterprises.

Frei began a land reform programme in 1967. This intended land to be distributed to 100,000 peasants over the next three years. However, by the end of Frei's presidency in 1970, only 28,000 new farm ownerships had been established. Although this was not insignificant, it was considered a failure by both the left and by Frei's own supporters.

Frei's government improved access to education. It also encouraged many squatter communities to build houses, which put the PDC and FRAP in competition for support from the inhabitants of shanty towns. Also under Frei, the voting age was lowered from 21 to 18, and the franchise (the people who were allowed to vote) was broadened to include people who were illiterate – about 10% of the population.

## Foreign policy

Frei followed a more independent foreign policy than previous presidents. He was more open towards developing and non-aligned countries, and less hostile towards the Soviet bloc. Frei restored diplomatic relations with the USSR and backed multilateral organisations (those made up of several countries). These included the Latin American Free Trade Association (LAFTA), the Andean Group, the Organization of American States (OAS) and the United Nations. Despite these moves, Frei remained popular in Washington, so US investment poured into Chile. Between 1964 and 1970, Chile received more aid per capita from the USA than any other Latin American state.

### Activity

Are there any contradictions or inconsistencies in Frei's policies from 1964 to 1970? Consider the following:

- Frei's criticism of Alessandri for over-dependency on the USA, in contrast to Frei's handling of the Chileanisation of copper
- Frei's attitude to land reforms versus that of his political backers
- possible contrasting attitudes in foreign affairs.

The USA considered Chile to be a country of political, strategic and industrial importance, and Chilean prosperity would be good for Washington. Within Chile, however, Frei caused resentment among both the conservative upper class and the Marxist left. Members of the right talked of defending their property; radicals on the left urged the illegal seizure of factories and farmland.

Frei was personally popular, and his Revolution in Liberty enjoyed some success. However, by following a centrist path Frei was accused by the right of being too friendly towards the left, while the left criticised his conservative views. Many Chileans also felt that Frei's loyalty to the USA undermined him. There was a sharp increase in anti-US sentiment in Chile, and growing resentment of US intervention in Chilean affairs. Ultimately, Frei's Christian Democrats did not meet the expectations they had raised in 1964.

What were the main problems for Frei's Revolution in Liberty? Why might some people have felt that he had not lived up to expectations?

# The 1970 election

The right, centre and left all put forward candidates for the 1970 election. Former president Jorge Alessandri led the right-wing National Party (PN), which had been established in 1965 as a coalition of conservatives and liberals. In the centre, the Christian Democrats sought to accelerate Frei's reforms with a progressive candidate, Radomiro Tomic Romero. The left nominated Salvador Allende – for the fourth time – and promised to put Chile on the road to socialism.

Allende's party was the Unidad Popular (Popular Unity, UP), a coalition of the Socialist Party and the Communist Party. It also included several minor parties, such as the much-reduced Radical Party, and even some Christian Democrats who had abandoned Frei. For many Chileans, this leftist coalition was similar to the Popular Front that had existed in 1936–41 (see page 184), except that its leader was now a Marxist. Allende campaigned well and attracted large crowds of supporters.

US president Richard Nixon and his national security advisor, Henry Kissinger, knew that Allende's victory would give Cuba an ally, thus changing the Cold War balance of power in the Americas. Nixon believed that if Marxism was allowed to take hold in the Americas in this way, it would damage US businesses and threaten national security. The US government therefore worked to prevent Allende's victory in the election. Kissinger commented: 'I don't see why we need to stand by and watch a country go communist due to the irresponsibility of its own people.'

Despite US efforts, Allende won the election with 36% of the vote. In the Cold War context of the times, the democratic election of a Marxist president shocked capitalist nations across the globe, but it also led to rejoicing in Cuba and Eastern Europe. In the seven weeks between the counting of the ballots and the formal announcement of the winner by Congress, Chile remained tense.

The US government, the CIA and Chilean right-wing groups all tried to discredit Allende and convince Congress to appoint Alessandri instead. One military plot (supported by the USA) was abandoned when the army commander-in-chief, General René Schneider, was accidentally killed during an attempt to abduct him. This event ensured military support for Allende's safe passage to office.

## SOURCE C

Allende's election as president followed a decade of increasing radicalisation, a decade in which it had become commonplace for Chilean economists to talk of the need for 'structural reforms'. The Christian Democrats contributed a great deal to this process ... in 1964 they even campaigned on the slogan of a 'Revolution In Liberty'.

*Roddick, J. F. 'Class Structure and Class Politics in Chile', in O'Brien, P. (ed.) 1978. Allende's Chile. Westport, USA. Praeger Publishers. p. 5.*

> What does Source C suggest about Allende's election? Does the text in the section about the 1970 election support or contradict this? Why was the USA so alarmed about Allende's election?

# Allende's Chile 1970–73

## Background

Allende won the 1970 election with a smaller percentage of the total vote (36%) than his defeat in 1964 (39%). Despite this drop in support, he was determined to introduce radical changes to Chile.

Allende's immediate strategy – like Castro in Cuba – was a price freeze combined with wage rises. This enhanced the middle classes and stimulated consumer spending. This benefited 95% of the population in the short term, because prices were low and employment rose. However, two disastrous years followed, during which it became increasingly difficult for Allende to find the right solutions to growing problems. The USA was particularly unhelpful towards Allende, but historians have also laid some of the blame on the USSR.

## Allende's problems

After a successful first year, Allende faced a number of challenges, and took several steps to improve his popularity.

- Allende made nationalisation of the copper mines a top priority; most people wanted this, and it was unanimously approved by the Chilean Congress.
- He also nationalised coal, steel and many private banks. Industrial and financial élites and landowners were angered by this move, and it caused alarm in the USA.

- The middle classes feared that the widening of state control under Allende might lead to small shops and businesses becoming Soviet-style workers' co-operatives. US propaganda did much to encourage this notion, creating an atmosphere of anxiety and growing opposition.
- A short economic boom was followed by major financial problems. Supply was much lower than demand, the economy shrank, and deficit spending rapidly increased. By early 1973, Chile was experiencing rapid inflation.
- As sales of copper declined, new investments and foreign exchange grew scarce. There were shortages of everyday goods, which badly affected the working classes.
- A thriving black market sprang up, which initially accepted the Chilean currency, escudos. However, the government printed more money and escudos eventually became worthless. Allende responded by distributing food directly to working-class neighbourhoods.
- Allende could do little to prevent the rapid decline of the Chilean economy. He did not dare impose austerity measures on the working class, and he was unable to get new taxes approved by Congress or borrow enough money from other countries.

## Allende's dilemma

Even in Cuba, where Castro had a level of power that Allende lacked, the transition to a socialist economy was difficult. Chile was still a multi-party democracy, in which the opposition controlled Congress. This put Allende in a difficult situation, but other forces also played a part in the dilemmas he faced.

The USA was cold towards Allende, although official diplomatic relations remained polite. Nixon damaged the Chilean economy by blocking loans and other financial aid from multilateral organisations. Nixon also approved increased aid to the Chilean military, aware of its indifference towards Allende. It has also been suggested that by 1973, the US and the CIA were working actively – although secretly – to destabilise and then remove Allende by funding opposition groups and encouraging a military coup.

The USSR also had an interest in Chile, and historian Robert Moss raises the question of Soviet involvement in the country when discussing a visit Allende made to Moscow in December 1972 (see Source D on page 198). Since 1970, Allende had received $400 million from the USSR, mainly in the form of aid for building projects and in credit that could only be spent on goods that were imported from the Soviet Union. During his 1972 visit, Allende hoped to receive further credits and loans from the USSR totalling $500 million.

The Russians clearly had an important stake in Chile. It was ... a test-tube demonstration of a Marxist government controlling a democratic society, and the success or failure of Allende's experiment would be certain to stir ripples in France and Italy – amongst the socialist intelligentsia if not among ordinary voters ... Chile was a much richer country than Cuba, with a major export commodity (copper) ... [but] Allende did not get much from Moscow ... he got limited aid ... and also $50m in military credits.

Moss, R. 1993. Chile's Marxist Experiment. *Newton Abbot, UK. David & Charles.* pp. 202–3.

The Soviets must have realised that if Allende actually used any of the military credits (by which the USSR would have supplied military equipment), he would have been widely criticised for aligning the country too closely with the USSR after breaking Chile's dependency on the US. This would probably have been fatal to his presidency.

Did Moscow think that Allende's survival was in doubt anyway, and choose to sacrifice him? The USSR had poured aid into Egypt for years without earning unfailing loyalty, so perhaps it was reluctant to be 'used' again. Some historians have argued that Allende alienated Soviet leader Leonid Brezhnev by refusing certain conditions he wished to attach to the aid. For example, the USSR demanded that Allende restructure the Chilean economy along Soviet lines.

Given that this was a time of emerging détente between the USSR and the USA, it has also been suggested that Moscow and Washington may have reached an understanding over Chile. Brezhnev had been promised a huge wheat shipment from the USA to help the USSR over a bad harvest. In addition, Nixon had visited Beijing – the first trip to Communist China made by a US president. Perhaps the USSR was anxious not to interfere in the Americas – and therefore in Chile – at this point in time.

### Discussion point

Was Allende 'sacrificed' by the Soviets? Carry out some further research on détente, US–USSR relations in the 1970s, and Allende's visit to Moscow in December 1972 – then discuss this question.

Allende knew that the USA dominated the Americas, and his government tried to maintain good relations with Washington even while Chile showed support to developing nations, some of which had anti-US regimes. In 1971, Fidel Castro visited Chile. While there, he organised huge rallies and offered advice to Allende. The USA and the Chilean political right saw this as proof that the 'Chilean way to socialism' was simply about putting Chile on the same path as Cuba.

*Fidel Castro and Salvador Allende greet supporters during the Cuban president's visit to Chile in 1971*

## Allende's overthrow

Over the next two years, Chile established diplomatic relations with Cuba, China, North Korea, North Vietnam and Albania. These actions all confirmed to Washington that Allende was a threat to US interests. By September 1973, the Chilean congress and judiciary were united against Allende, claiming that his government had ignored the Chilean constitution. On 11 September, the Chilean army launched an attack on the presidential palace. Before the assault, the commanders-in-chief – headed by General Augusto Pinochet – removed all officers who were sympathetic to the president.

During the course of this attack, Allende died. The manner of his death has been the subject of debate. Some people believe that Allende committed suicide with an assault rifle in the presidential palace after defending his government against the coup. However, it has also been suggested that he was killed during the assault on the palace – or even that he was deliberately sought out and murdered.

After the attack there was some resistance, but the military quickly gained control. Many Chileans thought the coup would lead to civil war, but instead there was a long period of brutal military dictatorship.

The bombing of the presidential palace during Pinochet's coup in 1973

## Historical interpretations

Most historians believe that the actions and attitudes of the USA contributed significantly to the Chilean coup that brought down Allende. No one has established beyond doubt that the USA was directly involved in the coup, although Stephen Graubard reports that in 1974 the *New York Times* published a story suggesting that US involvement was considerable. When asked about this at a press conference, Gerald Ford replied defensively, protesting that US involvement was nothing more than an effort to prevent Allende from suppressing opposition to his regime: 'The American interest involved nothing more than helping opposition newspapers and political parties – the essential components of a democratic society.' This is probably the closest we will ever get to an admission of involvement by the USA.

The USSR's reluctance to give Allende greater financial support in December 1972 has also been viewed as a key moment, so the reasons for Allende's downfall have been much debated. Was it mainly economic? Was it the result of interplay between social classes and political parties? Skidmore and Smith suggest that 'the worker-based Allende movement was unable to form an enduring coalition with the other strata in Chilean society ... hence its vulnerability'. Other historians have questioned why Allende failed to preserve democracy or achieve socialism.

Critics blame Allende for going to extremes – destroying the economy, ignoring the constitution and undermining the spirit of democracy. Right-wing critics, in particular, accuse the left of planning an armed takeover – a charge that was never proved. Others feel that the UP fatally drove the middle classes to active opposition. Combined with the USA's efforts to destabilise Allende and the USSR's failure to finance him, all these factors probably contributed to his downfall.

Many Chileans today believe that a variety of people and groups across the whole political spectrum helped destroy the democratic order by being too ideological, too unwilling to compromise or too disloyal. Certainly, a minority president facing foreign interference as well as growing opposition at home was unlikely to be able to uphold democracy and create socialism at the same time. Perhaps Allende was a victim of the Cold War – in the wrong place at the wrong time.

In contrast to most other nations in Latin America, Chile had a long tradition of civilian democratic rule before this coup. Military intervention in politics was rare in the country. Perhaps the bloodiness of the coup was due to the stability of the existing democratic system, which required extreme action to overturn it.

### SOURCE E

There can be no doubt that the profound economic crisis which beset Chile in 1972 and 1973 was a contributory factor to the coup of 11 September 1973. The widespread shortages, the necessity to queue for hours for certain basic goods ... and spare parts ... the frequency of strikes, and an uncontrollable inflation – all these helped to create a climate propitious for a military intervention to put an end to the 'chaos' ... but the roots of the crisis were political, and the solution to the crisis could only be political. It is only international agency and banking reports which try to pretend otherwise.

Roxborough, I., O'Brien, P. and Roddick, J. 1977. Chile: The State and Revolution. London, UK. Macmillan Press. p. 123.

What viewpoint does Source E on page 201 take over Allende's downfall?
What other possible causes of his failure might there be?

## Activity

Use the internet to find out more about Allende and the situation in Chile
between 1970 and 1973. What conclusions do you reach about the reasons
for Allende's failure? Compare your findings with other students. How far
did Allende bring about his own downfall?

# What was the impact of the Pinochet regime after 1973?

Few coups in Latin America have received so much international
attention as the one in Chile in September 1973. There was almost
universal condemnation of Augusto Pinochet. This was partly because
his action was both brutal and illegal, but also because his coup took
place in a democratic society. It also brought to an end an unusual
– perhaps even misguided – attempt to create socialism
through parliamentary and constitutional means.

*Augusto Pinochet (left)
and Salvador Allende
(right) in August
1973, shortly before
Pinochet's coup
against Allende*

## The junta takes charge

On the day of the coup, Pinochet – together with the heads of the air force, navy and police – issued an Act of Constitution. The act established a junta (military) government that immediately suspended the constitution and congress. It imposed strict censorship, a 9 p.m. curfew, banned the left-wing parties that had made up Allende's government, and halted all political activity. Effectively, a military dictatorship had come to power. The new government claimed that the coup had been necessary to save the Chilean economy, crush communism, prevent class warfare, restore law and order, and stabilise commerce and industry.

Once in power, Pinochet quickly consolidated his control and was made the head of the junta and 'supreme chief of the nation'. In January 1974, Pinochet announced that the military would remain in power for no less than five years. In making this claim, he broke with Chilean military tradition by not handing back power to civilians.

The junta introduced the National Security Doctrine, whose main aim was to defeat 'domestic enemies', who had infiltrated national institutions such as schools, churches, political parties, unions and the media. Marxists and left-wing intellectuals were at the top of the list. Army officers were awarded most government positions at both national and local levels. Once there, they issued decrees to restore order on the junta's terms.

## Human rights and social policy

Pinochet's regime did not hesitate to use repression in order to combat popular protest or unrest amongst the labour force. Indeed, the period immediately after the coup was particularly brutal and destructive. The armed forces pursued members of the UP as enemies to be crushed, not just as political opponents to be barred from office. Thousands of perceived enemies of the state were imprisoned and thousands more were murdered – possibly over 5000 – during the early days of the regime.

The Chilean national stadium in Santiago became synonymous with the brutality of Pinochet's government – it was used as a prison camp and interrogation centre. Around 12,000 people were detained there between September and November 1973, and the Red Cross estimated that 7000 prisoners occupied the stadium at one point. Survivors later spoke of detainees being tortured and threatened with death by shooting. Some were shot on the premises or taken to unknown locations for execution.

Universities and schools were also targeted, and all union activities were banned. Thousands were murdered, jailed, raped, tortured or exiled. Pinochet used his secret police to investigate and report to him on dissidents, who lived in fear of arrest – or worse. More than 20,000 Chileans went into exile to escape what Pinochet described as 'retribution for the crimes committed against Chile'. The Church and international human rights organisations denounced these violations. There were also occasional protests in the West and genuine anger in the Soviet bloc. Despite international condemnation, though, many people within Chile felt that Pinochet might be a positive force.

## Activity

Pinochet's National Security Doctrine lay at the heart of the regime's control over Chileans during the 1970s and 1980s. But what other means of control or influence did Pinochet's dictatorship use? What was everyday life like in Chile? Using books and the internet, find out how both supporters and opponents of the regime viewed Pinochet. Consider the following questions:

- Did Chile's relations with the USA keep Pinochet in power?
- How did Pinochet ensure army loyalty?
- Why did so many Chileans go along with the regime and even see Pinochet as a positive force?

## Theory of knowledge

### History and empathy

The historian R. G. Collingwood (1889–1943) said that historians should be concerned with 'the thought in the mind of the person by whose agency the event came about'. Pinochet claimed that the repression after his coup in 1973 was 'retribution'. However, is it ever possible for historians to empathise with the actions of a dictator like Pinochet? Should historians even attempt to do so?

## Pinochet and the international community

The USA originally supported Pinochet, since he maintained a free-enterprise economy and helped to stop the spread of a 'Marxist cancer from Cuba'. Despite Pinochet's repressive regime and his abuse of human rights, US aid to Chile increased during Pinochet's first three years in charge.

Relations between Chile and the USA declined when Jimmy Carter became president in 1977. Carter placed human rights at the centre of an ethical foreign policy, and was angered by the fact that Chilean intelligence services had been involved in the assassination of Allende's ambassador to the US, **Orlando Letelier**. Carter pressed Pinochet to extradite those implicated in the crime, but Pinochet refused. Carter cut aid to Chile, but this had little effect.

**Orlando Letelier (1932–76)** Letelier was a Chilean economist, political figure, and – during the administration of socialist president Salvador Allende – Chilean ambassador to the USA. As a refugee from Pinochet's dictatorship, Letelier accepted several academic positions in Washington, DC, where he was assassinated by Pinochet's agents in 1976.

### Activity

Find out more about the Letelier assassination. Why was Letelier so important to the Chilean government? What does his murder reveal about Pinochet's regime?

With the election of Ronald Reagan in 1980, relations with Chile improved once more. Reagan argued that anti-communist authoritarian regimes should not be undermined, and the US government sought to re-establish ties with Pinochet. As unrest grew across Central America throughout the 1980s, the US once again began to regard Chile as a Cold War barrier against the threat of communism.

Responding to international criticism, Pinochet held a tightly controlled plebiscite (public referendum) in 1978, calling for a yes or no vote for his 'defence of the dignity of Chile'. The government claimed that over 75% of voters supported Pinochet. Another controversial vote in 1980 approved a new constitution, which confirmed Pinochet's position until 1989. As a result of this, Pinochet's supporters believed that his dictatorship was fully within the rule of law. With Reagan in the White House and Chile back in favour with Washington, by 1981 Pinochet seemed untouchable.

During the 1982 Falklands War between Britain and Argentina, Chile gave support to Britain in the form of early-warning radar and intelligence about the movement of Argentinean forces. In return, Britain offered Pinochet a deal on the purchase of military aircraft. Part of the reason for Chile's support of Britain was that Chile and Argentina had almost gone to war over the possession of islands south of Tierra del Fuego in 1978, and the relationship between the two countries was still tense. The Chilean government was also concerned that if Argentina captured the Falklands (*las Malvinas*), it might attack Chile.

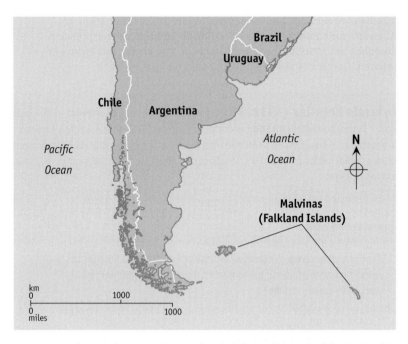

*A map showing southern South America and the Malvinas (Falkland Islands)*

However, these same fears led Chile to remain officially neutral during the conflict. Likewise, the British prime minister, Margaret Thatcher, did not want to be publicly associated with a military dictatorship that was widely condemned for human-rights abuses. The alliance therefore remained secret. After leaving office, Thatcher admitted that Pinochet had helped save many British lives. The operation to win back the islands, which came after Argentina invaded in April 1982, cost 255 British and 655 Argentinean lives.

> Why did Pinochet help Britain against Argentina?

## Economic policy

By 1975, Pinochet's regime had developed an economic policy of free-market reforms. This meant that the state had no control over areas such as means of production, prices and supplies. Pinochet wanted to make Chile a nation of proprietors, and relied on the so-called 'Chicago Boys' to create a model free-market economy, opening Chile to world business.

The Chicago Boys were technocrats (people who believe in a form of government in which science controls decision-making). These men trained at Chicago University under Professor **Milton Friedman**.

Their goal was to reduce import tariffs, cut inflation and government subsidies, privatise state-owned companies, introduce immediate free-trade policies and reduce the size of the public sector. Known as 'economic shock therapy', this was first applied in both Chile and Argentina.

**Milton Friedman (1912–2006)** An American economist, academic and author, Friedman led the Chicago University school of economics. During the 1960s, he promoted an alternative 'shock therapy' economic policy known as monetarism. His ideas were later adopted by Thatcher in Britain, Reagan in the USA and Pinochet in Chile. Friedman was awarded the Nobel Prize for Economics in 1976.

*Opponents of Pinochet's dictatorship in Chile demonstrate in Stockholm, Sweden, against Milton Friedman being awarded the Nobel Prize in 1976; they called Friedman 'the economist of oppression'*

Under Pinochet, the Chicago Boys also assumed importance in ministerial roles. Interestingly, the political activist Naomi Klein quotes Orlando Letelier, Allende's ambassador to the US, who argued that although the coup was described as military, it was 'an equal partnership between the army and the economists'.

What do you think Letelier meant by describing Pinochet's coup as 'an equal partnership between the army and the economists'?

The use of these tactics began an era of economic privatisation. Pinochet abolished the minimum wage, withdrew trade union rights, privatised pensions, state industries and banks, and lowered taxes on wealth and profits. Supporters called this 'the Miracle of Chile', due to the 35% increase in real per capita GDP from 1960 to 1980, and the significant reduction in inflation. However, opponents disputed this 'miracle', pointing out that unemployment increased from 4.3% in 1973 to 22% in 1983, while real wages dropped by 40%. Social spending cuts had serious consequences for public health and education programmes. Homelessness and malnutrition became more widespread, and the infant mortality rate increased.

Despite a passionate commitment to privatisation, Pinochet's largest nationalised asset – the state copper corporation, Codelco – remained untouched. Ironically, his regime received its greatest financial support from a state company nationalised by Allende. There was also corruption within Pinochet's own circle, as privatisation benefited his family and supporters. Throughout the 1980s, Chilean society grew increasingly unequal. Some people recovered their lost industrial and agricultural holdings as the junta sold off industries that had been absorbed by Allende. However, many firms lost out to multinational corporations buying into Chile. The business community that had largely backed Pinochet was often negatively affected.

This multinational 'invasion' came about because Pinochet's Chicago economists wanted a free-market economy moulded by international organisations and governments, rather than by private banks and Chilean companies. As Skidmore and Smith conclude: 'The financial crash of 1982, triggered by Mexico's de facto default on its foreign debt, hit Chile even harder than the rest of Latin America.' Pinochet presided over two recessions – one in 1975 (partly inherited from Allende) and one in 1982–83 (triggered by events in Mexico, but worsened by his economic policies). The economy did not begin to recover until 1986.

Today, Chileans remain more divided on Pinochet's legacy than that of any other political leader. Some see him as a brutal dictator who ended democracy and led a regime characterised by torture and nepotism. Others believe he saved Chile from the kind of Cold War conflict that engulfed Nicaragua and El Salvador.

According to statistics from the IMF and the World Bank, Chile has enjoyed greater economic progress since democracy was restored in 1990. However, this progress is perhaps less Pinochet's legacy and more related to the benefits of democratic government, freed from Cold War constraints and ideology.

# How far has Chile's political history since 1945 been determined by the USA and the Cold War?

US dominance in the Americas frequently influenced Chilean politics after 1945. González Videla purged the communists in his administration, and Ibáñez and Alessandri both supported Washington. However, tensions arose after Castro's revolution and during the rise of the Marxist left under Salvador Allende's leadership.

Although the left gained ground throughout the 1950s, the right maintained its electoral presence and bought time by expanding social welfare programmes. Public works projects were financed largely by the US, so the economy grew and unemployment dropped. Alessandri even tackled land reform – an issue that those on the right sought to avoid, but which was a driving force for the left.

However, anti-US sentiment was fuelled by Washington's attitude towards Castro and opposition to the war in Vietnam. US influence in Chilean domestic affairs was equally resented – a fact highlighted by the covert CIA operation to secure Frei's victory over Allende in the 1964 election. Frei's reformist politics had America's blessing, as he wanted to pre-empt the left, implementing reforms his own way – from the political centre. But this angered both Chile's conservative upper classes and the left. By 1970, Chilean politics were polarised and the USA's reputation there was tarnished.

Allende's election was viewed as a setback by Washington. National security advisor Henry Kissinger was concerned about the free election of a Marxist. With growing unease about Soviet influence in the western hemisphere – especially the Americas – Washington undermined Allende's democratically elected government.

Although the USA did not directly stage the bloody coup of 1973, it encouraged Allende's overthrow, providing assistance to Pinochet's pro-American, anti-communist military regime. Later, though, human-rights violations led many in the US Congress to oppose ties with Pinochet. Jimmy Carter publicly condemned Pinochet, while the assassination of Orlando Letelier contributed further to Chile's growing isolation.

After Ronald Reagan was elected in 1980, better relations were established, largely due to the USA's fear that undermining Chile might lead to a Marxist victory, as it had in Nicaragua. However, large-scale protests against Pinochet in 1983 were followed by bombings, popular unrest and economic decline. By November 1984, the USA had reached the conclusion that his regime was problematic. Chilean politicians of the centre-right felt that Pinochet's own ambitions stood in the way of a transition to civilian rule, and by 1989, Washington actively backed the opposition in its effort to obtain a fair electoral process.

This coincided with Mikhail Gorbachev's leadership in the USSR and his desire for openness, or *glasnost*. A series of Reagan–Gorbachev summits between 1985 and 1988 had a significant impact on the nature of international relations. Gorbachev's *glasnost* exposed the dominance of the Soviet Communist Party, and unintentionally set in motion events that would end both the Communist Party and the Cold War. As relations between East and West improved, the threat of revolution in the Americas receded.

Chile's state of emergency was lifted in 1988, and in 1989 the country held its first presidential election since 1970. Christian Democrat Patricio Aylwin was elected. He subsequently initiated modest economic reforms, whilst setting up a commission to investigate human-rights violations. In the post-Cold War era, anti-Americanism in Chile remains quite strong in military circles and the right. Many are still angered by what they believe was an about-turn by the USA – dropping Pinochet and switching its support to democratic parties.

Nonetheless, US influence in Chile since 1945 has been profound. Direct involvement may have been limited, but the US had an effect through trade, including the IMF, the Inter-American Development Bank, the World Bank, the OAS, and various cultural agencies.

Some have interpreted the turn towards democracy in Latin America – and notably in Chile – as a global triumph of US values, particularly in light of the collapse of the USSR. But perhaps this shift to democracy is really a belated expression of Chilean nationalism and a determination to rectify the state's failed experiment with socialism. Today, politicians and economists are aware that, realistically, Chile must come under a capitalist system, and exist in harmony with the USA and other nations in the Americas.

# End of chapter activities

## Paper 3 exam practice

### Question 1

Analyse the reasons for González Videla's purge of Chilean communists in the late 1940s.
[20 marks]

### Skill focus

Using your own knowledge analytically and combining it with awareness of historical debate

### Examiner's tips

Always remember that historical knowledge and analysis should be the core of your answer – aspects of historical debate are desirable extras. However, where it is relevant, the integration of relevant knowledge about historical debates or interpretations, with reference to individual historians, will help push your answer up into the higher bands.

Provided that you have read the question carefully, drawn up a plan, worked out your line of argument/approach and written your introductory paragraph, you should be able to avoid both irrelevant material and simple narrative. Your task now is to follow your plan by writing a series of linked paragraphs that contain relevant analysis, precise supporting own knowledge and, where relevant, brief references to historical debates and interpretations.

For this question, you will need to:

- give a brief explanation about the nature of the purge and about the role of the Chilean Communist Party
- supply a brief summary of the historical context (i.e. González Videla rewarding communists for their electoral support; the split between the socialists and communists; the rise of the AChA; US and Canadian Cold War experiences; rising tensions between the USA and USSR)
- outline what actually happened (i.e. when these events started, who was involved/affected, their results, e.g. Ley Maldita, communists outlawed)
- provide a consistently analytical examination of the reasons for the introduction, course and development of these events.

This particular episode of Chilean history in the context of the Cold War has been the subject of much historical debate. It will give you the chance to refer to different historians' views.

## Common mistakes

Some students, aware of an existing historical debate (and knowing that extra marks can be gained by showing this) sometimes simply write things like: 'Historian x says … and historian y says …' However, they make no attempt to **evaluate** the different views (for example, has one historian had access to more/better information than another, perhaps because he/she was writing at a later date?); nor is this information **integrated** into their answer by being pinned to the question. Another weak use of historical debate is to write things like: 'Historian x is biased because she is American.' Such comments will not be given much credit.

## Sample paragraphs containing analysis and historical debate

The following is a good example of how to use historians' views. The main focus of the answer is properly concerned with using precise own knowledge to address the demands of the question. However, the candidate has also provided some brief but relevant knowledge of historical debate, which is smoothly integrated into the answer.

González Videla won the 1946 election with communist support, and he rewarded them with government posts. However, the communists soon demanded a more hardline Soviet approach to policy, which caused a split in the main Chilean trade union, the CTCh. González Videla tried to prevent government discord, but the situation deteriorated with strikes and disorder. In response, he suspended civil liberties and declared a state of siege.

The Cold War was in its formative stages. Earlier in 1946, the Gouzenko spy scandal had rocked Canada and the USA. Washington wanted the Americas free from communist expansion, so Chile was a concern. González Videla expelled the communists from his Cabinet and then banned them completely under the 1948 Law for the Defence of Democracy.

> The Communist Party remained illegal until 1958. As
> if to emphasise cutting ties, González Videla severed
> diplomatic relations with the Soviet Union, Yugoslavia and
> Czechoslovakia. A crackdown followed on communists in
> public service. This ruined careers, and many communists left
> Chile. Roxborough, O'Brien and Roddick argue that González
> Videla wanted to encourage US business and bolster Chilean
> security by appeasing Washington. Others, like Hudson,
> interpret González Videla's purge differently ...

There then follows precise own knowledge and further historical debate about the reasons surrounding González Videla's purge.

## Activity

In this chapter, the focus is on writing an answer that is analytical and well-supported by precise own knowledge, and one that – where relevant – refers to historical interpretations/debates. So, using the information from this chapter, and any other sources of information available to you, try to answer **one** of the following Paper 3 practice questions using these skills.

Remember to refer to the simplified Paper 3 markscheme on page 219.

# Paper 3 practice questions

1   Assess the impact of Allende's policies and actions on Chile in the period 1970–73.

2   To what extent were Eduardo Frei's attempts at reform from 1964 to 1970 doomed to fail?

3   'Pressure from the USA was the reason for González Videla's outlawing of communism in Chile between 1946 and 1949.' To what extent do you agree with this statement?

4   Compare and contrast the social and economic policies of Allende and Pinochet in Chile between 1970 and 1983.

5   Analyse the influence of the Cold War on the foreign and domestic policies of Chile, 1945–81.

## Question 2

Why did Allende's socialist government fail in the period 1970–73?
[20 marks]

## Skill focus

Writing a conclusion to your essay

## Examiner's tips

Provided you have carried out all the steps recommended so far, it should be relatively easy to write one or two concluding paragraphs.

For this question, you will need to cover the following possible reasons for the failure of Allende's government:

- the interplay between social classes and political parties in Chile
- divisions within Allende's government between differing factions, some of which wanted provocative action while others preferred a legalistic approach
- the growing economic problems faced by Allende – including responses from both the USSR and the USA
- how Allende's foreign policy was viewed by people inside and outside Chile
- the alleged role of the USA and the CIA
- the reforms and legislation carried out by Allende
- the emergence of growing opposition
- the role of the army (Pinochet) and the judiciary
- mistakes made by Allende and his administration.

With questions like this, you will need to be specific – avoiding generalisations and giving precise information about a range of different factors. Also, such a question – which is asking for an analysis of several reasons – implicitly expects you to come to some kind of judgement about which cause(s) was/were the most important. You might even wish to argue that, in some respects, Allende's government did not fail, even though it was driven from power.

## Common mistakes

Sometimes, candidates simply rework in their conclusion what they have written earlier – making the examiner read the same things twice. Generally, concluding paragraphs should be relatively short: the aim should be to come to a judgement/conclusion that is clearly based on what has already been written. If possible, a short but relevant quotation is a good way to round off an argument.

Remember to refer to the simplified Paper 3 markscheme on page 219.

# Sample student conclusion

It is difficult to conclude why Allende's government had failed by September 1973. Several overlapping factors thwarted Allende. The left drew support mainly from the urban working class, but it never trumped a unified élite, able to gain the allegiance of middle-sector groups and key elements, such as shopkeepers and truckers. So Allende did not form a broad coalition with other groups. The UP was weakened by internal splits: the far left pressed Allende for radical action, whilst moderate communists knew that gradual reform was less likely to play into the hands of the right. 'Outside agencies' were crucial. The USA and its CIA contributed to Allende's demise, by undermining his administration and financing strikes. The USSR behaved enigmatically towards Allende when, facing severe economic problems, he visited Moscow to seek aid. Whilst Allende can be blamed to a degree, financial aid to Chile was blocked by the US and multilateral organisations. Finally, Allende had not lived a revolutionary life like Castro. As a lifelong parliamentarian, he had ceaselessly negotiated to create and preserve coalitions, but was ill-prepared for Pinochet, whose betrayal of Allende made him the traitor who cut off Chile's 'road to socialism'.

This is a good conclusion as it briefly pulls together the main threads of the argument (without simply repeating/summarising them), and then also makes a clear judgement. In addition, there is an intelligent final comment which rounds off the whole conclusion – and no doubt the core of the essay – in a memorable way.

## Activity

In this chapter, the focus is on writing a useful conclusion. Using the information from this chapter, and any other sources available to you, write concluding paragraphs for **at least two** of the following Paper 3 practice questions. Remember – to do this, you will need to create full plans for the questions you choose.

# Paper 3 practice questions

1   Analyse the effects of the Cold War in Chile from 1958 to 1973.

2   'Pinochet's economic policy brought prosperity and opened up Chile to world markets.' How valid is this statement?

3   'The main objective of Allende's government was to create "socialism with a human face".' To what extent do you agree with this statement?

4   Compare and contrast the governments of González Videla and Pinochet in Chile.

5   Assess the impact of external political factors on Chile in the period 1945–81.

# 8 Exam practice

## Introduction

You have now completed your study of the main events and developments in the Americas during the period 1945–81. You have also had the chance to examine several of the historical debates and differing historical interpretations that surround some of these developments.

In the earlier chapters, you encountered examples of Paper 3-type essay questions, with examiner's tips. You have also had some basic practice in answering such questions. In this chapter, these tips and skills will be developed in more depth. Longer examples of possible student answers are provided. These are accompanied by examiner's comments that should increase your understanding of what examiners are looking for when they mark your essays. Following each question and answer, you will find tasks to give you further practice in the skills needed to gain the higher marks in this exam.

## IB History Paper 3 exam questions and skills

Those of you following Route 2, HL Option 3 – Aspects of the History of the Americas – will have studied in depth **three** of the 12 sections available for this HL Option. *The Americas and the Cold War 1945–81* is one of those sections. For Paper 3, two questions are set from each of the 12 sections, giving 24 questions in total; you have to answer **three** of these.

Each question has a specific markscheme. However, the 'generic' markscheme in the IB *History Guide* gives you a good general idea of what examiners are looking for in order to place answers into the higher bands. In particular, you will need to acquire reasonably precise historical knowledge so that you can address issues such as cause and effect, and change and continuity. This knowledge will be required in order to explain historical developments in a clear, coherent, well-supported and relevant way. You will also need to understand relevant historical debates and interpretations, and be able to refer to these and critically evaluate them.

# Essay planning

Make sure you read each question **carefully**, noting all the important key or 'command' words. You might find it useful to highlight them on your question paper. You can then produce a rough plan (for example, a spider diagram) of **each** of the three essays you intend to attempt, **before** you start to write your answers. That way, you will soon know whether you have enough own knowledge to answer them adequately.

Next, refer back to the wording of each question. This will help you work out whether or not you are responding to all its various demands/aspects in your plan. In addition, if you run short of time towards the end of your exam, you will at least be able to write some brief condensed sentences to show the key issues/points and arguments you would have presented. It is therefore far better to do the planning at the **start** of the exam; that is, **before** you panic, should you suddenly realise you haven't time to finish your last essay.

## Relevance to the question

Remember, too, to keep your answers relevant and focused on the question. Don't go outside the dates mentioned in the question, or write answers on subjects not identified in that question. Also, don't just describe the events or developments. Sometimes, students just focus on one key word, date or individual, and then write down everything they know about it. Instead, select your own knowledge carefully and pin the relevant information to the key features raised by the question. Finally, if the question asks for 'causes/reasons' and 'results', 'continuity and change', 'successes and failures', or 'nature and development', make sure you deal with **all** the parts of the question. Otherwise, you will limit yourself to half marks at best.

## Examiner's tips

For Paper 3 answers, examiners are looking for well-structured arguments which:

* are consistently relevant/linked to the question
* offer clear/precise analysis
* are supported by accurate, precise and relevant own knowledge
* offer a balanced judgement
* refer to different historical debates/interpretations or to relevant historians and, where relevant, offer some critical evaluation of these.

## Simplified markscheme

| Band | | Marks |
|---|---|---|
| 1 | **Consistently analytical/explanatory** in approach, with very explicit focus on all demands of the question. **Understanding and evaluation of different historical interpretations**; good synthesis of **plentiful and precise own knowledge** with different interpretations/approaches. **Argument is clear, well-supported and well-structured** throughout. | 17–20 |
| 2 | **Clear/explicit focus** on all the demands of the question, with **consistently relevant analysis/explanation.** Very **detailed own knowledge**. Argument in the main is **well-structured and supported.** Some **awareness of different historical interpretations**, and **some attempts at evaluation.** | 14–16 |
| 3 | **Some relevant analysis/argument**, mainly linked to the question, with **relevant and precise supporting own knowledge. Reasonable structure, with some explanation** and **some awareness of different historical views** – but not all aspects of the question addressed. | 11–13 |
| 4 | Mainly **narrative in approach**, with **reasonably accurate knowledge**; but **limited focus**, and **no real analysis/ explanation. Some structure**, but **links to the question are mainly unclear/implicit.** | 8–10 |
| 5 | **Limited relevant knowledge**, with a **few unsupported comments/assertions. Not well-structured**; and **not linked effectively to the question**, which is not really understood. | 0–7 |

# Student answers

The following extracts from student answers have brief examiner's comments next to them, and a longer overall comment at the end. Those parts of student answers that are particularly strong and well-focused (such as demonstrations of precise and relevant own knowledge or examination of historical interpretations) will be highlighted in blue. Errors/confusions/irrelevance/loss of focus will be **highlighted in white**. In this way, you should find it easier to follow why marks were awarded or withheld.

# Question 1

'A lack of understanding was at the heart of the Cuban Missile Crisis in October 1962.' To what extent do you agree with this view?
[20 marks]

## Skills

- Factual knowledge and understanding
- Structured, analytical and **balanced** argument
- Awareness/understanding/evaluation of historical interpretations
- Clear and balanced judgement.

## Examiner's tip

Look carefully at the wording of this question, which asks you to consider the view that a lack of understanding by both the United States and the Soviet Union lay at the heart of the Cuban Missile Crisis. This means you need to show both how the statement is true **and** how it is not true. It is perfectly acceptable for you to challenge the view, as long as you support your arguments with relevant and precise own knowledge. All aspects of the question will need to be addressed in order to achieve high marks. And remember – don't just describe either what happened day by day in October 1962, or what Kennedy and Khrushchev did. What is needed is explicit analysis and explanation of the background to the crisis and of the actions during it, and how these do/do not demonstrate lack of understanding. You should also try to consider other factors that might explain how the crisis developed.

## Student answer

The Cuban Missile Crisis was undoubtedly influenced by a lack of understanding between Kennedy and Khrushchev. Both leaders were playing with high-risk stakes, but there were moments when neither seemed fully in control. Lack of understanding was crucial, but political, ideological and financial motives were also deeply rooted in this crisis, and require analysis. Ideological hostility to Castro's Cuba was demonstrated by the failed CIA-backed invasion at the Bay of Pigs in 1961, by the destabilising Operation Mongoose and by the trade embargo. Khrushchev's awareness of the USA's advantage in nuclear missiles –

*and their presence in Turkey – was compounded by his desire for prestige following Chinese criticism of his 'weakness' at a time of Soviet economic stagnation. Also, following the Vienna Summit and the building of the Berlin Wall, he believed Kennedy was weak.*

**Examiner's comment**

This is a clear and well-focused introduction, showing accurate topic knowledge and an appreciation of the existence of several factors that contributed to the crisis.

*To understand why these other factors were important, it is necessary to examine why Cuba had become an important part of the Cold War.* Castro's victory over Batista in 1959 led him to introduce radical agrarian land laws, limiting estates to 1000 acres; worryingly for Washington, he also banned foreigners from owning agricultural land. His appointment of the communist Nuñez Jimenez as head of the reform programme caused the US to liken Castro to Árbenz in Guatemala. This worried the USA because it was anxious not to have left-wing or communist states in Latin America or the Caribbean, which Americans considered their 'back yard', as per the Monroe Doctrine.

Post-war Cuba had very much been a playground for the rich and famous in America, with US companies dominating most Cuban industry and utilities. Fulgencio Batista – who had seized power in a coup in 1952 – led a divided society with little economic security, driven by the USA and over-dependent on sugar. Batista's influence and populism was based on a divided opposition and US backing. This angered many on the left, including Fidel Castro – who launched a coup against Batista in July 1953. With the rebellion's failure, Castro left for Mexico, to plot Batista's downfall and build a new revolutionary force, which became known as the 26 July Movement. Castro's decision to leave Cuba was wise, as it distanced him from island politics.

## Examiner's comment

Although there is some accurate own knowledge, this is mostly background material and not explicitly linked to the demands of the question. While making a brief reference or two to the historical context of Castro's revolution is a good idea, it is not wise to give too much information on this. What is needed is precise own knowledge of the relationship between Castro and Khrushchev between 1959 and 1961, and how this contributed to US hostility towards Cuba. The amount of detail provided about Cuba prior to Castro shows that this answer is slipping into interesting but irrelevant narrative.

In Mexico, Castro met Che Guevara, who became an important and effective recruit to the revolutionary band. So in 1956, they sailed for Cuba to lead a new rebellion. This effort was crushed when Castro's revolutionaries landed in the wrong place, and Batista's forces killed or captured many. They fled into the mountains in eastern Cuba, regrouping and planning Batista's downfall through guerrilla tactics.

Castro entered Havana on 8 January 1959, telling cheering Cubans that 'the revolution begins now'. There was a political vacuum, but a real desire for change. A major unifying factor was the wish to be free from US influence. This was quickly picked up in Washington, since the US was shaken by the Cuban revolution and knew it would be affected economically, due to US ownership of Cuban industries and most major tourist facilities. Castro himself was seen initially as an enigma and in the US, questions were asked. Was he a communist or just a nationalist? Was he anti-American or just pro-Cuban?

There are different theories about Castro. Dewart says that Castro's main aim was to carry out a badly needed redistribution of land, and that there is no evidence to suggest he was some sort of 'dedicated agent of international communism'. However, Aldred argues that Castro's success was the first time a Marxist–Leninist revolt had succeeded in controlling a state since Mao's revolution in China in 1949.

Mike Sewell takes a different angle, arguing that Castro's revolution overthrew the US-backed Batista, but then turned towards Marxism and a pro-Soviet alignment partly due to US sanctions and pressure. This came about when Castro nationalised US oil companies after they refused to process Soviet crude oil supplied by Moscow. The USA retaliated by totally cutting off imports of Cuban sugar, so Castro nationalised all US-owned companies. With a US embargo on almost all aspects of trade with Cuba, Castro established diplomatic relations and negotiated a trade agreement with Communist China. He had also secured a credit allowance of $100 million with Moscow to buy weapons and machinery, as well as getting an agreement from Khrushchev to purchase large quantities of Cuban sugar.

**Examiner's comment**

This section shows good awareness of historical debate, although these different interpretations about Castro's beliefs are merely mentioned, with little evaluation. However, the main point is that all this information is largely irrelevant – and will not score many marks. The candidate should have summarised this in a couple of sentences and is wasting time when he/she should be writing about the missile crisis. It is possible that this candidate has revised Cuba very well, but is not prepared to answer a question linking it with the USA. Remember – it is important to study *all* the bullet points set down in the IB *History Guide*, as each section will only have two questions set on it.

US reaction was to brand Castro's regime as communist. The land seizures and trade agreements appeared to confirm this, although these actions may have been misunderstood by the USA. Kennedy identified Castro's removal as a top priority, as seen by the failed invasion at the Bay of Pigs and Operation Mongoose. Castro also made sure that Khrushchev was aware of the US threat to Cuba. Moscow increasingly regarded Cuba as 'the soft underbelly of the Americas'. By 1962, Soviet equipment was pouring into Cuba, which was also being used as a tracking station for Soviet space shots. But when the USA launched a huge military operation in the Caribbean in March – Operation Quick Kick – Soviet monitors realised that Cuba could resist a US attack for no more than a week.

**Examiner's comment**

Again, there is accurate own knowledge in this paragraph – but this is not what the question requires. Despite an opening sentence that suggests the correct focus and analysis might now be applied, the candidate wanders off the point.

*So Khrushchev decided to place nuclear missiles on Cuba, also to counter US missiles in Turkey.* When Kennedy found out, it triggered the Cuban Missile Crisis.

[There then follow a couple more paragraphs giving detailed narrative of the events of October 1962, with reference to the 800-mile quarantine zone, Robert Kennedy's negotiations with the Soviet ambassador, and Khrushchev's telegrams.]

*The crisis had important consequences. Both leaders established a telephone 'hotline' to talk directly in a crisis, and in August 1963 a Partial Nuclear Test Ban Treaty was signed by the USA, USSR and Britain.* But to the USA, the crisis had reinforced the threat of communism spreading into its back yard, making it aware of Soviet influence in the region. This had important long-term consequences for the USA in Vietnam and in the Americas.

**Examiner's comment**

There is little development of an argument to suggest that something other than 'a lack of understanding' was at the heart of the crisis. Ideology and economics are mentioned, but only in passing.

## Overall examiner's comments

There is plentiful and accurate own knowledge in this answer, but unfortunately it is mostly irrelevant, with too much information about Cuba in the 1950s. While there are hints of analysis, it is mostly descriptive. The bulk of the answer is not really focused on the demands of the question. However, there are brief sections that are relevant, so the answer is probably good enough to be awarded a score in the middle of Band 4, perhaps 9 marks. The answer needed to focus on the various causes of the Cuban Missile Crisis, with specific reference to how much/little 'a lack of understanding' was at root, as opposed to other political, economic or ideological factors. Also, although there is some awareness of (irrelevant) historical debate in the answer, it is not evaluative.

# Activity

Look again at the simplified markscheme and the student answer.
Now try to draw up a plan focused on the demands of the question.
Then try to write several paragraphs that will be good enough to
get into Band 1, and so obtain the full 20 marks. As well as making
sure you address **all** aspects of the question, try to integrate into
your answer some references **and** evaluation of relevant historians/
historical interpretations.

# Question 2

Compare and contrast the domestic policies of Eduardo Frei and
Salvador Allende in Chile.
[20 marks]

## Skills

* Factual knowledge and understanding
* Structured, analytical and **balanced** argument
* Awareness/understanding/evaluation of historical interpretations.

## Examiner's tip

Look carefully at the wording of this question, which asks you to
compare and contrast the domestic policies of Frei and Allende.
Questions like this show how important it is to study **all** the bullet
points in the sections you study. If you only select a few of the named
individuals for detailed study, you could seriously limit your options in
the exam.

To answer questions like this in the most effective way, it is best to
structure your answer so that the comparisons/contrasts are brought
out **explicitly**. In other words, draw up a rough plan with headings
for 'comparisons' and 'contrasts' – then jot down where aspects
of their policies were similar under 'comparisons' and where/
how they were different under 'contrasts'. Remember – don't just
describe what their policies were; what is needed is explicit focus on
similarities **and** differences.

## Student answer

Eduardo Frei was president of Chile from 1964 to 1970 and Salvador Allende was president from 1970 to 1973. Frei and Allende were very different presidents of Chile – not least because Frei had the backing of the Roman Catholic Church, European Christian Democrats and the USA, and he gave up his position democratically. Allende was a Marxist, feared by the Church and by Washington. He was seen as a dangerous outsider, and was toppled in a bloody coup. However, there were some areas in domestic affairs where they were in broad agreement. They both felt that some major national issues needed wider consideration: improvements in health and education, fairer income distribution, reform of land-holding, and a more independent foreign policy. Crucially, they also both agreed on the need for greater Chilean control over the US-owned copper-mining industry. So there were both similarities and differences between Frei and Allende. To demonstrate this, I shall examine Frei's policies first, and then look at Allende's domestic policies.

### Examiner's comment

This introduction starts in a generally promising way, although the opening sentence is unnecessary. However, the final sentence in this paragraph is of some concern – such an approach will almost certainly result in a narrative of the two sets of policies with, at best, only a little implicit comparison/contrast. A narrative account without clear focus on the demands of the question is unlikely to get beyond Band 4 and gain more than 10 marks.

Frei's main domestic policies can be divided into two areas: political policies designed to maintain his power and retain the trust and backing of the USA; and economic and social ones – Frei's so-called 'Revolution in Liberty' – intended to transform Chile into a more modern Latin American state, yet doing so within a moderate, traditional Christian democratic framework.

As the 1964 Chilean election approached, the USA favoured Frei, and was worried that Allende might win the election, fearing a repeat of Cuba and the spectre of both a trade embargo and a new Soviet springboard in the Americas. The CIA later admitted to contributing over half of Frei's campaign expenses. Supporting him mainly through radio and print advertising, it aimed to create a 'Red Scare' – warning Chileans about Cuba and the USSR. Frei's 'Revolution in Liberty' campaign did initially cause concern, but the USA felt assured that its reformist elements had all the characteristics of a moderate programme favoured by the Alliance for Progress, set up in 1961 by Kennedy. The US and the IMF therefore continued to give Frei extensive financial backing and political support.

**Examiner's comment**

This paragraph contains precise information, clearly the result of solid revision. However, it is mainly background material, with little on Frei's actual policies.

Frei did much to tackle poverty and by 1970 the wage and salaried sector received close to 51% of GNP, compared with 42% in 1964. This positive redistribution of wealth was encouraged by government policies, particularly in the rural sector, where wages rose by 40% in real terms. Between 1964 and 1970, total enrolment in education increased by 46%, while around 250,000 houses were built, mostly for the poor. A wealth tax was introduced, while a property tax reassessment was carried out, in order to make the taxation system more progressive. Taxes as a percentage of GNP increased from 12% to 21% by 1970. The social reforms introduced by Frei led to a huge increase in public spending, and investment in education, agriculture and housing went up considerably. Frei's 'Revolution in Liberty' made its mark very quickly.

**Examiner's comment**

Again, there is a lot of commendable own knowledge, some of it dealing with aspects of Frei's social and economic policies. However, this answer is turning into a descriptive account of Frei's actions – there has been no attempt so far to address the key issue of similarities/ differences with Allende.

One of Frei's most significant economic achievements was the 'Chileanisation' of copper, which he undertook using a centrist approach. Chile took 51% ownership of US-controlled mines, principally those of Anaconda and Kennecott. Critics complained that the companies received too generous terms – having invested little in Chile – and retained too much ownership. Nevertheless, copper production rose, and Chile received a higher return from the enterprises, thereby validating Frei's approach. Frei enacted tax reforms that made tax collection more efficient than ever before, and pushed through changes to strengthen the presidency, which would later be used by Allende. Electoral regulations changed – the voting age was lowered from 21 to 18 and the franchise was given to people who were illiterate (about 10% of the population).

While remaining friendly to US investors and politicians, Frei developed a more independent foreign policy, receptive to developing and non-aligned countries, and less hostile to the Soviet bloc. He restored diplomatic relations with Moscow and most of its allies, whilst giving strong Chilean backing to multilateral organisations. These included the Latin American Free Trade Association (LAFTA), the Andean Group, the Organization of American States (OAS) and, naturally, the United Nations. But Frei was still popular in Washington, so US aid and investment continued to pour in. From 1964 to 1970, Chile received more aid per capita from the USA than any other Latin American state.

**Examiner's comment**

Again, there is plenty of accurate own knowledge, some of which highlights the policies Frei pursued. However, apart from a brief reference to Allende, no comparisons/contrasts with Allende's political style and policies have yet been made, and the answer strays into Frei's foreign policy.

[There then follow two more paragraphs on Frei's main economic and social policies, touching on a 70% increase on spending on housing, the fostering of local self-help organisations, the creation of Mothers' Centres, sports associations, resident's communities and youth clubs. However, there is still nothing on Allende's domestic policies.]

*Frei's policies were pragmatic and enabled Chile to move into the 1970s as a more modern country. Frei was personally popular and his Revolution in Liberty was not without success. However, by being centrist, he was accused by the right of pandering to the left, while the left – including Salvador Allende – criticised him for being too conservative.*

Many Chileans felt that Frei's undoubted loyalty to Washington cancelled out much of the reform undertaken. Frei caused resentment among Chile's conservative upper class as well the Marxist left. Those on the right talked of forming paramilitary units to defend their property, while radicals on the left urged the illegal seizure of factories, building plots and farmland. *Allende would come to power with this discontent as a backdrop to his domestic policies, which he intended to pursue more radically.*

### Examiner's comment

This is a good conclusion – about Frei! However, it is not a supported judgement or conclusion as there is **nothing** about Allende's policies in the body of the essay – the only real reference to his taking power in 1970 comes here in the conclusion.

## Overall examiner's comments

Although there is precise and accurate own knowledge, this essay is basically a narrative of Frei's domestic policies. If the candidate had written about Allende in the same way, then the answer would have reached Band 3 and earned 11 marks – even though it hasn't really addressed the demands of the question. However, because it **only** deals with Frei, it can only be awarded a mark in Band 5 and receive 7 marks at most. To reach Band 3 or higher, the answer would need **some explicit and well-structured treatment of comparisons and contrasts, with consistent analysis of both similarities and differences.**

## Activity

Look again at the simplified markscheme and the student answer above. Now draw up a plan, with a structure focused on the demands of the question. Then try to write your own answer, making sure you consistently make comparisons and contrasts between both Frei and Allende – so that the answer can reach Band 1 and obtain the full 20 marks.

# Question 3

To what extent did Canada develop a foreign policy independent to the USA during the Cold War between 1945 and 1963?
[20 marks]

## Skills

- Factual knowledge and understanding
- Structured, analytical and **balanced** argument
- Awareness/understanding/evaluation of historical interpretations.

## Examiner's tip

Look carefully at the wording of this question, which asks the extent to which Canada's foreign policy was 'independent' of the USA during the 18-year period identified in the question. Both aspects of the question – the extent and what is meant by 'independent' – will need to be addressed if high marks are to be achieved. Remember, don't just describe what happene – explicit analysis and explanation are needed, with precise supporting own knowledge. There are also some relevant historical debates around this subject that could be made part of the answer.

## Student answer

Canada was rich and politically stable in 1945, and as one of the Allies and a founder member of the United Nations, it became a minor power, with many Canadians wanting to play a more influential international role. During the Cold War, which affected Canadian domestic and foreign policy, Canada became a founder member of NATO. As part of this Western alliance against communism, Canada provided the single-largest component of European air defence. Indeed, Canada emerged as a middle-ranking player on the world stage, with Lester Pearson's independent mediation during the 1956 Suez Crisis being a high point of Canadian foreign policy. But although Canada was supportive of the USA, by 1963 the relationship had changed following disagreements over the presence of US nuclear missiles in Canada and during the Cuban Missile Crisis. Historians *have debated the degree to which Canadian and US foreign policy differed, and have argued whether or not there was any independent strand to Canada's foreign policy. Or perhaps Washington was merely annoyed because Canada dared to voice differences of opinion? This essay will examine such a debate.*

**Examiner's comment**

This is a clear and well-focused introduction, showing a good appreciation of all the demands of the question, an awareness of historiography, and indicating that an analytical approach is likely to be followed.

*If we define foreign policy as 'the diplomatic policy of a nation in its interactions with other nations', and then define independent as 'free from the influence, guidance, or control of others or of outside forces', it can be argued that Canada adopted an á la carte approach to independent foreign policy. Squarely behind the USA in the fight against communism, Canada was still content to disagree when appropriate.*

*Canada was privately concerned about its own geographical and political situation, as the next-door neighbour to atomic superpower America. Would Canada always be the downtrodden younger brother in the relationship between these two allies? Might a fearful anti-communist USA try to push Canada into defence operations and backlash military action? Canadian governments believed that a multilateral relationship was the best safeguard – one that brought Canada and the USA into close alliance, but in partnership with the democracies of Western Europe and with freedom to disagree.*

**Examiner's comment**

Overall, this is a good attempt to define and resolve the parameters of the question, and there is an explicitly analytical overview. The student should now go on to select examples both for and against the notion of Canadian independence.

Canada was drawn into the Cold War at an early stage with the Gouzenko spy scandal in February 1946. Coinciding with the decline in relations between the USSR and the West, Canadians felt that the Cold War was on their doorstep. Outside events such as the Berlin Blockade, Soviet nuclear capability and the communist takeover of China in 1949 all meant that developing an independent foreign policy was not really a priority for the government. Canadian assistance in the Berlin Airlift and Louis St Laurent's signing up to NATO prove that Canada sought collective security against a ideological enemy, although undoubtedly under US leadership.

Even here, though, an independent stance was developed by St Laurent. He saw NATO as an opportunity to help Canada's economic position and reasoned that in order to contribute internationally and to manage its own political problems, then Canada needed economic security. He fought hard to obtain a clause requiring members to co-operate economically and not just band together in a military alliance; to strengthen the social aspects of these Atlantic nations in an attempt to bring internationalism to the fore. He succeeded despite British and US uncertainty, although in reality NATO became a military alliance. Nevertheless, Canada had – to an extent – set the terms, and NATO membership had benefits for Canada, giving it a say in NATO policy and enabling dealings with the USA in a multilateral context. So hints of independence are visible here.

### Examiner's comment

Again, this is a mainly well-focused section, with analysis and balance, showing examples of Canadian submission and independence of action/desire. Here there is good supporting own knowledge, although the student wanders off the point on occasion.

[There then follow several good paragraphs – with detailed supporting own knowledge – analysing Canada's differences with the USA over tactics in Korea, Lester Pearson and Suez, Diefenbaker's criticism of Britain, then his disagreement with the USA over the Bomarc missiles, Kennedy and the OAS, and finally Cuba. The candidate selects examples, arguing both for and against independence in foreign policy. However, there is still no mention or evaluation of different historians' views.]

In conclusion, there were clear signs of an independent streak in Canadian foreign policy, especially after 1956. Canada's politicians were not too nervous to voice a difference of opinion with their mighty neighbour. But after the Cuban crisis came the realisation that Canada – like many other countries – was relatively powerless in comparison to both the USA and USSR. Thus, Canada was locked into an alliance with the USA. Suez, Bomarc, Berlin and Cuba had focused people's attention on the Cold War and increased doubts about the wisdom of the superpower stand-off. Such doubts grew in Canada under Pierre Trudeau, and this is when Canadian foreign policy really became more independent.

### Examiner's comment

The conclusion attempts to balance the argument and ends on a well-focused and analytical note.

## Overall examiner's comments

This is a good, well-focused and analytical answer, with some precise and accurate own knowledge to support the points made. The answer is good enough to be awarded a mark in Band 2 – probably 15. However, to get into Band 1, the candidate needed to provide some specific reference to historians' views/historical interpretations. The answer shows an awareness of the existence of a historical debate, referring to it in the introduction. However, no critical evaluation of these interpretations is made, and no names are mentioned.

## Activity

Look again at the simplified markscheme and the student answer above. Now try to write your own answer to the question, and attempt to make it good enough to get into Band 1 and so obtain the full 20 marks. In particular, make sure you are aware of the main historical debates about this topic – and incorporate some critical evaluation of them in your answer.

# Further information

Sources and quotations in this book have been taken from the following publications.

Aldred, John. 2010. *Aspects of International Relations 1945–2004*. Cheltenham, UK. Nelson Thornes.

Beal, John R. 1964. *Pearson of Canada*. New York, USA. Duell, Sloan and Pearce.

Bethell, Leslie. 1993. *Cuba: A Short History*. Cambridge, UK. Cambridge University Press.

Bothwell, Robert. 2007. *Penguin History of Canada*. London, UK. Penguin.

Bottaro, Jean and Stanley, John. 2011. *Democratic States*. Cambridge, UK. Cambridge University Press.

Boyer, Paul, Clark, Clifford et al. 2008. *The Enduring Vision: A History of the American People Vol. II*. Boston, USA. Houghton Mifflin.

Bragg, Christine. 2000. *Vietnam, Korea and US Foreign Policy 1945–75*. Oxford, UK. Heinemann.

Cavell, Richard (ed.) 2004. *Love, Hate and Fear in Canada's Cold War*. Toronto, Canada. University of Toronto Press.

Chafe, William H. 2003. *The Unfinished Journey: America Since World War II*. New York, USA. Oxford University Press.

Dewart, Leslie. 1964. *Cuba, Church and Crisis*. London, UK. Shed and Ward.

Dobell, Peter. C. 1972. *Canada's Search for New Roles*. Oxford, UK. Oxford University Press.

Edwards, Oliver. 1997. *The USA and the Cold War*. London, UK. Hodder & Stoughton.

Gaddis, J. L. 2005. *The Cold War*. London, UK. Penguin.

Graubard, Stephen. 2009. *The Presidents: The Transformation of the American Presidency from Theodore Roosevelt to Barack Obama*. London, UK. Penguin.

Iacovetta, Franca. 2006. *Gatekeepers: Reshaping Immigrant Lives in Cold War Canada*. Toronto, Canada. Between the Lines.

Jones, J. M. 1955. *The Fifteen Weeks*. New York, USA. Random House.

Kapcia, Antoni. 2000. *Cuba – Island of Dreams*. New York, USA. Berg.

Klein, Naomi. 2007. *The Shock Doctrine*. London, UK. Allen Lane.

Levine, Paul and Papasotiriou, Harry. 2005. *America Since 1945*. Basingstoke, UK. Palgrave Macmillan.

Mace, Gordon and Therien, J. P. 1996. *Foreign Policy and Regionalism in the Americas*. Boulder, USA. Lynne Riener Publishers.

McCauley, Martin. 2004. *Russia, America and the Cold War*. London, UK. Pearson Longman.

Moss, Robert. 1993. *Chile's Marxist Experiment*. Newton Abbot, UK. David & Charles.

Murphy, Derrick, Cooper, Kathryn and Waldron, Mark. 2001. *United States 1776-1992*. London, UK. Collins Educational.

O'Brien, Philip (ed.) 1978. *Allende's Chile*. Westport, USA. Praeger Publishers.

Paterson, David, Willoughby, Susan and Willoughby Doug. 2001. *Civil Rights in the USA 1863–1980*. Oxford, UK. Heinemann.

Phillips, Steve. 2009. *A World Divided: Superpower Relations 1944–90*. London, UK. Pearson.

Pike, Frederick B. 1963. *Chile and the United States 1880–1962*. Notre Dame, USA. University of Notre Dame Press.

Rayner, E. G. 1992. *The Cold War*. London, UK. Hodder Murray.

Roberts, J. M. 1981. *Pelican History of the World*. London, UK. Penguin.

Roxborough, Ian, O'Brien, Philip and Roddick, Jacqueline. 1977. *Chile: The State and Revolution*. London, UK. Macmillan Press.

Schulzinger, Richard. D. 2002. *US Diplomacy Since 1900* (5th edition). Oxford, UK. Oxford University Press.

Sewell, Mike. 2002. *The Cold War*. Cambridge, UK. Cambridge University Press.

Skidmore, Thomas and Smith, Peter. 2001. *Modern Latin America* (5th Edition). New York, USA. Oxford University Press.

Smith, Denis. 1997. *Rogue Tory: The Life and Legend of John G. Diefenbaker*. Canada. McFarlane, Walter & Ross.

Smith, Gaddis. 1986. *Morality, Reason and Power: American Diplomacy in the Carter Years*. New York, USA. Hill and Wang.

Thomas, Hugh. 1977. *The Cuban Revolution*. London, UK. HarperCollins.

Todd, Allan. 2011. *The Cold War*. Cambridge, UK. Cambridge University Press.

Whitaker, Reg and Hewitt, Steve. 2003. *Canada and the Cold War*. Toronto, Canada. James Lorimer & Co.

# Further reading

In addition to the publications listed opposite, the following titles are recommended for further reading on the topics covered in this book.

## 1 Introduction
Phillips, Steve. 2001. *The Cold War*. Oxford, UK. Heinemann.

## 2 The USA 1945–61
Gaddis, J. L. in Griffith, Robert and Barker, Paula (eds). 2001. *Major Problems in American History Since 1945*. London, UK. Houghton Mifflin.
Hanhimaki, J. M. and Westad O. D. (eds). 2004. *The Cold War*. Oxford, UK. Oxford University Press.
Logevall, Fredrik. 2001. *The Origins of the Vietnam War*. London, UK. Pearson Education.
McCauley, Martin. 1995. *The Origins of the Cold War 1941–1949*. London, UK. Longman.
McCullough, David. 1992. *Truman*. New York, USA. Simon and Schuster.

## 3 The USA and the Cold War 1961–81
Dallek, Robert. 2003. *John F. Kennedy: An Unfinished Life*. London, UK. Penguin.
Dunbabin, John. 1994. *The Cold War*. London, UK. Longman.
Giglio, James N. 1992. *The Presidency of John F. Kennedy*. Kansas, USA. University Press of Kansas.
Hanhimaki, Jussi M. and Westad, Odd Arne (eds). 2004. *The Cold War*. Oxford, UK. Oxford University Press.
Hobsbawm, Eric. 1999. *Age of Extremes: The Short Twentieth Century 1914–1991*. London, UK. Michael Jones.
Karnow, Stanley. 1983. *Vietnam: A History*. London, UK. Penguin.
Munton, Don and Welch, David. 2007. *The Cuban Missile Crisis: A Concise History*. Oxford, UK. Oxford University Press.
Todd, Allan. 2009. *Democracies and Dictatorships: Europe and the World 1919–1989*. Cambridge, UK. Cambridge University Press.
Vadney, T. E. 1992. *The World Since 1945*. London, UK. Penguin.

## 4 Canada and the Cold War 1945–63
Macleod R. C. 1994. *Police Powers in Canada*. Toronto, Canada. University of Toronto Press.
Whitaker, Reg and Marcuse, Gary. 1994. *Cold War Canada: The Making of a National Insecurity State 1945–1957*. Toronto, Canada. University of Toronto Press.

## 5 Canada and the Cold War 1964–81
Bothwell, Robert. 2007. *Penguin History of Canada*. London, UK. Penguin.
Macleod R. C. 1994. *Police Powers in Canada*. Toronto, Canada. University of Toronto Press.
Whitaker, Reg and Marcuse, Gary. 1994. *Cold War Canada: The Making of a National Insecurity State 1945–1957*. Toronto, Canada. University of Toronto Press.

## 6 Cuba and the Cold War 1945–81
Munton, Don and Welch, David. 2007. *The Cuban Missile Crisis: A Concise History*. Oxford, UK. Oxford University Press.
Patterson, James T. 1996. *Grand Expectations: The United States 1945–74*. Oxford, UK. Oxford University Press.
Todd, Allan and Waller, Sally. 2011. *Authoritarian and Single-Party States*. Cambridge, UK. Cambridge University Press.

## 7 Chile and the Cold War 1945–81
Harmer, Tanya. 2011. *Allende's Chile and the Inter-American Cold War*. Chapel Hill, USA. University of North Carolina Press.
Haslam, Jonathan. 2005. *The Nixon Administration and the Death of Allende's Chile: A Case of Assisted Suicide*. London, UK. Verso.

# Index

# Acknowledgements

The volume editor and publishers acknowledge the following sources of copyright material and are grateful for the permissions granted. While every effort has been made, it has not always been possible to trace all copyright holders. If any omissions are brought to our notice we will be happy to include the appropriate acknowledgement on reprinting.

## Picture credits

Cover Getty Images; p. 10 Getty Images; p. 15 Time & Life Pictures/ Getty Images; p. 17 Time & Life Pictures/Getty Images; p. 21 Library of Congress; p. 27 Getty Images; p. 29 Time & Life Pictures/Getty Images; p. 34 Army Signal Corps/John F. Kennedy Library and Museum; p. 40 Bettmann/Corbis; pp. 46–7 US Army; p. 55 Getty Images; p. 57 Popperfoto/Getty Images; p. 66 Bettmann/Corbis; p. 76 Getty Images; p. 86 The Granger Collection/Topfoto; p. 87 Bettmann/Corbis; p. 98 Time & Life Pictures/Getty Images; p. 99 AP/Topfoto; p. 104 Time & Life Pictures/Getty Images; p. 107 Time & Life Pictures/Getty Images; p. 110 Bettmann/Corbis; p. 118 Time & Life Pictures/Getty Images; p. 125 Time & Life Pictures/Getty Images; p. 128 Bettmann/Corbis; p. 130 Getty Images; p. 136 Bettmann/Corbis; p. 138 AP/Press Association Images; p. 146 Bettmann/Corbis; p. 157 Bettmann/Corbis; p. 158 AFP/Getty Images; p. 159 Madelaine Répond/Corbis; p. 161 Ullsteinbild/Topfoto; p. 168 Bettmann/Corbis; p. 174 AP/Press Association Images; p. 187 Bettmann/Corbis; p. 191 AFP/Getty Images; p. 192 Bettmann/Corbis; p. 199 AP/Press Association Images; p. 200 La Tercera/Reuters/Corbis; p. 202 AFP/Getty Images; p. 207 Gamma-Keystone via Getty Images.

Produced for Cambridge University Press by
White-Thomson Publishing
+44 (0)843 208 7460
www.wtpub.co.uk

Series editor: Allan Todd
Development editor: Chris McNab
Reviewer: Nigel Haworth
Editor: Sonya Newland
Designer: Clare Nicholas
Picture researcher: Sonya Newland
Illustrator: Stefan Chabluk